The American West in
2000

The American West in 2000

Essays in Honor of Gerald D. Nash

Edited by
RICHARD W. ETULAIN
and
FERENC MORTON SZASZ

Published in cooperation with the Center for the Southwest
University of New Mexico

University of New Mexico Press
Albuquerque

Library of Congress Cataloging-in-Publication Data

The American West in 2000 : essays in honor of Gerald D. Nash / edited by
Richard W. Etulain and Ferenc Morton Szasz.— 1st ed.
    p.   cm.
Includes index.
    ISBN 0-8263-2943-8 (cloth : alk. paper)
    1. West (U.S.)—Civilization—20th century.   2. West (U.S.)—History—1945–
3. Nash, Gerald D.   I. Etulain, Richard W.   II. Szasz, Ferenc Morton, 1940–

F595 .A54 2003
978´.033—dc21

                                   2002154216

Contents

Preface

After Gerald D. Nash retired in the mid-1990s from full-time teaching at the University of New Mexico, he returned occasionally to campus to chat with his longtime colleagues in the Department of History. Frequently these conversations turned to classic and new historical writings about the recent United States and the American West and sometimes, at our instigation, to Nash's shaping role in those fields. Historiography, historical methods, and philosophies of history always intrigued him. On one occasion, as we chatted about these subjects, we asked Nash if he would allow us to celebrate his academic contributions—through a scholarship, a research fellowship, or a collection of essays in his honor. Two years before his untimely death in November 2000, Nash expressed his preference for a festschrift.

This volume follows Nash's wishes. After eliciting a list of potential contributors from Nash, we wrote to several colleagues, at the University of New Mexico and elsewhere, and to his former students to ask if they might contribute to this volume. Following Nash's suggestion, we requested that all contributors focus their articles on historical subjects in the post–World War II American West. Here is the result. Taken together, these essays provide a valuable overview of important topics in recent western American history.

The introduction to this collection, by Nash's longtime colleague Ferenc M. Szasz, illustrates the wide, clear impact that Nash's ideas have had on his colleagues and students. Then follows Nash's brief but illuminating autobiographical piece, which traces his life from his natal Germany through his years of academic training and on into his lengthy career of research and teaching. Next Margaret Connell-Szasz, a former student and later Nash's colleague at the University of New Mexico, contributes an interest-whetting sample of her comparative work on Native American and Celtic cultures. Another of Nash's students, Arthur Gómez, draws on his experience in the national park system to provide a valuable essay on tourism and the national parks, past and future. The next essay, on the Bureau of Reclamation, is by long-term friend Donald J. Pisani, a leading authority on water and irrigation policies in the American West.

The following three articles are contributions by Nash's students. One of his doctoral students, Marjorie Bell Chambers, herself a political activist, provides an overview of western women rallying for their political rights in the years since 1960. Then Carol Lynn MacGregor extracts information from her recently completed dissertation to furnish an illuminating summary of cultural life in Boise, Idaho, from 1950 to 2000. Another of Nash's doctoral students, Christopher J. Huggard, supplies a rewarding discussion of conflicts between mining developments and environmental policies in the recent West.

The final four essays are from Nash's colleagues. The first, by Ferenc Szasz, building on his extensive studies of religion in the United States and the American West, analyzes several major trends in organized religion in the recent West. Roger W. Lotchin follows with a probing discussion of urban sprawl in late-twentieth-century western cities. Moving outward, Gene M. Gressley, perhaps Nash's closest professional colleague, contributes a sweeping, provocative overview of the contemporary West in world perspective. The final essay, by coeditor Richard W. Etulain, surveys the impact of Nash's scholarly publications, especially those in the field of twentieth-century American western history.

During his long, distinguished career, Gerald D. Nash made several major contributions to the study of modern American and western American history. This collection of essays on the recent American West testifies to the extensive impact that he has had on shaping the contours of these historical fields.

—Richard W. Etulain

Introduction

A s noted in Richard W. Etulain's preface, this book of essays on the American West since 1945 is dedicated to the memory of University of New Mexico historian Gerald D. Nash (1928–2000). During his thirty-four-year career at the university—1961–95—Nash taught more than 15,000 undergraduate students. In addition, he directed scores of master's theses and doctoral dissertations on various aspects of American history, especially the history of the American West. Along the way he chaired the History Department from 1974 to 1980 and edited *The Historian,* the journal of Phi Alpha Theta, from 1974 to 1984. He attended virtually all the Western History Association gatherings and served as the WHA's twenty-eighth president in 1990–91. His inaugural address was titled "The Great Adventure: Western History, 1890–1990."

While donning and doffing these historical hats, Gerald Nash also found time to write or edit more than fifteen books on a variety of themes. He penned studies on national oil policy, California bureaucracy, Franklin D. Roosevelt, and American economics—to name just a few—but he is probably best known for his work on the twentieth-century American West. Indeed, he pioneered in the creation of the modern West as a distinct field of academic study. His *The American West in the Twentieth Century* (1973) provided the first overview, and in *The American West Transformed: The Impact of the Second World War* (1985) and *World War II and the West: Reshaping the Economy* (1990) he continued to argue for the importance of the federal government and various levels of bureaucracy as crucial shapers of the modern western landscape. The Nash thesis—the idea that ever since World War II the American West has served as the nation's "cultural pacesetter"—still engenders lively debate. He considered the excesses of the New Western History as his particular bête noire. A prodigious scholar, Nash remained exceptionally active during his retirement years. His *The Federal Landscape: An Economic History of the Twentieth-Century West* was published in 1999, whereas his final book, *A Brief History of the American West Since 1945* appeared in September

2000, only two months before his untimely death from pancreatic cancer. In short, Gerald D. Nash was the consummate professional historian. His colleagues, friends, and students held him in the highest regard.

In spite of all the time he spent in the public eye, Gerald Nash remained a private, almost shy person. In many ways he carried the manners and mores of his Berlin childhood into his adult years. Strangers found him formal, almost courtly in his bearing, and he always maintained a distinct sense of propriety in his dealings with other people.

But beneath Nash's outward formality lurked a puckish sense of humor. He ran department meetings with a wry understanding of human nature and academic foibles. He possessed a delightful sense of classroom theatrics that gave him a campuswide reputation. His classes attracted students from every discipline.

The students appreciated his clear, concise lectures that usually contained three major points with various subpoints, and they especially relished his marvelous sense of the ridiculous. Indeed, his classroom humor bordered on the outrageous. So dramatic was he that his teaching assistants likened his wit to that of comedian Jerry Lewis.

Three examples will have to suffice: (1) In a class on western history, Nash would solemnly peer over his half glasses and say: "Based on his reading of the 1890 census, Frederick Jackson Turner argued in 1893 that the door had closed on the American frontier." Long pause. "Rather like this," whereupon he would march out of the class and ostentatiously slam the door. (2) In treating the complex international world of the 1920s and 1930s, Nash would remark: "The theme for today is relatively simple: the U.S. was strongly isolationist between the two world wars." Dramatic pause. "Having said that, I guess we might as well go home." (He starts to pack up his things as the students squirm uncomfortably.) "But wait." Another long pause. "A good historian needs to prove his points," and then he would launch into his lecture/discussion on the main reasons for the mood of isolation. Toward the end of the class period, he would remind the students—in a reference to Albuquerque's major intersection of I-25 and I-40 (termed "the Big I")—that "the real 'Big I' of the interwar years was 'Isolation.'" (3) When Nash cotaught the course The United States During the Era of World War II, he always devoted considerable attention to the Japanese attack on Pearl Harbor. He remained especially critical of General Walter Short, the army commander of the Hawaiian Islands. Since Short lived in constant fear of sabotage from the Hawaiian Japanese, he ordered that U.S. aircraft be positioned wingtip to wingtip behind high fences, all patrolled by armed guards. Thus the planes were sitting ducks when the actual attack arrived from Japanese aircraft carriers. "It's easy to remember the general's name," Nash would remind the students, as he was "short on brains."

Gerald Nash enjoyed remarkably good health all through his career. It was not until the October 2000 gathering of the Western History Association in San Antonio that colleagues and friends learned of his terminal illness. Word spread quickly, and over the next four weeks more than fifty people phoned or wrote the Nash household—several from Europe—to offer their final farewells.

When the coeditors of this volume began to contact Nash's former students and colleagues regarding a possible festschrift, they asked the contributors to assess the role that Nash had played in their own careers and in the shaping of their understanding of western history. The responses were extensive, thoughtful, and, in many cases, moving.

Here are some excerpts: of the former students, Arthur Gómez (National Park Service) recalled how Nash had helped him broaden his regional understanding to grasp the national significance of local concerns. Gómez also noted how Nash's writings had helped shift the historical emphasis in U.S. history from a North-South axis to an East-West one, thus legitimizing the field of modern western history as an area of scholarly inquiry.

Christopher Huggard (NorthWest Arkansas Community College) fondly remembered how generous Nash had been with his time. Huggard spent many hours conversing in his office and praised Nash for guiding him into his current area of research: the study of natural resources and the consequences that emerge from the overutilization of the gifts of nature.

Marjorie Bell Chambers (Union Institute) credited Nash with inspiring her to run for public office and helping her preside over the Los Alamos County Council meetings, as well as serve on various New Mexico, federal, and presidential advisory boards. Nash's written and spoken words, Chambers reflected, "are frequently with me, not only while researching or teaching history, but unexpectedly on an airplane, ironing clothes, or arguing with a television commentator."

Carol MacGregor (Boise State) was especially taken by Nash's persistent emphasis on the role of irony in western history: Why is it that the land of rugged individualism has been so dependent on the federal government for support in the twentieth century? She concluded that she will ever "continue to appreciate his balanced view and professional methodology."

Margaret Connell-Szasz (University of New Mexico) began as a Nash student but later became a colleague. As she noted:

The breadth of his knowledge, combined with the particular worldview that he carried from his prewar European childhood, lent him an air of the paterfamilias. Since he was on Mesa Vista Hall's second floor, a few doors down the hall, I often observed him in his office, sitting directly across from a graduate student, listening intently, fully engaged through the critical compassion that characterized this relationship. Those in this position always sensed his concentrated focus. His bemused perspective on things gave an unexpected dimension to conversations. Thus he suggested one day that those relegated to the second floor were in dire need of a fireman's pole that might enable them to accelerate their descent down to the history office, on the ground floor. The humor, the brilliance, and the compassion were a rare combination that left their marks on many students and colleagues.

His long-term friend Roger Lotchin (University of North Carolina) pointed to the crucial emphasis that Nash placed on the interaction between war and society, as well as his recognition of the generally optimistic character of twentieth-century western history. He also observed that Nash's views on the New Western History have often gotten under people's skins, at times (perhaps inadvertently) forcing them into a more articulate defense of their positions.

Donald J. Pisani (University of Oklahoma) remarked how Nash centered modern western history on public policy and bureaucracy. "Bureaucracy is little studied by historians of the West," Pisani wrote; "they don't know much about how the federal, state, and local governments actually operate, and their lack of attention to day-to-day decision making is one reason so many books distort the power of the federal government." Pisani also gave Nash credit for restating the traditional view that good history should be based on thorough archival research and a profound respect for the integrity of the past. Nash insisted that scholars acknowledge the autonomy of history itself. He remained profoundly skeptical of any attempt to turn history into an "extended morality play."

Gene Gressley (University of Wyoming, emeritus) argued that Nash's influence has been "all pervasive" in his own scholarship, especially in the realms of economic policy and the role of federalism in the modern West. Said Gressley: "Simply and elementally put, the historiography of the twentieth-century West for a number of years was Gerald Nash. . . . [His] uncanny ability as a synthesizer, his pithy and witty comments are unexcelled today or yesterday in western history."

Ferenc M. Szasz (University of New Mexico) was Nash's colleague for twenty-eight years. He recalled the numerous World War II classes that they cotaught and how effective Nash was in challenging students to think through their conclusions. Szasz also fondly remembered the countless student committees and professional programs on which they served together. Among the most memorable of the latter was the 1973 Taos Women's Conference on Communication. Drawing on his own experience with Nazi Germany, Nash expounded on the fragility of the American experiment of democratic republicanism. If the heart of the American political system ever decays, he warned, it will still retain the traditional rhetorical and symbolic veneer of former years. As he reminded his audience, a republic demands eternal vigilance.

Richard W. Etulain (University of New Mexico) has probably been Nash's closest departmental colleague for the last fifteen years. Nash dedicated his final book to "Richard W. Etulain, Historian of the West" and in early October confessed to Etulain that "you have enriched my life." Writing on H-Net, Etulain praised Nash's "great professionalism and his moral standards." Over the last several years, Etulain and Nash coedited several books and book series, including the Modern American West series, published by the University of Arizona Press. In so doing they engaged in endless discussions over the trials and tribulations of the history profession. Often Etulain would jest, "Well, we're just fanatics about history, Jerry," and this sentiment always brought forth an amused nod of approval. Nash and Etulain agreed that the ever-changing field of history was worthy of such devotion.

Philosopher Ralph Waldo Emerson once observed that a teacher affects eternity, for he never knows where his influence stops. Surely this is true for Gerald D. Nash. His many works on the history of the West will be read well into the present century. His graduate students, now teaching all across the nation, carry forth his passion for archival research and historical accuracy. Scholars continue to debate the Nash thesis. And thousands of former University of New Mexico undergraduates, now deep into their varied careers, can still vaguely recall that the "Big I" of the 1930s was "Isolation" and that General Walter Short was "short on brains."

—Ferenc M. Szasz

Autobiography: Roads to the West

Gerald D. Nash

Like many historians of the American West, I was not born in the region but came to it from somewhere else. Probably my road to becoming a western historian was longer and more indirect than that of many others. For the last forty years, however, more than one-half of my adult life, I became an adopted New Mexican, which gave me a vantage point for viewing the western experience in the twentieth century.

My journey began in Germany. Without question, the accidents of birth provided me with particular perspectives. In my own case, I have always eschewed narrow provincialism and maintained a global view. Moreover, I have always harbored a passionate belief in human rights and the functions of historians to illuminate those rights. Undoubtedly such beliefs influenced my work as a historian.

My life began in Berlin, Germany, where I was born in 1928 into a Jewish middle-class family. My father was a businessman engaged in the lumber trade. Our family had deep roots in Germany. The original family name at one time was Nashon, an ancient Hebrew name already noted in both the Old and New Testaments of the Bible. Over the centuries it had been Germanized to Nachschoen. With the dissolution of the ghettos in early-nineteenth-century Europe most Jews were forced to adopt new names, but apparently the Nashons were able to retain the German version of their original Hebrew name. My youth coincided with the rise of Hitler and Nazism.

I spent the first nine years of my life in Nazi Germany. We lived in Berlin, the last few years near the Rathaus Schoeneberg. That was made famous by President John F. Kennedy in 1961 when in a speech in front of the Rathaus, he proclaimed, "I am a Berliner." My family left Germany in October 1937, and after a stay in Palestine we came to the United States in March 1938.

Our arrival in America required many adjustments. My father decided to shorten our name since the German version was hard to pronounce for English speakers. As he searched for some kind of livelihood he decided to remain in New

York City, at least in the immediate future. This was still the era of the depression, and jobs were hard to find, especially for a foreigner. Once my father did have a serious inquiry from the Duke City Lumber Company in a seemingly faraway place, Albuquerque, New Mexico. We pored over maps on the kitchen table to find the location of this distant town. But this job, and no others, materialized in 1938. Everything was so different in the United States. In Germany my father had often bought timber from noblemen. I still remember accompanying him on some of these trips, waiting outside their castles in the car. In such surroundings a child's imagination ran wild with images of castles, nobles, dukes, and royal forests, just as in fairy tales. Well, in America there were no dukes or medieval castles. It was a very different world.

We settled in a small apartment in Washington Heights, a New York City neighborhood that quickly became an enclave of German-Jewish refugees in the 1930s. I entered the local public school in the third grade. Mine had been a somewhat irregular peripatetic educational experience until then. Moreover, I was completely ignorant of the English language. The school officials were extremely gracious and assigned me a fellow student to guide me into the new language and culture. My parents and I were profoundly grateful. What other country on earth would make such efforts? My parents attended night school to improve their English while I, like most children, learned it in about a year or so. Bilingual programs were unknown at the time.

Between 1938 and 1940 our savings were rapidly depleted, and my father's search for a sales position in the lumber industry was futile. Given these circumstances, my father decided what we needed most was a roof over our heads. One could skimp on other necessities like food. So in 1940 he made the decision to lease a town house that had just been subdivided into studio apartments. We moved to the new address, 316 West 103rd Street in Manhattan, a rather upscale neighborhood near Riverside Drive. The address is noteworthy because this was the house that George Gershwin had just recently built for himself, his parents, and his brother Ira. George Gershwin died in 1937, and the estate sold the house, which was converted to rentals. We moved there in 1939, and some beautiful pieces of furniture left by the Gershwins still graced the building. The cellar contained hundreds of phonograph records and sheet music left by the Gershwins. We knew that they were famous, of course, but we did not know what to do with the bulky materials they left behind. Eventually we disposed of these belongings because of lack of space. We lived in somewhat cramped quarters.

During the next six years the Gershwin house became a haven for quite a few German refugees, some famous, some not so famous. Life was not easy, but certainly interesting. Before us passed a kaleidoscope of the European emigration. It included well-known conductors like Jasha Horenstein, visitors like pianist Artur Rubinstein, psychiatrists, physicians, scholars, businesspeople, and even a few bookies. While later historians wrote extensively about the influence of the Frankfurt school of historians and sociologists, I met some of them as a child.

I also remember Saturday afternoons between 1939 and 1941. That was when members of the German-American Bund—the contemporary neo-Nazis of that time—would come to picket the building across the street, the Masters Hotel. Their venom was directed against Congressman Sol Bloom, who lived there and at the time was chairman of the House Committee on Foreign Relations. He opposed isolationism, and even worse from their perspective, he was Jewish. Whenever I and my friends passed along the street, they screamed anti-Semitic epithets. It seemed like the old country that we had just left.

Other memories of that old country crept up. One of our tenants was a waiter at the famous old Astor Hotel in Times Square. He never hid his pro-Nazi sympathies in conversations with my father. One day in 1940 five sullen men from the FBI appeared in the lobby of our house to arrest him. It seemed he was part of an important espionage ring at the Astor. Soon we had a new vacancy because he was deported. German espionage also took other forms. Occasionally the mailman delivered postcards from Germany addressed to Georg Sylvester Viereck, who lived in the apartment building next door. Viereck was quite well known as the leading German poet living in the United States. As a staunch nationalist during World War I, the federal government had imprisoned him at that time for sedition. He had not changed his extreme pro-German nationalistic views by 1941, when he was charged again with sedition and imprisoned. We were convinced that the mail delivered to us in error contained coded messages from Germany.

In 1941 my father finally found a sales position in the lumber industry and left management of the building to my mother. Meanwhile I attended the local public schools in a new neighborhood, which had a typical New York City ethnic mix of the time. This included youngsters from Irish, Italian, Jewish, and African American backgrounds. In middle school I began a number of small jobs, including serving as school representative for the *New York Times,* which I sold to about thirty to forty seventh and eighth graders. In 1942 I was fortunate in securing admission to Stuyvesant High School, then as now one of the finest in the nation. Its programs were oriented toward science, but I already was interested in history.

Upon graduation from high school I entered Washington Square College of New York University. The choice was dictated by the financial necessity of living at home during the college years. I had also been admitted by the City College of New York, but my father's boss's son was a professor at New York University. He was a specialist on ancient Mediterranean shipping, and I had an interest in history. During my four years there he paid no attention to me. The college had an interesting array of scholars. Sidney Hook in the Philosophy Department was already very famous. In history, the subject in which I declared a major, Wallace K. Ferguson was a noted Renaissance expert while Oscar Falnes was well known in Scandinavian and modern European history. I found Leo Gershoy's courses on the Enlightenment and the French Revolution absolutely brilliant. Among Americanists Thomas C. Cochran was well known. The department also had a large number of lesser known but dedicated teachers. They offered stimulating courses on colonial America, the history of the South, and a good course on the

American West, taught by Ray Watkins Irwin, which opened new vistas for me. My minor in political science focused on public policy, public administration, and comparative government. I graduated in 1950 and was elected to Phi Beta Kappa, somewhat to the surprise of my father's boss's son, who was chapter adviser.

Until this time my entire experience in the United States had been confined to New York City. I was really ignorant regarding the rest of the United States and quite innocent. I felt strongly that I needed to learn more about the rest of the country firsthand. I knew very little about American colleges and universities as well. Moreover, I required financial aid, which in those days was rather sparse. After I had done some searching, Ohio State University offered me a fellowship, but I spent only one quarter there. The first problem there was to find suitable housing. Unfortunately, Columbus in the 1950s was a city with virulent anti-Semitism. Most landlords in the university area did not rent rooms or apartments to Jewish students. My experience was not unique. Each year, I learned, several hundred Jewish students, unaware of local mores like me, returned to their homes or went elsewhere because they could not obtain suitable housing. The administration at Ohio State University openly supported such discrimination. The official directory of university-approved housing for students listed all of the private individuals without indicating that virtually all were "restricted," which in the language of the time meant no Jews. When it came to the issue of racial or ethnic discrimination, I certainly had firsthand experience. I did quite well in my courses there but decided that I did not relish the atmosphere. When a decade later Ohio State University offered me an instructorship, it took me less than two minutes to decline it.

On my return from Columbus, I enrolled in the graduate faculties at Columbia University. At the time it had a distinguished history faculty. I listened to exciting lectures by Allan Nevins, Henry Steele Commager, Richard Morris, Dumas Malone, Richard Hofstadter, and the unforgettable Garrett Mattingly. His courses on the expansion of Europe and on the Renaissance and Reformation were unusually brilliant. At the time there were more than 400 candidates for the master's degree in history at Columbia.

Meanwhile my courses on southern history at New York University had alerted me to a neglected topic. I was drawn to the career of John H. Reagan of Texas, the only member of the Confederate cabinet about whom by midcentury no one had written a biographical study. Actually, the political significance of Reagan was much greater after the Civil War. He became a U.S. congressman in 1874 and a U.S. senator in the 1890s. My interest in him revolved about his crusade for national railroad regulation in the 1870s and 1880s and role as the cosponsor of the Interstate Commerce Act of 1887. That became the topic of my M.A. thesis. There was a problem—his personal papers were at the University of Texas, and I lacked funds to go there. Fortunately my seminar director was John A. Krout, who was also the provost at Columbia University. He approved my topic and arranged for the microfilming of the collection. It turned out not to be as full as one would have liked. Still, within a year after receiving my degree I was able to publish three articles about the subject, stemming from the research.

The thesis directed my attention to politics in the West because Reagan was actively involved in forming congressional coalitions between the South and the West. His activities led me into a lifelong interest in the history of public policies in the West. Such an interest could obviously be pursued better at a western rather than an eastern university. Moreover, I could not continue graduate studies without some financial aid. Both became available at the University of California at Berkeley. Thus in 1952 I headed west to the Bay Area to study for a doctorate and to learn more about the West. At Berkeley, I was fortunate in securing special guidance from John D. Hicks, the well-known author of *The Populist Revolt,* who supervised my dissertation. I took courses with, among others, Carl Bridenbaugh, Henry May, Kenneth Stampp, and Walton Bean. Bridenbaugh served as chair of my Ph.D. orals committee. I served as teaching assistant to Henry May. In the 1950s Hicks was directing his students to the history of twentieth-century California, which he felt had been largely neglected. Himself a former student of and successor to Frederic L. Paxson, he had an interest in twentieth-century U.S. and western history. Under his gentle prodding I chose a topic dealing with the history of public policy in California. It seemed at the time that perhaps the topic could be expanded to the entire West in the future. Several studies of public policies had recently been published dealing with Massachusetts and Pennsylvania, but nothing on a western state. The dissertation dealt with the role of state government in California's economy, 1849-1911, and was extended to 1933 when it was expanded into a book in 1964. The work was based on hundreds of volumes of state documents in the state records center as well as records still in the files of state agencies. The records of the State Harbor Commission, for example, were in random heaps in the attic of the San Francisco Ferry building. As a minor I chose public administration. I was extremely fortunate to study under Dwight Waldo, the leading figure in administrative theory during the past half century. He had a keen interest in administrative history as well. I served as his research assistant for three exciting years, helping him with the many books and essays he was publishing during this period. I also served as a research assistant in the School of Librarianship at Berkeley, working with Edward Wight, a wonderful gentleman who was a specialist in county administration and finance. I believed then, as I do now, that these varied assignments provided greater breadth than being confined solely to history.

Once I received the doctorate in 1957, I embarked on a teaching career. My first position was at Stanford University in the then well-known Western Civilization program. It was terrific for students and for the faculty. To be sure, the first weeks were a little difficult since my knowledge of Neolithic times and ancient Egyptian art was limited, but I had to field sharp questions from the students. They were also having fun with inexperienced instructors. But once we got to ancient Greece and Rome, to Hebrews and Christians, we moved right along. I learned a great deal. The instructorship was for a four-year period. But after one year I received a very good offer from Northern Illinois University in De Kalb to teach American history on a tenure track position. I relished that opportunity and packed my books and boxes of notes into my old Buick and headed for the Chicago area.

I quickly fell in love with northern Illinois. It seemed so very much the heartland of America and was reminiscent of an older rural nation that was fast disappearing. Northern Illinois University had been a state college for many years and had only recently been transformed into a university. Adlai Stevenson, whom I greatly admired, had only recently been governor of the state and had dedicated the library at the institution. Growth and expansion were everywhere. For the young faculty, which was being recruited from major universities, it was an exciting time, and presented an opportunity to mold a new university. I lived in Chicago, did research in the extensive collections of the Newberry Library, and commuted to De Kalb several times a week to teach my classes. It seemed like the best of all possible worlds. To me Chicago was a very exciting city, in some ways more so than New York City, where I had grown up.

Just as I was happily settling down in Chicago the Stanford History Department was in the process of creating a new junior position in American history and invited me to return as a visiting assistant professor and candidate for the job. I was really quite hesitant to leave Illinois. But my mentor, John D. Hicks, insisted that I take advantage of this possible opportunity. So with some reluctance therefore I resigned my position and loaded up the car to head west. By this time the car knew the way without much direction from me. At Stanford that year I taught American economic history and the history of California. Meanwhile the chairmanship of the department changed. Thomas A. Bailey, who had recruited me, stepped down, and Gordon Wright from the University of Oregon took over. Wright intended to make the post a senior position and secured funds from the Coe Foundation to support his endeavors. He was especially eager to attract David Potter from Yale University, one of the most brilliant historians in the nation. Eventually Potter agreed to come, and the junior opening evaporated.

During my second year at Stanford, I had also gotten to know Professor Frank Freidel well. He was on leave from Harvard University and was spending a year at the Behavioral Sciences Center at Stanford. Freidel also served as a scout for Oscar Handlin, who was gathering postdoctoral fellows at his new Center for the History of Liberty in America. Handlin was interested in the topic of my dissertation, which fit into some of the broad themes he was pursuing. After some negotiation he offered me a postdoctoral fellowship so that I could turn my dissertation into a book for Harvard University Press. He also wanted me to write a book on the income tax. It was time to turn around and head east for this new venture. I was getting to know the country better.

At that time Handlin was a star in American history, and the center's activities were exciting. The year at Harvard was interesting. Handlin carefully edited my manuscript at least three times, and I followed his suggestions. I was not aware of any disagreements, nor were any ever uttered.

Although the appointment had possibilities of renewal, I decided to reenter the job market. Just a few weeks before the opening of the fall semester in 1961 a visiting position opened up at the University of New Mexico. By now I was leery of visiting positions since I had been burned. Hicks and Armin Rappaport at Berkeley were urging me on the chair, Edwin Lieuwen, who had also received his doctorate at Berkeley. Handlin and Freidel had recently been in the Southwest and urged me to take advantage of the opportunity. By this time I was not sure whether I was in control of my own destiny or whether it was being determined by others. Still somewhat naive, I turned my old Buick around and headed west.

It did not take me long to feel at home in New Mexico, which seemed to me a special kind of place. The beauty of the land and the ethnic mix made it distinctive. At the time it still had a special western atmosphere as well. That fall the department conducted a national search for a regular tenure track position and then offered me the job, which I accepted gladly.

I also developed a special liking for the students at the University of New Mexico. Some came from ranch country and had that special blend of self-confidence, modesty, freshness, and openness that was distinctly western. It was a unique form of sophistication. It was a refreshing contrast to some of the self-conscious pseudo-sophistication sometimes found on the East and West Coasts. In those days at least one-fourth of the students also came from out of state, some from prep schools in the east. Others were easterners or middle westerners seeking adventure in the Wild West. Graduate students were attracted by the American Studies program directed by George Arms, a nationally known literary scholar with whom I worked closely. I remember my first M.A. candidate, Alexander Evarts, grandson of Grover Cleveland's secretary of state. The History Department was still small, consisting of eight colleagues and myself. Only two were specialists in American history. Thus in these early years I taught a wide range of courses, including U.S. Social and Intellectual History, U.S. Diplomatic History, U.S. Economic History, Twentieth-Century America, and American history surveys. The surveys had more than 600 students but counted as one course. A typical semester load also included seminars in twentieth-century U.S. history and in assorted topics in the American Studies program. The 1960s were a busy time and were also characterized by rapidly increasing student enrollments and a doubling of the faculty.

During this decade I also gained diverse teaching experience. I spent summers at the University of California, Davis (teaching California history), at the University of Maryland, and in 1965 at the Institute of Governmental Studies at Berkeley. During 1965–66 I returned to my alma mater for one year to teach in the graduate faculties at New York University, filling in for Vincent P. Carosso, a good friend.

By the 1960s I decided to broaden my horizons and to extend the California experience—first emphasized by Professor Hicks—to the entire trans-Mississippi West. Much of the region's history in the first half of the twentieth century had not been explored by historians. American history survey textbooks largely ignored the development of that region, the fastest-growing area in the United States. They dutifully described the frontier movement and Indian wars in the nineteenth century. Thereafter the West dropped out of sight. The situation had not changed much by 2000.

Here was a clear gap in American historiography. Obviously no one person could fill it, but one could try to call attention to the subject. In my endeavors my wife provided me with much help and support. We were married in 1967, and in later years our daughter pitched in as well. In the 1960s I made two efforts to work in the field after publication of my first book. One was a history of U.S. oil policies, an account of public policies affecting a major western resource. The other was a general history of the twentieth-century West, the first such effort. In 1999 it was translated into Japanese and enjoying good sales there. I suspect that personal reasons had much to do with my editing a book on Franklin D. Roosevelt, whom I admired greatly. To maintain my national perspective, I edited an anthology, *Issues in American Economic History*. It was in print for over twenty years and underwent three editions. I followed my main interest in two books on the impact of World War II on the West. The possibilities of that subject had been suggested to me by a volume on the Great Depression and World War II that I published with St. Martin's in 1979.

By the 1980s directions in American historiography were changing. A new generation came to focus largely on social and environmental history, especially on race, class, gender, and environment. Increased specialization was also characteristic of much of the writing of this period. These changes affected not only choice of subjects but method of presentation. As the centennial of Frederick Jackson Turner's famous essay "The Significance of the Frontier in American History" approached, it seemed a good time to take stock of the field. Most important, however, was the influence of my colleague Richard W. Etulain, an inveterate mover and shaker in western history, who urged me to deliver the Calvin Horn Lectures in Western History at the University of New Mexico in 1990. As I pondered his suggestions, it seemed that such lectures could well focus on changes in the writing of western history over the course of a century. The result was *Creating the West*. Professor Etulain and I had already edited a book of fine essays on the twentieth-century West before he asked me to prepare an appropriate volume for the lecture series.

The 1960s were a turbulent time at the University of New Mexico, as they were on many campuses. I remember leaving the library one evening in 1970 and walking straight into the arms of a crowd led by Jane Fonda. She was leading them in a Vietnam protest march on the president's house. I had expected to see Jane Fonda on a movie screen, but certainly not outside the university library. Whether I liked it or not, I was engulfed by the marching crowd and pondered the role of chance in history. When the National Guard came to maintain order on the campus, a number of protesters spent the nights in the corridors of the History Department, along with stretchers and first-aid kits, should they be needed. Fortunately they were not. Some of our classes were disrupted during these disturbances by roving bands of protesters who were determined that regular classes should not meet. At the time I participated in several teach-ins in the hope of calming tempers. These were times when emotions ran high.

By the 1970s the size of the department had tripled over what it had been fifteen years earlier. University enrollments increased dramatically to 25,000. The department maintained a special focus on Latin American and western and southwestern history. Edwin Lieuwen and Donald Cutter were well known in their respective fields, and the number of graduate students swelled to about 200. Our location made the emphasis natural. Specialization was now much more feasible than before. I taught courses dealing with the twentieth century, including a new one on the twentieth-century West, which proved to be popular. Opportunities arose for me to move to larger universities in the Midwest, but I ultimately decided to remain in the Land of Enchantment.

During the 1970s my research time was more limited. I served as department chair between 1974 and 1980 and also as editor of *The Historian,* the national journal of Phi Alpha Theta, which came to the university for a decade after 1974. I found the editorial duties scintillating because the journal embraced not only American but also European history, in which I had a broad background. I have always been more sensitive to Central European affairs than many Americanists. I found the editing challenging and enjoyed the contacts with hundreds of scholars, who graciously volunteered their expertise to serve as readers. We received more than 200 manuscripts each year, although we could publish only about fifteen of these. Our authors included well-known established historians as well as younger faculty in the profession. It was a rewarding experience and one on which I look back with a sense of accomplishment.

In 1980 the department's specialization in western history was greatly augmented by the coming of Richard W. Etulain, already a leading scholar in western literary and cultural history. He brought a new dimension and an enthusiasm and breadth that greatly expanded the visibility of western history at the University of New Mexico. During this decade we developed one of the largest and most diversified faculties in western history in the nation. Paul A. Hutton joined the staff with expertise in the frontier; Ferenc M. Szasz turned his interests to science in the West; John Kessell succeeded Cutter in teaching about the Spanish Borderland; Margaret Connell-Szasz focused on American Indian history. With such talent we had a comprehensive graduate program. At least one-half of the graduate students in the department specialized in some aspect of western history. The university administration encouraged the trend by providing funds for the Center for the American West, which Richard W. Etulain directed with an active program of publications and conferences.

In 1990 I spent a year in Germany to fill the George Bancroft Chair in American History at the University of Goettingen. My primary motivation in going there was to be of service to my adopted land since I could teach American history in the German language. To a lesser extent, I was curious about a reunified Germany. I had declined earlier opportunities to teach in Germany because I was disinclined to mingle with people who had lived during the Holocaust or chose to ignore it. By 1990 I hoped that many of these people would be gone, and certainly I had no grudge against a new generation. At Goettingen, I gave courses and seminars on

American economic development and found the German students receptive. Professor Hermann Wellenreuther, my host, also insisted that I deliver the traditional inaugural lecture in German. I did that on the same spot where Heinrich Himmler, head of the Gestapo, had made a major speech in 1934. In addition I was useful to the U.S. Information Agency in giving dozens of talks and offering seminars for teachers in Germany and Austria, appearing on television programs, and lecturing at other universities. Tact and discretion led me to avoid the topic of World War II since Germans of all ages were disinclined to listen to discussions of that subject by an American. On the other hand, there was great interest in American Indians. Invariably discussions turned to American mistreatment or removal of Indians and minorities. Comparisons with German policies in this sphere were not appreciated. I was especially useful to the U.S. Information Agency in the former East Germany. Very few teachers there could understand English since teaching of the language had been prohibited under communist rule.

U.S. intervention in the Gulf War aroused very strong protests in Germany. After initial American actions crowds rioted on the main streets of Goettingen for four days and nights, smashing shop windows and shouting anti-American slogans. Students closed the university in protest and forced cancellation of all classes. Since I could mingle as a German, I asked one blond maiden among the protesters who authorized her to block my way to class. The people, she replied, we represent the people. I had heard such a refrain before. Meanwhile U.S. consuls urged Americans not to speak English on the streets. Directors of U.S. Information Agency centers throughout Germany avoided their offices for at least one week since many of their windows were broken. In Goettingen protesters blocked main streets for at least four days and occupied the railway station. Trains could not enter or leave, interrupting service between Hanover and Frankfurt. For several nights we sat in our apartment near the campus and listened to the shouting at mass meetings, saw the bonfires, and heard the shattering of glass. Somehow it brought back memories of the Nazi era for me, and I wondered how much had really changed.

Nevertheless, the year in Germany was interesting. Some of the best was still there, such as the academic stature of universities like Goettingen and the work of philosophers like Karl Jaspers and Juergen Habermas. At the same time, the attitudes of many Germans had not changed that much. The German war veterans' magazines I read in doctors' offices were as chauvinistic in 1991 as they had been in 1944. I had no problems in moving about in German society. Since the younger generation had rarely met a German Jew, inasmuch as their elders had exterminated most of us, it was easy for me to blend. I attended quite a few rallies of young Germans, especially left-wing groups, who had a special hatred of Israel. Yasser Arafat was their hero, and many of the schoolchildren in Goettingen wore Yasser Arafat shawls and dress. I'm sure the children did not really understand the significance of their garb. It puzzled me at first. But after a while I realized that perhaps it reflected the anti-Semitic strains of adults even when there were no Jews in evidence. The children may not have understood, but

I did. At the end of my appointment I was glad to return to the United States. I felt that I had been of service to the United States, especially the U.S. Information Agency. I liked my German students, and several opted to write theses in western history, generally of high caliber.

Looking back on the road I have traveled in western history, I felt that in some small way I had contributed to development of the field of twentieth-century western history. In 1960 it was rather exotic; by 2000 it was being explored by a new generation of younger scholars. I have no illusions. The books of one generation, after a period of time, are often ignored, reviled, or forgotten. It was always thus. Yet something of the past does endure.

The Cultural Renaissance in Native American and Celtic Worlds: 1940-2000

Margaret Connell-Szasz

In the mid-1990s a popular American mail-order music company known as Green Linnet issued a well-received album titled *The Celts Rise Again*. At about the same time, a new talk show, sponsored by American Indian Radio on Satellite, hit the National Public Radio airwaves under the title *Native America Calling*. In the late fall of 1999, a 696-page history of Scotland, *The Scottish Nation, 1700–2000*, by T. M. Devine, director of the University of Aberdeen's Research Institute of Irish and Scottish Studies, became a best-seller in Scotland and a selection of the American History Book Club.[1]

Although these incidents might appear to be isolated, in reality they symbolize a movement that was sweeping across Native America and the Celtic lands of Ireland, Scotland, and Wales. A cultural renaissance was running at high tide. Perhaps the shattering of the Soviet Union in 1991 played a role in this movement. As historian J. M. Roberts put it, "The end of the Cold War posed questions of identity throughout eastern Europe; people everywhere looked to the past for clues to who they were." Elsewhere "countries considered anew how distinctive in their political arrangements ought they to be . . . if Basques were to be distinguished from Spaniards-or the Scotch [*sic*] and Welsh from the English, or the Northern from the Southern Irish?"[2] This cultural renaissance swept beyond the former Soviet Union and the Celtic Fringe of Europe. It also reached the North American continent, where entities like the Navajo Nation, the Yakama Indian Nation, and the Crow Nation felt the ramifications of the crumbling of the Soviet monolith. In what appeared to be a global spin-off effect, the Soviet collapse raised universal questions about the historic relationship between dominant cultures—the United Kingdom and the United States—and the cultures that lay within. In some instances this cultural renaissance accompanied the resurgence of various forms of nationalism.

The nationalism that emerged during the 1990s, however, was rooted in the rebellious 1960s, when a generation turned against the conservative milieu of the cold war era. In the Native American and Celtic worlds, the decade of the 1960s empowered these early cultural stirrings that reflected the dissatisfaction of a people long subjected to outside and internal pressures. This essay will assess the cross-Atlantic links between the Celtic and Native American worlds as each pursued a cultural renaissance mingled with nationalism during the final decades of the twentieth century.

Words on the Land

N. Scott Momaday, the well-known Kiowa author, writes: "Words, as they are carried from one generation to the other solely by means of the human voice, are sacred. Nothing is so potent as the word; . . . and nothing is so close to beauty."[3] In the Celtic and Native American traditions culture has always moved across the generations through the expression of the oral word. The pattern continued with the generations of the late twentieth century.

In this manner the poet has recently reemerged as the voice of the cultural renaissance. On both sides of the Atlantic, the people of these sometimes submerged cultures have rebelled against the sterile world of contemporary life by reemphasizing their historic connections with the earth. No Native American nor Gaelic voice has expressed this tie more eloquently than that of the poet. Encapsulating ancient bardic traditions, these poets have restored, through the power of word, the tattered relationship between humans and the earth. It is fitting that their highly respected voices introduce the theme of the cultural renaissance.

Among Native Americans, Cherokee poet Gladys Cardiff reminds us of earth's connectedness with her people's lengthy heritage.

Where fire burns in the hollow sycamore
smoke like a vague feather lifting
up from the island,
and the world is cold,
where all the animals wait
on the river's edge
while Water Spider weaves
a *tusti* bowl, and steals
across the waves
wherein the little crucible
she carries on her back
an orange piece of the Thunder's gift,
there all the fires
of hearth and harvest,
the conflagrations to come,
the everlasting fire of the sacred mounds,
leap into being.[4]

Across the water in Ireland, Louis MacNeice, born in Ulster but a longtime resident of London, similarly speaks of the pull of his native land that draws the being like an irrepressible magnet.

> In doggeral and stout let me honour this country
> Though the air is so soft that it smudges the words
> And herds of great clouds find the gaps in the fences
> Of chance preconceptions and foam-quoits on rock points
> At once hit and miss, hit and miss

> For the western climate is Lethe,
> The smoky taste of cooking on turf is lotus
> There are affirmation and abnegation together
> From the broken bog with its veins of amber water,
> From the distant headland, a sphinx's fist, that barely grips the sea,
> From the taut-necked donkey's neurotic-asthmatic-erotic lamentings,
> From the heron in trance and in half-mourning
> From the metred mountain weeping shale.[5]

From the pen of Scots-Gaelic poet Sorley MacLean (Somhairle MacGil-Eain), respected as the father of the twentieth-century Scottish Gaelic renaissance, comes this vivid impression of the western Highlands. His homeland was on the Isle of Raasay, tucked into the eastern shoreline of the Isle of Skye.

> I am going through the Creagan Beaga
> in the darkness alone
> and the surf on Camus Alba
> is a sough on smooth shingle.
>
> The curlew and the plover
> are crying down about the Suil;
> and southeast of Sgurr nan Gillean,
> Blaven and the stainless moon.[6]

Finally, T. H. Parry-Williams, a gifted bard of Wales (1887–1975), reflects in this excerpt on the mystic attraction of his homeland and the connection that could not be broken.

> I've since had it with listening to the croon
> of the *Cmry*, indeed, forever moaning their tune.
> I'll take a trip, to be rid of their wordplay with tongue and pen,
> Back to where I once lived aboard my fantasy train.
> And here I am then. Thanks be for the loss.

Far from the fanatics' talkative fuss.
Here's Snowdon and its crew; here's the land, bleak and bare;
Here's the lake and river and craig, and look, over there,
The house where I was born. But see, between the earth and the heavens,
There comes over me, so it seems, a sort of faintness;
And I feel the claws of Wales tear at my heart.
God help me, I can't get away from this spot.[7]

For each of these poets it was the land that drew them back through a meta-phorical journey. For many others, whether Native American or Celtic, the land echoed a similar pull. In North America, post–World War II urban Indians fled their recently adopted metropolitan enclaves to return to their reservations. From the 1950s and 1960s forward, they journeyed from Los Angeles to Dinétah, the Navajo Nation; from Denver to Cheyenne River, a Lakota reservation in South Dakota; and from Seattle across the Cascade Mountains to the Yakama Indian Nation. Traveling via midnight flights, by car, or by ubiquitous pickup, they joined their kin groups and participated in ceremonies, dances, and hunts—before reluc-tantly retreating to the city.

Among the Celts, the magnetic draw of Gaelic land and kin possessed a sim-ilar magic, drawing Gaelic Aberdonians along the North Sea to the Inner Hebrides, exiled Irish Londoners back to Ulster and Cork, Welsh urbanites from Liverpool to Caernarfon. Traveling via train or ferry, by car or jet, they, too, joined family groups, went hill walking, or participated in the *Eisteddfod,* the annual cul-tural fest of Wales, which celebrates Welsh literature, including the selection of a Chair for Bardic Poetry.[8]

Background

In the years immediately after World War II, Native Americans struggled against the legislation introduced under the auspices of the postwar federal assimilation policy. During the 1940s and 1950s, Congress and the Bureau of Indian Affairs (BIA) "terminated" the "trust relationship" between certain targeted tribes and the federal government, thereby removing their treaty-guaranteed benefits. Especially crucial were those guarantees related to health care and education. Congress also threatened other tribes with a similar fate. This policy had a dis-astrous impact on the Menominee of Wisconsin, whose trust relationship was later reestablished, and the Klamath of Oregon, along with a number of other smaller groups. By President John F. Kennedy's administration in the early 1960s, therefore, most Native American groups were fearful of similar consequences, and they remained on their guard when the government considered the intro-duction of yet another federal policy shift.

On the other side of the Atlantic, post–World War II Scotland and Wales wres-tled with the contemporary ramifications of their historic union with England, a union that had endured in Wales from the sixteenth century forward and in

Scotland from the Union of the Parliaments in 1707. Reassessing the bitter heritage of England's military defeat of Wales in the 1280s, Welsh historian John Davies wrote recently:

> Henceforth the fate of the Welsh ... would be to live under a political system in which they and their characteristics would have only a subordinate role, a fact which would be a central element in their experience until this day and hour.[9]

For the Scots, Welsh, and English, the years immediately following World War II, dubbed the "age of austerity," saw the introduction of the British welfare state that both the Labour and Conservative parties would support until the late 1970s. Labour's welfare state legislation, exemplified by the creation of the National Health Service, was mitigated by the severe rationing that all of Britain endured until the early 1950s. For Scotland and Wales, the austerity of these years notwithstanding, the postwar economy brought virtually full employment.

Despite the seeming affluence of this era, the economies of Wales, Scotland, and the Irish Republic still lagged behind that of England, and it was this economic reality that propelled hundreds of thousands of Scots, Welsh, and Irish citizens to flee their homelands. In Scotland, more than half a million people emigrated in the 1950s. By the end of the decade some 400,000 Irish had moved abroad, and less than 3 million people remained in the Irish Republic. In Wales, the pattern was reversed. Thousands of English people moved into the tiny country, altering the ethnic patterns of many communities and concentrating the native Welsh along the southern rim—the old coal-mining region—and in the northeast.[10]

The demographic changes in Native America echoed the Irish and Scottish exodus pattern. Following the impetus of job-seeking Indians during World War II, the migrations of Indians to postwar urban America, both voluntary and federally directed, shifted the balance between reservation and off-reservation populations. Before the war, one in ten Indians lived in cities. But the Native American wartime experiences shared by those who were enlisted in the armed forces as well as other Indians who were employed in defense plants began to turn the tables. Within a decade after the war, one in four Indians lived in the urban Indian enclaves of Los Angeles, Chicago, Seattle, Phoenix, Denver, Minneapolis, and Albuquerque. By the end of the 1990s almost two-thirds of all American Indians and Alaska Natives had chosen an urban environment.

Like their counterparts in North America, the Irish, Scots, and Welsh also chose to migrate to cities during these years. Attracted by jobs and the magnetic appeal of city life, they fled the isolation of Connemara for Galloway, they retreated from the jobless western Highlands and Hebrides to Glasgow, and they abandoned the villages of interior Wales for the southern coastal towns of Cardiff and Swansea.

Although these migration patterns reflected economic realities on both sides of the Atlantic, the separation of people from their homelands did not necessarily sever the ancient social connections. In a sense, by moving into cities, Indians were reclaiming a broader geographical heritage. Throughout Native America from the 1960s forward, urban Indian enclaves often served as seedbeds for political activism and as focal points for the cultural renaissance as well. Poets, artists, and musicians, as well as members of the American Indian Movement (AIM), the controversial Red Power organization founded in Minneapolis in 1968, all reflected an urban Indian experience. Indian Country, once attributed exclusively to rural reservations, proved to be "anywhere Indians were living," which meant most of the continent. And in their urban enclaves Indians often nourished the cultural roots that had long sustained them. When I met an urban Navajo friend on the jogging track recently, I learned that her father, who lived back on the Rez, had reminded her, "Remember, always run East, always run East . . . toward the Dawn." Thus she carried the spiritual dimension of her Navajo running tradition into an urban, off-reservation setting.

Urban Scots, Welsh, and Irish maintained similar rural traditions. Those who migrated to the central belt of Scotland—stretching from Glasgow to Edinburgh—to Belfast or Dublin, to Cardiff or Swansea, brought with them their village and rural patterns of living, often maintained through their religious affiliations and their kinship networks. In the cities they emulated their rural counterparts, turning for camaraderie to select urban pubs, which rapidly emerged as social gathering centers for these rural immigrants.

Activism in the 1960s and 1970s

By the 1960s and 1970s many of these Celtic and Native American peoples had come to a crossroads. On either side of the Atlantic, the frustrations engendered by persistent colonialism had been compounded by domestic political resistance and an international shift in economic and political power. These internal and external forces were the catalyst for change, leading the people to search within their own heritage for unique responses to altered circumstances. Despite obvious differences, their responses also reflected basic similarities. Whether they were Celtic or Native American, they expressed their deepest feelings through music and art, poetry and story. They also maintained their commitment to cultural continuity. And they reacted in a variety of ways to the dominant political structure by reasserting the legitimacy of their historic rights for sovereignty. In Native America this movement found its political voice through the process dubbed "self-determination"—the essence of which was tribal control of their own programs. In Scotland and Wales, it became known as "devolution"—the core of which was Scottish/Welsh control over their own regional domestic concerns.

From the path-breaking American Indian Chicago conference of 1961, where Native youth and their Elders (a term of respect within Native communities) crafted the historic "Declaration of Indian Purpose," a document that was intended as a guide for the federal Indian policy of President Kennedy, to the Indian self-determination legislation of the 1970s, this era witnessed a remarkable change as Indians came into the consciousness of mainstream America.[11] During these crucial years some 42,000 Indians served in Vietnam. Others erupted in political activism, confronting the mainstream in well-publicized, sometimes violent encounters that drew media reporters like locusts. These events began with the Pacific Northwest "fish-ins" of the early 1960s and the occupation of Alcatraz from 1969 to 1971, merging into "The Longest Walk" and the brief occupation of the BIA headquarters in Washington, D.C., in 1972. A year later, the confrontation that achieved the highest profile came with the shoot-out at Wounded Knee on the Oglala Lakota Pine Ridge homeland in South Dakota. Increasingly these events attracted the television news cameras that would bring Indians and their grievances into the public spotlight.

The high visibility of these clashes eclipsed in the public mind the struggles of those Indians who seemed less newsworthy but who were equally determined to follow an alternate path toward sovereignty, one that led to peaceful encounters with members of the U.S. Congress. The apogee of their success was the passage of the Indian Self-Determination Act of 1975. This revolutionary legislation would remold the historic pattern of relations between Native nations and the U.S. government by reintroducing government-to-government relations—a historic pattern dating to the eighteenth century—through a process known as "contracting" and dubbed "638" by Indian Country, a reference to the fact that the law was denoted as PL 95–638. Under 638's guidelines, Native nations or other Native entities negotiated contracts with the federal government that provided for Native administration of their own programs in areas such as education and health. Indians themselves directed and continue to direct these contract programs under 638.

The courts also played a role in the struggle for Native American sovereignty. In 1979 the U.S. Supreme Court handed down a long-awaited decision on Native fishing rights in the Pacific Northwest. This ruling, which upheld the "Boldt decision" (*U.S. v. State of Washington*, 1974), reconfirmed Indians' right to "fifty percent of the catch," a reference to the percentage of fish caught in the Columbia River and other rivers in the region. The Supreme Court's ruling was the first substantive legal corroboration of fishing rights for these Natives, who include the Yakama Indian Nation, the Puyallup, the Nisqually, and others. Their position was grounded firmly in the treaties negotiated in the 1850s.[12]

The significance of these actions taken during the 1960s and 1970s cannot be overestimated. For the first time since the Battle of the Little Bighorn, the Apache wars, and the Wounded Knee Creek massacre of 1890, the continent resounded with Native voices alerting the federal government of the United States that the time had come for the earliest people of the land to reassert their rights. The Native cultural renaissance would spring in part from this reassertion of Native political sovereignty, energizing the movement, giving it spiritual force, and perhaps even shifting its direction.

The political and social unrest that disrupted America in these decades affected both sides of the Atlantic. Disruption on university campuses spread across Ireland, hitting Northern Ireland especially hard, and moved across the Irish Sea to Wales and Scotland as well. Within these societies, the demographic phenomenon of the "baby boomers" jostled against the materialistic culture that characterized the rising affluence of the day. Here the sexual revolution, compounded by the ebbing of Catholic Church control in the Irish Republic as well as the increasing secularization within Wales and Scotland, also spurred the growth of a youthful subculture.[13]

Welsh youth led the way, but their leadership in the movement to preserve the traditional Welsh cultural heritage was echoed in Scotland, where an "army of eager young canvassers and volunteers" working for the Scottish National Party (SNP) "proved more than a match for the moribund local Labour party organization." In 1967, these young Scots helped to bring about the remarkable election victory of Winnie Ewing, the SNP candidate in Hamilton, a community just outside Glasgow. In the long run this victory of the 1960s would prove to be a linchpin in the successful Scottish vote of 1998 that secured Scottish devolution.[14] In Scotland and Wales in particular, the political, economic, and social changes sweeping across their lands during the 1960s and 1970s would also help to shape the forthcoming Celtic cultural renaissance.

The Welsh and the Scots had shared in the economic benefits accruing from the British Empire from the heyday of its power through World War II. Only a decade or two after the war, however, when the empire began to crumble, the ties of patriotism that had once engendered support for Britain as a world power sharply declined. The independence of India, secured shortly after the war, and the flight of the former African colonies was one matter. Striking closer to home was the discomforting awareness that by the late 1950s the economic thermometer of Europe registered well above that of Britain. By the 1960s the citizens of some of Europe's smaller nations were beginning to enjoy a higher standard of living than their British counterparts. Compounding Britain's decline in economic status, in 1963 French President Charles DeGaulle persuaded the Common Market, forerunner to the European Union, to reject the United Kingdom's application for membership.[15]

The dismembering of the vast British Empire, symbolized at the end of the twentieth century by Britain's dramatic withdrawal from Hong Kong, was merely one stimulant to Scottish and Welsh nationalism. In each country the path to sovereignty reflected unique historical circumstances. In both Scotland and Wales the respective nationalist parties—Plaid Cymru in Wales and the SNP in Scotland—derived new energy through the Labour-dominated political scene in the 1960s and 1970s. Plaid Cymru won its first victory in a by-election in Carmarthen in 1966 when Gwynor Evans defeated the Labour candidate. The SNP was equally successful the following year in Winnie Ewing's election victory in Hamilton.

By the 1980s, however, the Welsh had developed a strong sense of nationalist pride. This appeared in the Welsh language revival movement and also in the creation of a Welsh office in Westminster, which would eventually contribute to the revival of the city of Cardiff as the Welsh capital and adopted home of the Welsh yuppie, who was dubbed the cypy. Early in the decade Welsh nationalism was further reflected through the establishment of Radio Wales and Radio Cymru as well as the creation of a Welsh television channel.[16]

During these transition years Scotland saw the rapid decline of its Conservative Party, a change that evinced the shifting mood of Scottish politics. The historic tension between Catholic and Protestant, dating from the Scottish reformation of 1560, was beginning to be diluted. This shift occurred in part because of greater educational opportunities, but it also reflected the erosion of discrimination against Catholics in skilled occupations. Although the impact would not be felt immediately, by the late 1990s it would bear fruit with the Scots' disastrous defeat of the Conservatives.[17]

Scotland would test its commitment to nationalism and devolution in an economic breakthrough that pitted the northeastern Scottish port of Aberdeen against the capital of London. As one scholar has noted, "From 1967 the ports of eastern Scotland started to fill up with odd-looking vessels, high-prowed and low in the stern, like floating lorries: tenders for oil-drilling rigs. Old shipyards and warehouses sprouted the insignia of international oil and engineering companies. . . . The hunt was on for North Sea oil. It had started over a decade earlier. . . . By 1965 gas was being piped from the sea off East Anglia. . . . As pressure on world supplies increased, the rigs were towed north to the treacherous waters off the north-east coast."[18] By the end of 1970, British Petroleum had discovered a large oil field 120 miles northeast of Aberdeen.

The issue of ownership of the oil fields arose quickly. The SNP immediately seized the leadership in the debate by embarking on a campaign based on the argument, "It's Scotland's Oil!" Arguing shrewdly, the party declared that the profits should not be sent to the wealthiest region of Britain—the Southeast; rather, they should remain in Scotland. Assessing the contemporary mood among Scots, Christopher Harvie writes, "To an extent not appreciated by politicians in the south, it presented the Scottish economy with as many problems as opportunities, problems which ultimately brought, as no other issue did, the whole concept of the Union into question."[19] Across the Atlantic, the tremendous economic potential of Indian gaming would raise equally troubling issues of economic equity among Indian nations, intensifying the questions of tribal sovereignty and tribal-state-federal power dynamics.[20] Both devolution in Britain and self-determination for Native Americans in the United States were molded in part by economic concerns.

The issue of oil field ownership in Scotland merged into a more dramatic political feud that erupted between Scotland and England and, to a lesser degree, between Wales and England, with the election of Margaret Thatcher as prime minister in 1979 and the return to power of the Conservatives (1979–97). Thatcher, the "great friend" of Ronald Reagan, remained in office until 1990, when she was succeeded by John Major, who, contrary to all the pundits and pollsters, was elected on his own right in 1992. Prime Minister Thatcher and President Reagan presided over an era that was aggressively friendly to business.

One journalist noted that the American president launched the "greed is good" decade.[21] But Reagan's failure to demolish the programs of Franklin Delano Roosevelt's New Deal and Lyndon Baines Johnson's Great Society was outmatched by Thatcher, who made considerable headway in dismantling Britain's thirty-year-old Labour-based welfare state. Scottish historian T. M. Devine writes that "Thatcherism came to mean monetary control, privatization, the liberalization of free markets, reduction in trade union power, and a concern to inspire a national revival of the virtues of self-help in a people too long inclined to state supported welfare subsidies."[22]

Despite the severe impact on the Scottish and Welsh economies brought about by Thatcherism, Conservative support among the Scots and Welsh did not drop precipitously until the Tories introduced in 1987 a scheme for supporting local authority finances through a flat-rate community charge, known as the "poll tax." The Scots' disaffection with the Tories multiplied when they learned that they had been selected as guinea pigs for the new venture—the tax would first be levied north of the border. Although the poll tax was eventually defeated, the damage to the Conservatives was irreparable. Devine argues that "more than any other single policy, the poll tax drove home the message to many Scots that they were being ruled by an alien government."[23] In short, for the Scots, Prime Minister Thatcher came to personify the evils of the British constitutional system itself.

In May 1997, when Tony Blair and the Labour Party finally routed the Conservatives, the Tories in Wales lost their last remaining seat to the Liberal Democrats; in Scotland, the Tories failed to salvage any of their remaining ten seats.[24] During his election campaign Blair had promised Wales and Scotland another vote on devolution. On the day of the Labour victory, many politicians predicted that "the Tory wipe-out in Wales and Scotland . . . makes resistance to devolution all but impossible."[25] Only four months later, in September 1997, their predictions proved accurate. In both countries the people went to the polls to cast their "aye" votes for the proposed Welsh Assembly in Cardiff and the Scottish Parliament in Edinburgh. The *Manchester Guardian Weekly* thrust the events into historical and cinematic perspective: "Scottish voters marked the 700th anniversary of William 'Braveheart' Wallace's most famous victory last week by voting overwhelmingly for the historic return of their Parliament to Edinburgh—complete with tax-raising powers. [The] vote . . . presaged the biggest shake-up of British politics since the Irish Free State was established in 1922."[26]

In the spring and summer of 1999 the Welsh and the Scots elected their respective Assembly and Parliament members and opened their new governing bodies. *The Economist* observed that these elections "confirmed the new shape of British politics. The two-party battle between Labour and the Conservatives, which has dominated British political life since the 1920s, has been definitively broken in Scotland and Wales. In both countries, the elections on May 6th produced Nationalists as the main rivals to Labour."[27] In the Edinburgh-based *Scotland on Sunday,* William Paul saw deeper historic roots: "The Scottish parliament, which self-destructed in a long ago age, when modern history had scarcely begun, has been recreated in the final year of the 20th century." Paul then drew on an earlier historic moment: "To paraphrase the suitably historic 1320 Declaration of Arbroath [during Robert the Bruce's reign], it was not for glory or for riches that the devolutionists fought, but for democratic accountability, a concept so roundly abused during 18 years of uncompromising Thatcherite rule from London that no politically aware Scot can now give it up."[28] In 1999, with the opening of the Scottish Parliament and the Welsh Assembly and the advent of Welsh and Scottish control over their own affairs, devolution had finally come to pass.

With the arrival of devolution in Scotland and Wales as well as the beginning of self-determination in Indian Country, a measure of sovereignty had come to the subordinate groups on both sides of the water. Throughout the late twentieth century, the sovereignty struggle was closely entwined with the cultural renaissance. The symbiotic relationship that they shared meant that each helped influence the other to form a newly crafted entity. It could be argued that the renaissance actually sprang from the assertion of sovereignty. A closer view suggests that the two forces were so closely interconnected that it has become impossible to assess which was the primary source of change.

Merging of Nationalism and Cultural Renaissance

In North America the Native cultural renaissance emerged largely, though not exclusively, through the urban Indian experience. Natives whose parents had moved to cities in the post–World War II years began to reassert their heritage through literature, music, and art. At the same time that Indian activists were engaging in the fish-ins and the occupation of Alcatraz, the future leaders of the cultural renaissance began to make their voices known. On some occasions, the urban cultural reawakening was linked with a university. Albuquerque's Native renaissance, which included well-known figures such as Simon Ortiz (Acoma), Leslie Marmon Silko (Laguna), Joy Harjo (Creek), Geary Hobson (Cherokee), and Louis Owens (Choctaw-Cherokee-Irish), was centered in part around the University of New Mexico.

Whether the Indian renaissance voice was urban or rural, the link between Native and the land remained central to the creative voice. During the Pacific Northwest fish-ins Clarence Pickernell (Quinault) wrote of the Quinaults' care for the earth. Spoken from the heart, his words served as commentary on the relationship between these Northwest Coast people, who live where the continent meets the Pacific Ocean, and their homeland.

> Listen to Ocean, for he speaks wisdom.
> He sees much, and knows more.
> He says, "Take care of my sister, Earth,
> She is young and has little wisdom, but much kindness."
> "When she smiles, it is springtime."
> "Scar not her beauty, for she is beautiful beyond all things."[29]

Pickernell's words provided the poetic dimension for the power struggle over Native fishing rights in the region. Through his poetry he linked the struggle for sovereignty through political activism with the struggle for cultural voice through creative expression.

In a similar fashion, the bards of Scotland, Ireland, and Wales have expressed their opinions on contemporary political power struggles. In the early 1970s, when the SNP was clamoring for some semblance of separate Scottish economic control over the oil lying under the North Sea, playwright John McGrath's 7:84 Theatre Company carried the antiestablishment message through performances of *The Cheviot, the Stag and the Black, Black Oil*. Mincing no words, the cast sang this refrain:

Oil, oil, underneath the sea
I am the Lord of the Oil said he,
And my friends in the Banks and the trusts
all agree,
I am the Lord of the Oil—Tee Hee.
Now all your Scotties need have no fear
Your oil's quite safe now the trouble-
shooter's here,
So I'll trust you, if you'll trust me,
'Cos I'm the ex-director of a trust company.[30]

The issue of devolution also struck a chord with the Celtic poets. Fearghas MacFhionnlaigh's lengthy bilingual poem (Gaelic-English) "A'Mheanbchuileag" ("The Midge"), written before Scotland's affirmative vote to restore its parliament, assailed Scottish willingness to remain within the British Empire. Here is a brief excerpt:

You chose captivity in the English zoo
In order to void vulnerability.
However, the Zoo-keeper is growing old now,
and the cages are falling apart through rust.
Practically every exhibit has escaped but yourself.
You were always loyal.
Though maybe you are a little timid about freedom,
about a world with no imperial whistle.[31]

On both sides of the Atlantic, poets emerged as the sometimes abrasive, sometimes provocative voice for these cultures. Their numbers multiplied after the 1960s. Among the many gifted Irish poets, Seamus Heaney, who was born in Northern Ireland, remains the most extraordinary. Winner of the Nobel Prize for Literature in 1995, he remains the bardic voice for twentieth-century Ireland. He has published over a dozen volumes of poetry, including *Opened Ground* (1998) and, most recently, a widely praised translation of *Beowulf* (2000). Like his Native American counterparts, he, too, is bound to his homeland, as expressed in this segment from his poem "Land."

I stepped it, perch by perch
Unbraiding rushes and grass
I opened my right-of-way
through old bottoms and sowed-out ground
and gathered stones off the ploughing
to raise a small cairn.
Cleaned out the drains, faced the hedges
often got up at dawn
to walk the outlying fields.

I composed habits for those acres
so that my last look would be
neither gluttonous nor starved.
I was ready to go anywhere.[32]

Like their Celtic counterparts across the water, the poets of Indian Country have guided the Native creative expression in recent decades. They speak of their ancestors and of ancient ways; they reveal strong anger, sometimes couched in ironic humor. They address the painful, unresolved issues of the entwined history of Native Americans and Outsiders. In this manner they provide a poetic cathar-sis, reopening the wounds of the past generations and reminding Native political activists of the power of words. Rooted across the expanse of "Turtle Island" (the Americas of Native-origin stories), they underline the variety of Native cultures. Their voices range from the pulsing beat of Joy Harjo's "She Had Some Horses"— a poet and musician who has described herself as wanting "to put ideas into the framework of words"—to the whimsical, often biting wit of Simon Ortiz, whose best-known collection is *Woven Stone,* to the multifaceted Linda Hogan (Chick-asaw), author of fiction, plays, and poetry.[33] Famed Navajo writer Luci Tapahonso tells stories in her poetry, pulling memories often expressed in Navajo (Diné) from those many generations living within the Navajo four sacred mountains. In an excerpt from her poem "It Has Always Been This Way," she writes:

This is how we were raised.
We were raised with care and attention
because it has always been this way.
it has worked well for centuries[34]

Like Luci Tapahonso and other writers of Indian Country who used the power of words to craft a creative counterpart, in both Native tongues and English, to the movement for self-determination, the Welsh authors molded their cultural renaissance toward a celebration of their dual linguistic heritage of Welsh and English. Saunders Lewis, well-known Welsh nationalist, was, like Linda Hogan, versed in many literary genres. Creating in Welsh and English, he authored plays, novels, poetry, journalistic pieces, and criticism. Since the postwar expansion of bilingual schools in the urban, English-speaking districts of Wales, "a generation of Welsh speaking city dwellers" has created a new audience for Welsh writers.[35]

Alan Taylor, well-known columnist for *Scotland on Sunday,* argued in 1999 that the renowned late-eighteenth-century Scottish Enlightenment had returned two centuries later. Describing Scotland's contemporary movement as "the Scottish efflorescence," Taylor wrote that "there has been a re-emergence of Scottish culture and self-confidence which has made its mark on a world platform. As in the days of [Sir Walter] Scott, the world of Scotland's writers are read internationally."[36]

A few of the noted Scottish literary figures of the 1990s include Iain Banks, whose most recent work is *The Business* (2000); Iain Rankin, an Edinburgh mystery writer whose Detective Inspector John Rebus has become "more familiar to many readers than their relatives"[37]; and A. L. Kennedy, prizewinning novelist and short story writer, whose latest work is *Everything You Need* (2000). By the end of the 1990s, however, the most popular Scottish writer was J. K. Rowling, whose tales of the youthful magician Harry Potter flew off the charts—see, for example, *Harry Potter and the Philosopher's Stone* (1997). With the exception of Iain Rankin and the daring Harry Potter, however, along with well-known novelist Rosamund Pilcher, in the 1990s the works of most Scottish novelists were not readily available in the United States. In a similar fashion, only acclaimed contemporary Irish novelists such as Maeve Binchy have become well known throughout the Atlantic community and across North America. Although contemporary American Indian authors had gained considerable fame in academic circles, their works were not best-sellers across the water.

American Indian novelists did not come into their own until the publication of N. Scott Momaday's novel *House Made of Dawn,* which won the Pulitzer Prize in 1969. Since then, Native American novelists have enriched the Indian literary renaissance with dozens of works. In addition to Momaday's, some of the best-known of these include *Ceremony,* by Leslie Marmon Silko; *The Surrounded,* by D'Arcy McNickle; *Love Medicine,* by Louise Erdrich (Chippewa); and *The Lone Ranger and Tonto Fist Fight in Heaven,* by Sherman Alexie (Spokane–Coeur d'Alene), which appeared in a film version as *Smoke Signals.*

Native journalists have similarly helped to shape the cultural renaissance by expanding tribal newspapers from a modest regional approach to national coverage. In the late twentieth century the two major newspapers were *The Lakota Times,* edited by Tim Giago, foremost Native journalist of this era, which evolved into the popular *Indian Country Today,* and its Great Lakes counterpart, *News From Indian Country,* edited by Paul DeMain. By the end of the century, both papers maintained staff members in Washington, D.C. Mark Trahant (Shoshone-Bannock), a well-respected journalist and newspaper editor who began writing a column for the *Seattle Times* during the 1990s, addressed the role of Native

Americans in print and visual media in his study *Pictures of Our Noble Selves: A History of Native American Contributions to News Media* (1995). In his research, Trahant discovered twenty-five Native American radio stations in tribal communities across North America. Some of these stations were broadcasting in Native languages.[38]

In the 1990s Native radio also moved from regional coverage to a national focus. Early in the decade tribal radio stations inaugurated a Native talk show, *Native America Calling*. Based at KUNM, the National Public Radio station in Albuquerque, it beamed its conversations throughout Indian Country, from Point Barrow, Alaska, to the Lakota nations in South Dakota. An equally important radio feature inaugurated in this era was *National Native News*, which reported stories from Indian Country through five-minute broadcasts appearing on many public radio stations. Radio coverage in an indigenous language, as one Hebridean Scot pointed out to me, is more important than television because people listen to the radio while they are otherwise engaged, whether at work or in the home. If this argument holds some truth, then the Gaelic, Welsh, and Native American radio coverage introduced in the late twentieth century offered a significant means of communication previously unavailable not only for isolated communities, but also for urban areas.

The cultural renaissance moved in a multiplicity of directions, incorporating a wide range of expression. A ubiquitous issue arose with the troubling question of language recovery, an especially complex theme in Scotland with its dual language heritage of Gaelic and Scots, but one that also carried widespread ramifications in many Native American communities, which have recently faced a new challenge with the "English only" movement affecting some western states. Native and Celtic expression in the arts also deserves a separate chapter that would include the impact of the Institute of American Indian Art, founded in Santa Fe in 1962, the National Museum of the American Indian, under construction in Washington, D.C., and the National Museum of Scotland, which opened in Edinburgh in 1999, to name a few institutions that reflect on this compelling theme. Another dynamic dimension of the renaissance has emerged with the revival of traditional music and the incorporation of the traditional with contemporary music forms. One of the individual leaders in this field, Scottish Highlands fiddler Alasdair Fraser, has urged a return to early Highlands music styles. Fraser became a frequent performer at the Highland/ Celtic Games circuit that began to encompass North America in the late twentieth century, a phenomenon that paced the Celtic revival on the American side of the Atlantic.

More widely known within the music renaissance were the universally popular Celtic music groups such as The Chieftains, U2, The Tannahill Weavers, Altan, and Runrig. The Gaelic Rock performances of Runrig, a group led for many years by Donnie Munro, pioneered the Gaelic music renaissance in Scotland and spearheaded the sentiment toward devolution. Runrig, along with U2, the acclaimed Irish group, also carved out a niche in the environmental movement through the powerful lyrics of their tunes. From the 1970s forward, Native American

musicians and musical groups dominated Native airwaves and were featured performers at powwows and other gatherings. Among the best known of these artists
are Buffy Ste. Marie (Cree), Ulali, Indigenous, Joanne Shenandoah (Mohawk), and
Joy Harjo's group, Poetic Justice. At the same time Native playwrights began to
come into their own, pioneered by Hanay Geiogamah (Kiowa) and William S.
Yellowrobe, Jr. (Assiniboine). During the late 1960s, local Native theater across
North America, in Toronto and New York as well as Seattle and Albuquerque,
began to attract audiences. By the year 2000 Native American Public Telecommunications, an institution based in Lincoln, Nebraska, would draw on the
work of some of these artists along with other leaders from Indian Country to
craft a proposal for a six-part multimedia series titled *Native America in the Twenty-
First Century.*

In both the Native American and Celtic cultural renaissance, education played
a significant role. In Indian Country, the late-twentieth-century movement for
self-determination in education originated in the Navajo Nation, where in 1966
the Navajo Nation's Rough Rock Demonstration School was founded and in
1969 the first tribal college, Navajo Community College (NCC, now known as
Diné College), opened. The movement was contagious. Within a decade after
the founding of NCC, the American Indian Higher Education Consortium had
secured the passage of the Tribal College Act of 1978, which promised federal
funding for these institutions. By the end of the century more than thirty tribal
colleges (including those with four-year programs and graduate degrees) had been
founded within the United States and Canada.[39]

In Wales and Scotland the cultural renaissance ignited an interest in national
history. John Davies's masterful volume, *A History of Wales* (1993), first published
in Welsh as *Hanes Cymru* (1991), illustrates this need among the Welsh. The lifelong efforts of Scottish historians such as Nigel Trantor, the highly successful pop-
ularizer of Scottish history, also began to come into their own in this era. *Scotland
on Sunday* urged the nation to take seriously the advice of the Scottish National
Party to offer "more Scottish history in schools," thereby enabling Scots to "wake
from a 300-year dream, realizing that they were once an independent nation and
can be so again."[40] As if in response to this plea, and echoing the energy of the
tribal colleges of North America, one of the remote Gaelic-speaking regions of
Scotland, the Highlands and Islands, began to lay plans for its own college system. The University of the Highlands and Islands, Pròiseact Oilthigh na
Gaidhealtachd's nan Eilean, was scheduled to open at various locations early in
the new century, foreshadowed by the Gaelic language center, Sabhail Mòr
Ostaig, which had already opened on the Isle of Skye.

On both sides of the water the Renaissance continues into the twenty-first
century. Through the arts, education, music, poetry, and story, the Celtic and
Native American people have begun to express the creative dimension of their
search for political and cultural sovereignty. Drawing on their unique heritage,
they have reminded themselves and alerted outsiders of who they are and who
they are likely to become in the new millennium.

Notes

1. This essay is dedicated to the memory of Gerald D. Nash.
2. J. M. Roberts, *History of the World: 1901–2000* (New York: Viking, 1999), 778–79.
3. *Harper's Anthology of 20th Century Native American Poetry*, ed. Duane Niatum (San Francisco: Harper & Row, 1988), xx.
4. Gladys Cardiff, "Where Fire Burns," ibid., 159.
5. Louis MacNeice, "Western Landscape," *Modern Irish Poetry: An Anthology*, ed. Patrick Crotty (Belfast: The Black Staff Press: 1999), 85. MacNeice (1907–63) was born in Belfast to County Galway parents and grew up in County Antrim, the ancestral home of the Coleman branch of my family. He spent most of his career in England, beginning as a lecturer in classics and moving on to become a respected critic and radio dramatist at the BBC.
6. Sorley MacLean, "Creagan Beaga," in *O Choile gu Bearradh, From Wood to Ridge, Collected Poems in Gaelic and English*, ed. Sorley MacLean (London: Vintage, 1991), 239.
7. T. H. Parry-Williams, "This Spot," trans. Joseph P. Clancy, in *A Private Language? A Dip Into Welsh Literature*, ed. Marion Eames (Llandysul, Cenedigion, Wales: Gomer Press, 1997), 168–69.
8. For a history of the *Eisteddfod*, see Dilwyn Miles, *The Secret of the Bards of the Isle of Britain* (Llandybie, Wales: Gwasg Dinefwr Press, 1992).
9. John Davies, *A History of Wales* (London: Penguin Books, 1993), 161. Davies was writing five years before the Welsh voted in favor of a Welsh Assembly. Wales came under the English monarchy of Edward I in 1282, but the two countries were not united (through the auspices of a unilateral English power play) until 1536. Scotland and England came under a single throne in 1603 in the reign of James VI and I, but the Union of the Parliaments did not occur until 1707, 171 years after the Welsh-English Union. Like Ireland, which lost its parliament when the Act of Union passed in 1800, the Scottish Parliament voted itself out of existence, even though the people of Scotland opposed the decision. Both countries retained representation in Westminster. Ireland became a Free State in 1922 and a republic in 1949 under the constitution crafted by President Eamonn de Valera in 1937. Northern Ireland emerged from the contentious legislation and treaty negotiations between 1920 and 1922 that led to the creation of the Irish Free State. James Lydon, *The Making of Ireland: From Ancient Times to the Present* (London and New York: Routledge, 1998), 176–77, 350–55, 388.
10. T. M. Devine, *The Scottish Nation: 1700–2000* (London: Allen Lane, Penguin Press, 1999), 570; Lydon, *The Making of Ireland,* 391; Davies, *A History of Wales,* 631–32.
11. On the Chicago conference, see Stan Steiner, *The New Indians* (New York: Harper & Row, 1968), 36–38. On the legislation of the 1970s, see Margaret Connell Szasz, "Introduction," in Estelle Fuchs and Robert J. Havighurst, *To Live on This Earth: American Indian Education* (Albuquerque: University of New Mexico Press, 1983), xiii–xx.
12. Fay G. Cohen, *Treaties on Trial* (Seattle: University of Washington Press, 1986), 3–17, 107–17. In *American Indian Sovereignty and the U.S. Supreme Court* (Austin: University of Texas Press, 1997), 186, David E. Wilkins argues that Indian activism of the 1960s and 1970s, combined with political and legal victories, "sufficed to provoke a sizable backlash among disaffected non-Indians."
13. On the degree of secularization in late-twentieth-century Scotland, see Joseph M. Bradley, *Ethnic and Religious Identity in Modern Scotland* (Aldershot: Avebury, 1995), 186–96. A more sanguine view appears in Devine, *The Scottish Nation,* 582–84. On this theme in Wales, see Davies, *History of Wales,* 641–43. James Lydon traces the changing position of the Catholic Church in the Irish Republic in *The Making of Ireland,* 390–91, and on Northern Ireland's increasing sectarianism, 393–94.
14. Devine, *The Scottish Nation,* 577.
15. The Republic of Ireland was rejected in the previous year. Both were accepted a decade later, Ireland in 1972 and the United Kingdom in 1973.
16. Davies, *A History of Wales,* 666–67, 680–81.
17. For differing perspectives on the issue of secularization in Scotland, see Bradley, *Ethnic and Religious Identity in Modern Scotland,* 188–96; Devine, *The Scottish Nation,* 583–84; and "Scottish Sectarianism, Empty Threats," *The Economist,* 18 October 1997, 57–58.

18. Christopher Harvie, *Scotland and Nationalism: Scottish Society and Politics 1707 to the Present*, 3d ed. (London and New York: Routledge, 1998), 183–84.

19. Ibid., 184–85.

20. In *Indian Gaming, Tribal Sovereignty and American Politics* (Norman: University of Oklahoma Press, 2000), 42, W. Dale Mason argues that "the story of Indian gaming parallels" the "movement toward devolution of federal programs to state governments and significant federal budgetary constraints [that] are once again threatening not only Indian programs but also tribal sovereignty itself."

21. Martin Kettle, "Washington Diary" *The Guardian Weekly*, 25–31 January 2001.

22. Devine, *The Scottish Nation*, 591.

23. Ibid., 603–4. Devine notes that when the tax was announced, "the leaders of the three largest Scottish churches condemned it as 'undemocratic, unjust, socially divisive and destructive of community and family life.'"

24. In Scotland the Conservative defeat was described as "a disaster of biblical proportions,'" whereas in Wales the defeated Conservative MP said the experience was "like being hit by a tidal wave.'" *Manchester Guardian Weekly*, 11 May 1997.

25. Ibid.

26. The Scottish vote was twofold, first for the parliament itself and second for its tax-raising powers. The Welsh vote for an assembly was more limited and did not include tax-raising powers. *Manchester Guardian Weekly*, 21 September 1997.

27. *The Economist*, 15 May 1999, 59.

28. *Scotland on Sunday*, "Election 99," 9 May 1999.

29. Clarence Pickernell, "This Is My Land," quoted in Cohen, *Treaties on Trial*, v.

30. John McGrath, *The Cheviot, the Stag and the Black, Black Oil*, presented by 7:84 Theatre Company (The Old School, Breakish, Isle of Skye: West Highland Publishing Company, 1977), 31. The play was performed in Edinburgh and Aberdeen and "was the highlight of the SNP's conference at Oban [a port northwest of Glasgow and the jumping-off point for the Inner Hebrides] in August." Harvie, *Scotland and Nationalism*, 185–87. Harvie points out that the attack in these lines was levied against "Lord Polwarth, Chairman of the Bank of Scotland and of the Scottish Council, who was brought into the government in March 1973 as 'oil supremo,' [and] who seemed to sanction a lash-up of big business, government, Scottish institutions and multinationals" (186).

31. Fearghas MacFhionnlaigh, "A'Mheanbchuileag," "The Midge," in *An Aghaidh Na Siorraidheachd: In the Face of Eternity, Eight Gaelic Poets*, ed. Christopher Whyte (Edinburgh: Polygon, 1993), 103.

32. "Land," in Seamus Heaney, *Opened Ground, Selected Poems, 1966–1996* (New York: Farrar, Straus and Giroux, 1998), 49.

33. *Albuquerque Journal*, 27 May 1990.

34. Luci Tapahonso, "It Has Always Been This Way," in *Saanii Dahataat: The Women Are Singing* (Tucson: University of Arizona Press, 1993), 17–18 (excerpt on 18).

35. Davies, *A History of Wales*, 645.

36. Alan Taylor, "And the Nominees Are," *Spectrum Magazine, Scotland on Sunday*, 5 September 1999, 20.

37. Ibid.

38. Mark Trahant, *Pictures of Our Noble Selves: A History of Native American Contributions to News Media* (Nashville: The Freedom Forum First Amendment Center, 1995), 22.

39. *Tribal College Journal* is the best source of information on the tribal colleges.

40. *Scotland on Sunday*, 5 September 1999.

Will the Circle Be Unbroken?: Tourism and the National Park System in the Twenty-First-Century West

Arthur R. Gómez

Picture this. Sunrise breaks over the corrugated majesty of northern Arizona's Grand Canyon, casting its thin vale of amber light across the vast chasm until the canyon's walls radiate with the brilliance of vermilion red. The silence of early dawn, normally punctuated by the chatter of restless birds and the cautious steps of an occasional deer or rabbit, is suddenly disrupted by the unmistakable clatter of motorized vehicles. The morning of November 17, 1996, was not a typical day at Grand Canyon National Park. As park service officials and their staff prepared to execute the first ever federally mandated public closure of the popular natural wonder, Arizona's governor, Fife Symington, accompanied by a thirteen-vehicle convoy of National Guardsmen, arrived at the park's south entrance. Somewhat startled but not intimidated, park superintendent Rob Arnberger greeted the governor, saying, "Would you like to visit the park?" "I'm not here to visit," Symington replied curtly, "I'm here to take over."[1]

What prompted this modern-day, mechanized reenactment of the notorious gunfight at the O.K. Corral? First, the park service only months before had survived a congressionally led attempt to reduce the national park system from its then 373 units to a mere fifty-two of the so-called jewels of the system. Second and more important, with the beginning of the new fiscal year the agency faced imminent financial disaster. In November 1996, a Republican-dominated Congress, mindful of its party's pledge to balance the national budget through closer scrutiny of annual federal expenditures, delayed passage of appropriations legislation for fiscal year 1997. The budgetary crisis occurred just as the National Park Service (NPS) reeled from a comprehensive internal reorganization that had begun in 1995, one aimed at reducing the size of the agency by 1,300 employees in two years. Thus the congressional impasse appeared to hit the NPS hardest among all of the five federal land-management agencies. In the wake of the impending financial and administrative catastrophe, Director Roger Kennedy ordered the temporary closure of all the national parks. The unprecedented systemwide shutdown on the eve of the Christmas holiday season touched off the armed showdown between the state of Arizona and the NPS.[2]

The near constitutional crisis at the entrance to the Grand Canyon dramatically underscored the importance of federally managed lands—in this case the national parks—to the regional economies of the West. Despite what some critics labeled "theatrics" on the part of Governor Symington and Superintendent Arnberger, the incident clearly demonstrated the extremes to which state officials were prepared to go in order to voice their indignation over the federal government's decision to make public lands inaccessible. Not since 1962, when President John F. Kennedy threatened to federalize the National Guard in reaction to Governor Ross Barnett's refusal to admit James Meredith to the University of Mississippi, had a state executive so blatantly challenged the authority of the federal government. Fortunately, tensions subsided without serious consequences, and the Arizona Guardsmen withdrew to Phoenix. Soon thereafter, a spokesperson for the governor admitted that the state was trying only to make the park service "take them seriously with a show of force."[3] Symington's antics, however, were not appreciated. Mindful of the tragedy that had befallen federal employees in Oklahoma City just months earlier, the NPS could ill afford complacency in the face of the state's challenge to federal authority.

In many respects, the incident at Grand Canyon was the direct consequence of the constant pressure brought to bear upon the natural and cultural amenities of the West. Growing tourist visitations to federal, state, and municipal attractions, especially during the past decade, has made the notion of their closure for any reason unacceptable to the tax-paying public. In an earlier work, *Quest for the Golden Circle* (1994), I extolled the virtues of scenic, heritage, and recreational tourism, which had forged the economic profile of the Four Corners Region during the previous three decades. I enthusiastically predicted that tourism, the universally accepted panacea for regional economic revival, "ensured a healthy economic prognosis for all of the [Four Corners] municipalities."[4]

If population growth at the expense of economic diversification, development at the cost of an increasingly diminished western land base, and recreation that exacts a heavy toll on environmental quality are the prerequisites for regional economic stability, then my optimism for the future of the Four Corners has been dramatically tempered. In recent years, several western historians have called into question the issue of the long-term benefits of tourism vis-à-vis its insidious and all too often irreversible effects. Most prominent among this cadre of scholars is University of Nevada–Las Vegas historian Hal Rothman, who argues persuasively that tourism is in effect a "devil's bargain," an unhealthy compact in which municipalities, resolved to reverse the boom-and-bust cycle in their favor, often compromise community integrity in the cause of economic revitalization. "Tourism typically fails to meet the expectations of communities and regions that embrace it as an economic strategy," Rothman writes. "Regions, communities and locales welcome tourism as an economic boon, only to find that it irrevocably changes them in unanticipated and uncontrollable ways."[5]

The traumatic overdevelopment of the West, clearly evident during recent decades, appears to validate Professor Rothman's disturbing proposition. In a strange twist of fate, many of the irreversible conditions that can be attributed to rampant tourism in the Four Corners area have threatened the very scenic and recreational amenities that initially attracted visitors to the region. During the period 1985–95, for example, tourist visitations to the twenty-six national park units within the Four Corners periphery increased from 11.7 million to 17.9 million visitors. Premier southwestern parks such as the Grand Canyon, Zion, and Bryce Canyon doubled their total visitations during this time. Smaller units such as Arches and Capital Reef National Parks in southern Utah and Navajo National Monument in northern Arizona also increased their total visitations by 40 percent or more. Notably, Mesa Verde National Park in southwestern Colorado witnessed a meager 1 percent increase from 656,300 in 1985 to 663,800 ten years later. The outbreak of hantavirus on the nearby Navajo Reservation, followed by a devastating fire in the park, appears to have temporarily impeded tourist interest in the famous archeological park.[6]

More ominous still are the visitor projections for the immediate future. In 1970, the date I purposefully selected to terminate *Quest for the Golden Circle,* the U.S. Census Bureau reported the population of the United States as 203.3 million inhabitants. Notably, 1970 was the year in which environmentalists worldwide commemorated the first Earth Day. In that same year, the nation's parks reported slightly more than 172 million visitations, approximately 85 percent of the American population. By the twenty-fifth anniversary of Earth Day in 1995, coincidentally the year that the National Park Service announced its reorganization plans, the Census Bureau reported 266.7 million people resident in America, a 31 percent increase. National park attendance for that year was an estimated 281 million visitors. In other words, attendance within the then 368-unit national park system for the first time exceeded the overall population of the country.[7] Increased visits to America's historic icons and great natural wonders will likely continue unimpeded as the national park system advances through the twenty-first century.

What has accounted for the recent mass convergence on the nation's parks? Concurrent with an escalating national population, Americans are experiencing not only greater leisure time but also have the money to enjoy it. One disillusioned booster from southern Utah recently had this to say about the so-called me generation: "We [City of Moab] began promoting just as the relatively frugal World War II generation began passing on its vast wealth to its spendthrift offspring in the largest transfer of disposable income in history." The average effective population of Grand County, Utah, for eight months out of the year is about 16,000 residents. During the peak summer months, however, tourists outnumber the local population three to one. These statistics are common throughout the Four Corners Region and indicate that the baby boomer generation has found a fertile playground among the scenic surroundings of the desert and mountain Wests. In some Four Corners municipalities, this cadre of transient residents, which I have caustically dubbed "elitist environmentalists," proclaim themselves the chief defenders of the western landscape. In my judgment, however, their resolve is more often intended to benefit their own recreational pursuits.[8]

Second only to increased leisure time as a factor in the recent surge in tourist visitations is the ease with which the public can now access the national parks. Generally speaking, the federal system of highways opened the West to unrestricted motor vehicle travel. The present ongoing cosmetic face-lift to the nation's interstate system, stimulated in anticipation of the fifty-year anniversary of the Federal Aid Highway Act of 1956, is intended to accommodate even greater numbers of vehicles at higher rates of speed than ever before. Concurrently, once inaccessible areas that were serviced only by dirt or graveled thoroughfares—those designated as secondary roads in 1956—today enjoy the luxury of surfaced highways. Finally, since the mid-1960s, the national park system, up to this time consisting almost exclusively of the most scenic natural and predominately isolated landscapes west of the 100th meridian, has become increasingly urbanized. With the exception of the Alaska parks that were established under the Jimmy Carter administration in the 1970s, the NPS's post–World War II expansionism has encouraged a park system in which at least half of its newest units have been established within or near national population centers. The combination of increased leisure time, excess money, and improved accessibility has resulted in year-round—as opposed to seasonal—tourism that has become the norm even within the most remote communities of the West.[9]

This seemingly relentless "rush" to federal parklands comes at a time when the agency under whose stewardship they have been placed has undergone its most strenuous period of budget cuts and staff reductions. The results of this paradox have placed enormous administrative constraints on the National Park Service. The recent, disastrous Cerro Grande fire in Los Alamos, New Mexico, has even called into question the venerable federal agency's ability to continue to care properly for the resources entrusted to it. "The national parks have become victims of their own popularity," laments one concerned parks system advocate. Indeed, traffic jams, overcrowded campgrounds, increased vandalism and crime, overflowing sewer lines, trampled landscapes, and deteriorating roads and trails are some of the residual consequences of America's love affair with its national park system. Because the majority of the great scenic parks were established either before or shortly after World War II, when total annual visitations numbered less than 20 million, most have not benefited from a systemwide revitalization since the agency marked its fiftieth anniversary in 1966. As a result, original infrastructures in the parks have either seriously deteriorated or failed entirely.[10]

At a time when visitor overcrowding has jeopardized safety as well as reduced the opportunity to enjoy an optimum park experience, the NPS undertook the most comprehensive reorganization in its history. Spurred by Vice President Al Gore's National Performance Review, the effort was designed to make the federal government more efficient by doing "more with less." As noted earlier, the plan called for a 1,300-employee reduction of the NPS's 19,000 full-time positions in slightly more than two years. Decentralization was the hallmark of the agency's downsizing effort. The idea was to place decision making "closer to the ground" by vesting greater administrative responsibility in the park superintendents rather than a central office in Washington, D.C., or the ten existing regional offices. Ideally, superintendents could feel more at liberty to work with local communities and municipal governments in the management of resources in which they all shared a collective interest.

During the fourth annual joint meeting of the Association of National Park Service Rangers and the Association of National Park Service Maintenance Employees, held in Durango, Colorado, in the fall of 1994, the more than 500 men and women in attendance expressed grave reservations about the impending reorganization. Most worried that the much touted streamlining outlined in Director Kennedy's plan would turn out to be "nothing more than a glorified shrink wrapping of an agency already accustomed to doing more with less." Of greater concern, more than 50 percent of the park ranger force earned $25,000 or less annually and were assigned to live in park housing that one resident ranger described as a "national disgrace." Many present at the Durango meeting queried how, given these appalling conditions, could Washington expect the parks to endure additional funding cuts and staff reductions? For these reasons, when the park service moved forward with its downsizing plan and offered early retirement incentives such as bonus buyouts, the majority of the 425 employees who accepted the offer to leave during the first year came from the parks, and not the regional offices as had been anticipated. In 1980 the agency reportedly fielded one park ranger for every 59,000 visitors. In 1996, park managers estimated one ranger in the field for every 80,000 visitors, hardly sufficient to handle safely and effectively the flood tide of national and international tourism.[11]

Clearly the specter of increased visitations in the wake of a collapsing infrastructure and a downsized organization poses an immediate threat to the scenic, historical, and archeological amenities in the national parks throughout the West. Accordingly, threats to the Four Corners' units have become manifest in a variety of ways, some so innocuous that park managers have failed immediately to perceive them. Human-induced seismic disturbances, the result of sonic booms, nearby petroleum and mineral explorations, road construction, increased vehicular—and to a lesser degree pedestrian—traffic have caused serious structural damage to many fragile resources placed under federal stewardship. Sadly, some threats within the various national parks have been agency induced. Vibrations that today threaten the ruins in Chaco Culture National Historic Park in northwestern New Mexico, for example, result directly from increased vehicular traffic. In 1985, the park service succumbed to public pressure to pave the only road leading into and out of Chaco Canyon in order to better accommodate the growing number of recreational vehicles that entered the park. One critic summarized the downside of improved visitor access, saying, "The world's largest industry sent 30 million visitors to the national parks of the Colorado Plateau, and the more beautiful and beloved an area is, the more it's threatened." Equally destructive to walls and foundations are helicopter overflights, an enormously popular method by which tourists can view previously inaccessible ruins. The frequency of these flights threatens the stability of park resources, the result of propeller reverberation.[12]

Less damaging than seismic disturbances but nonetheless irritating, helicopter overflights have become especially intrusive among many of the Southwest's premier natural parks. The monotonous flutter of helicopter propellers that today permeates the red rock canyons of northern Arizona and southwestern Utah abruptly destroys the ambiance of these normally tranquil and scenic landscapes. What local residents near Canyonlands and Arches National Parks in southern Utah refer to as an "aerial invasion of privacy" has become more than a simple nuisance: helicopter overflights have jeopardized the safety of unsuspecting hikers and climbers below. In 1994, for example, two rock enthusiasts were nearly killed while repelling down a 1,000-foot cliff in Castle Valley, northeast of Moab. As a helicopter hovered near the climbers to enable passengers to take close-up photographs, the force of the prop wash slammed them against the face of the cliff. In another incident, one day hiker in Canyonlands National Park, whose hearing was disrupted by the harsh clatter of helicopter noise, failed to heed the familiar warning of a rattlesnake poised to strike. Park Superintendent Walt Dabney best summarized the frustration of his staff and the park's patrons when he remarked, "We have no air force, no anti-aircraft guns, and no authority."[13]

Since 1985, the issue of aircraft overflights has dominated the attention of park managers in the Grand Canyon. National Park Service officials estimated that forty-two tour companies representing five states (Arizona, California, Nevada, Utah, and New Mexico) offered aerial tours over the famous natural wonder. During the peak summer months, the number of park overflights—fixed wing and rotary—in the park averaged 10,000 per month; it was a lucrative enterprise to touring companies, who earned an estimated $110 million a year in tourism revenue. The noise pollution within the canyon, however, became so intrusive that NPS leadership, with the unflinching support of park superintendents throughout the Southwest, appealed to Congress to pass legislation restricting, or in some cases eliminating altogether, aircraft overflights. Aircraft noise, they argued, represented more than an annoyance. The virtually uninterrupted overflights destroyed the "natural quiet" in the park, thus degrading not only the park's ambiance but also the pedestrian visitor's enjoyment.

Using the Grand Canyon as the prototype for proposed congressional legislation, Congress passed the National Parks Overflights Act (PL 100–91) in 1987. This act charged the park service and the Federal Aviation Administration (FAA) jointly to develop guidelines for flight rules that would "substantially restore the park's natural quiet." After nearly a decade of contentious debate between the two agencies, the new flight rules were made public on July 31, 1996. The plan established five "flight-free zones" within the Grand Canyon that encompass about 87 percent of the park. Although aircraft overflights would be allowed in the remainder of the park, air corridors were modified so as not to conflict with hikers on backcountry trails. Finally, the new regulations established minimum flight altitudes of 5,000 feet above sea level for authorized air tours and 8,500 feet for all other commercial and military aircraft. In taking the initiative to address the issue of ever-increasing noise levels in the Grand Canyon, the National Park Service, in partnership with a second responsible federal agency, hopes to restore natural quiet—defined in the new flight rules as "50% or more of the park restored to the natural, ambient sound conditions for 75 to 100% of the day"— in all of its western parks.[14]

The problem of aircraft overflights in recognized protected areas is not restricted to commercial aircraft. Indeed, one recent challenge to the time-honored military training overflights in northern New Mexico originated not with the NPS, but with the American Indian community of Taos Pueblo. Although tribal governors Henry Lujan (1975) and Tony Reyna (1982) previously contested military overflights of their pueblo, the appeal to the U.S. Air Force had little effect until 1992, the year UNESCO named the thousand-year-old village to its World Heritage List.[15] Cited in the nomination as "a living cultural heritage of outstanding value to humanity," the northern New Mexico pueblo joined a prestigious list of national and international properties—the Pyramids, Victoria Falls, the Acropolis, and seventeen of America's most famous national parks. Notably, Taos Pueblo is the only World Heritage site within the Western Hemisphere to be selected as a "living" cultural heritage site. The World Heritage Committee distinguished Taos Pueblo as such because the community had experienced nearly a millennium of continuous occupation.[16]

On May 20, 1994, at the request of Taos Pueblo war chief Vincent Lujan, representatives of various federal agencies, including the NPS, the Bureau of Land Management (BLM), and the FAA, in addition to military officials from Cannon Air Force Base (AFB), near Clovis, New Mexico, and Tinker Air Force Base, near Oklahoma City, met in Taos to discuss the issue of supersonic overflights. Although the military made clear its willingness to cooperate with the Taos people to the fullest extent possible, they reminded those present that the air corridors, in use since World War II, served national defense objectives. The time-tested flights could not be arbitrarily changed, advised Colonel Thomas Runge, fighter training supervisor at Cannon AFB. Low-flying fighter aircraft traditionally had used the well-suited flight corridors near the pueblo to test low-altitude radar equipment, employed in every American armed conflict from World War II to the Persian Gulf War.

Although former tribal governor Tony Reyna fully appreciated the military's defense posture and respected the duty of the U.S. Air Force to serve and protect the nation, he rebuked the military officers present, noting that he personally "did not need a lesson in patriotism." Governor Reyna, a surviving member of the infamous Bataan Death March, argued that he had faithfully served his country, as had many other members of Taos Pueblo. He reminded the air force that the nation was at present not engaged in a global military conflict; rather, the issue at hand was the blatant disruption of the sacred and cultural traditions for which the World Heritage Committee had honored the entire pueblo and its surrounding lands. "Low-flying, supersonic overflights," Reyna admonished, "have inflicted structural damage to the surface structures in the pueblo and have caused seismic disturbance to underground ceremonial kivas." Routine military overflights, the Taos Pueblo elders unanimously concluded, had seriously undermined the daily ceremonial practices for which the pueblo had received international acclaim in 1992.

In a scenario reminiscent of Custer's Seventh Cavalry realizing—all too late—that they should never have charged into the valley of the Little Bighorn, the U.S. Air Force officers retreated from their national defense posture and profusely apologized to Governor Reyna and the Taos people. Colonel Runge promised to investigate the possibility of altering the current flight paths away from the village and the Blue Lake Wilderness Area, 48,000 acres of traditionally sacred lands north of Taos. Although not a national park, Taos Pueblo, because of its World Heritage status, is entitled to the same protection afforded other historic properties under the provisions of the National Historic Preservation Act (1966 as amended). For this reason, the Santa Fe Regional Office of the National Park Service endorsed the pueblo's request that the military and the FAA seek alternative flight paths in northern New Mexico. In a second meeting held in Clovis in October 1994, the air force announced its intent to reroute its low-level, radar training flights several miles north and east of Taos Pueblo.[17]

Efforts to protect seemingly undefinable boundaries such as air space, air quality, and ambient sound conditions within the national park system, and other associated resources entitled to legal guarantees under the provisions of the National Historic Preservation Act, underscore the obvious dilemma prompted by unabated tourism in the West. Today there are increasingly fewer places within our nation's parks where the average visitor can enjoy the mythical "wilderness" experience without interruption from low-flying observation aircraft, intrusive snowmobiles, the ubiquitous all-terrain vehicle (ATV), or, as occurred in southern Utah's Arches National Park, a golf enthusiast who reveled in driving buckets of fluorescent golf balls across the Colorado River into the park. In their determination to attract more visitors and to satisfy the demands of tax-paying citizens, national parks in the Four Corners have jeopardized their community self-esteem. Houseboats in Glen Canyon National Recreation Area, for example, so dominate the water corridors of Lake Powell that an oil residue produced from their huge outboard motors is visible a half mile or more from shore near the popular geological feature known as Rainbow Bridge, in the Utah sector of the recreation area.

Are there measures that national parks can take to minimize the impact of tourist visitations on their cultural and natural resources while still satisfying the congressional mandate issued to the National Park Service in 1916 "to provide for the benefit and enjoyment of the people"? Clearly, some superintendents have taken a proactive posture in addressing the issues of overcrowding in their parks. In an innovative approach, whereby visitors themselves help to resolve the problem, Arches National Park developed a public survey to determine what park officials have labeled "social crowding." Visitor opinion resulting from the survey determined that zero to twelve people at any one attraction in the park is conducive to an "optimum" visitor experience, twelve to thirty is marginally acceptable, and more than thirty people in the same location is "an unacceptable viewing experience." Just as a municipality might assign residential, commercial, and industrial zoning, park managers have imposed "protection" zones throughout the park with varying degrees of stringency. In an unprecedented effort to minimize visitor impact at the zero-to-twelve sites, the superintendent ordered that parking spaces nearest these attractions be removed.[18]

Similarly, at Mesa Verde National Park in southwestern Colorado, park officials have initiated a ticket system for those sites—Cliff Palace, Spruce Tree House, and Balcony House—that are consistently overcrowded. The nominal charge for a ticket today averages $1.75 per person and generates additional income for the park to maintain the most heavily impacted archeological sites. More important, the ticket system enables park rangers to exercise a measure of control over how many visitors view the sites at any one time. The tickets, which may be purchased in advance at various localities inside and outside the park, establish a maximum number of visitors per tour and vary the hours that the sites may be visited throughout the day. In this manner, park rangers have some assurance that their presentations will be better heard and therefore better appreciated by smaller, more attentive numbers of people. The program, in existence since 1995, has received overwhelming support from neighbor communities such as Cortez and Mancos, in addition to accolades from park visitors.[19]

Thus during the past decade, the most ominous threats to the national park system have evolved internally, largely in response to the federally imposed reorganization, as well as externally, the result of excessive visitor overcrowding. At every turn, the National Park Service mandated decisive organizational modifications to accommodate these challenges. At the park level, innovative solutions, such as protection zones or ticket sales, plus the recent initiative to become more self-supporting through the recovery of 80 percent of all entrance and user fees to be used in revitalizing the park's infrastructure, have empowered managers with greater control in the protection of the resources placed under their stewardship.[20] As a result, in the face of such menacing difficulties, the NPS has appeared malleable in its effort to seek solutions to these lingering problems.

What the NPS was not prepared for, however, was the virulent assault on the once sacrosanct system of national parks that originated on the floor of the 104th Congress. This attack threatened the existence of the agency as we know it today. Utah congressman James V. Hansen (R) and Colorado representative Joel Hefley (R) spearheaded the movement among western Republicans to reform radically the national park system. Since the establishment of Canyonlands National Park in 1964, there has been little love lost between Utah's multiple-use advocates and the conservation-minded Democrats in the White House. This acrimonious federal-state relationship worsened with former president Bill Clinton's grandiose proposal to set aside huge parcels of public lands in southern Utah and northern Arizona.[21] Bolstered by his colleagues Senator Orrin Hatch (R), Utah's senior congressional leader, and Senator Robert Bennett, the son of former senator Wallace Bennett (R), who had led the antifederalist campaign to prevent the creation of Canyonlands National Park in the mid-1960s, Representative Hansen in essence proposed the dismantling of the national park system.

On January 4, 1995, Hansen cosponsored a bill that Hefley and Minnesota congressman Bruce Vento (D) introduced to the House. The bill, known as the National Park System Reform Act (H.R. 260), proposed a comprehensive review of the national park system's then 368 units to identify those units "not worthy of the designation national park." Once passed, the law would require the director of the NPS to prepare within one year a plan, including goals and objectives, that would "carry the Park Service into the next century." The plan should specify the criteria used for the selection and retention of all of the system's urban and non-urban parks. The proposed legislation mandated the park service to identify in a report to Congress "all units of the System that do not conform with the revised park criteria from the new plan."

In his capacity as chairman of the House Subcommittee on National Parks and the second-ranking Republican on the House Committee on Resources, Congressman Hansen, in his personal contribution to H.R. 260, called for the establishment of the National Park System Review Commission. The eleven-member, politically appointed commission would recommend, subject to data compiled in the NPS director's report to Congress, specific units of the national park system to be designated for closure, privatization, or sale. The only exclusions, promised Hansen, would be an estimated fifty-four units, the so-called crown jewels of the system, including the Grand Canyon, Yellowstone, and Yosemite National Parks. Amazingly, some of the nation's most revered historical monuments— Independence Hall, the Statue of Liberty, and Mount Rushmore, as well as national icons such as the Lincoln, Jefferson, and Washington Memorials—were not exempt from scrutiny.[22]

Critics of H.R. 260 were indignant at the suggestion that an appointed commission, not the full Congress, primarily responsible for the parks' creation, should determine the value of the nation's parks to the American public. One editorial in the *Salt Lake Tribune,* Hansen's home state newspaper, likened the proposed parks commission to the controversial Base Realignment and Closure Commission created to determine the peacetime utility of military bases across the country. "National parks were created for purposes of preservation and posterity," the editorial argued, "not for the ever-shifting requirements of national defense." Presumably, the parks had an unchanging value and thus "should not be exposed to the whims of an independent commission." Acknowledging that not all units of the National Park Service met the standards of a Yellowstone or a Gettysburg Battlefield, the editorial stressed that Congress still retained its authority to decommission a park, citing the congressional deauthorization of the John F. Kennedy Center for the Performing Arts in 1994 as a prime example.

Although some journalists supported the notion that the National Park Service should undergo a strenuous self-examination, most agreed that it made little sense to set up a mechanism for park closure before all methods to increase park revenues had been exhausted. "National parks are not at all like military bases," one observer concluded; "they need more creative ways to stay open." In effect, critics of the Hefley-Hansen panacea for the ills of the national park system shifted the blame to a parsimonious, Republican-dominated Congress. *The New York Times*, for example, argued that in the past twenty years, Congress—not the National Park Service—had established more than eighty new parks while refusing to give the Interior Department money to do its job.

The Miami Herald echoed support for the *Times*'s accusations. The Republican budget resolution scheduled for debate that summer, noted the Florida daily, proposed to cut the National Park Service's annual budget request by 21 percent for fiscal year 1996. At this rate, the service would have 36 percent less money to maintain its parks by the year 2002. Meanwhile park visitations were expected to increase from 267 million in 1995 to an estimated 300 million by the turn of the century. "The real culprit," chided the *Times*, "is Congress." Echoing the charge to the NPS to leave its parks "unimpaired for the enjoyment of future generations," one newspaper asserted: "Congress wrote the language, and Congress needs to clean up the mess it created."[23]

Not surprisingly, Representative Hansen rebutted the media's challenge to his parks closure idea. He stood firm in his objection to the way the Park Service evaluated its prospective and existing national parks. The Utah delegate cited numerous examples in which the public expressed skepticism toward the national park system. Foremost among the questionable parks was Steamtown National Historic Site in Pennsylvania, the subject of widespread disapproval for having no obvious historical link to the railroad industry. Others denounced Wolf Trap Farm in Virginia as more of a venue for the performing arts than a site of outstanding historical significance. Another example, Santa Monica National Recreation Area (near Los Angeles), had the reputation of a city park rather than the distinction of a national preserve. Only a handful of federal units, in Hansen's estimation, aspired to the true definition of national park; most of those, he acknowledged, appeared to be in serious financial distress.

Discussion of the woeful financial condition of the national park system became a frequent topic among the leading newspapers. According to *The New York Times*, expenditures needed to repair roads, sewer, and water facilities at the Grand Canyon alone were estimated at $350 million. A conservative cost estimate for the entire national park system, including perennial repairs to its 22,000 historic buildings, was a staggering $4 billion. Clearly the park service's 1995 budget allocation of $972 million, which barely offset the agency's operating costs, seemed minuscule when compared with the parks' extensive maintenance backlog. Dismal financial prospects such as these, Hansen concluded, justified his plan to reduce the number of national parks from 368 to a mere 54 premier parks. The money saved from the closure or privatization of more than 300 "less popular" parks could be applied toward the operation and maintenance of the higher-profile units.[24]

The most persuasive voice in opposition to the Hefley-Vento-Hansen proposal came from New Mexico representative Bill Richardson (D), who later resigned his House seat to accept appointments to the United Nations and, more recently, to the Department of Energy. An ardent conservationist, Richardson expressed dismay that H.R. 260 appeared to focus more on park closure than park reform. First, he contradicted the notion that the proposed legislation would save money. "We could deauthorize all of the 30-plus units designated since 1980," Richardson said, "yet we would save less than 2 percent of the NPS's annual operation and maintenance budget." Further, he challenged Hansen's concept of the fifty-four-park exemption, noting that many of the country's most treasured historical landmarks would be in jeopardy of decommissioning or closure. "What makes the Statue of Liberty any less worthy than Yellowstone or Grand Canyon National Parks?" the New Mexican queried. Before his departure from Congress, Richardson prevailed upon his colleagues to strike out sections 102 and 103 of the proposal, which dealt with management review and the Park Closure Commission. Toward this end, Richardson sought to replace the adversarial document with a new bill intended to generate increased revenue for the national park system through concession reform and entrance fee legislation.

Bent on reforming the system, not gutting it, Bill Richardson introduced H.R. 2181 in August 1995, appropriately named the Common Sense National Park System Reform Act, as a countermeasure to what had come to be known simply as the Hansen Bill. The legislation proposed to increase park entrance fees from the standard $3 per carload—the same admission charged since 1916—to a still affordable $10. More substantive was the language that required park concessionaires to contribute a portion of their annual gross receipts, beyond the nominal 2.8 percent, into a Park Improvement Fund; these proceeds would be expended only on long-neglected repairs within the parks.[25]

The H.R. 260 bill came up for a vote before the floor of the House on September 18, 1995. The proposal resoundingly failed passage by a vote of 231 opposed to 180 in favor. Predictably, the Utah delegation voted along partisan lines: Republicans Hansen and Waldholtz voted yes while Bill Orton, the state's lone Democrat, dissented. For all of its defects, H.R. 260 contained redeeming qualities. First, it articulated the need for the National Park Service to standardize the criteria by which the agency designates its new units. In an official Interior Department news release posted the following day, Secretary Bruce Babbitt acknowledged the wisdom of at least this part of the reform bill. "I believe that there should be good criteria for establishing new national parks." He pledged further, "I would be willing to work with Congress to ensure the quality of future additions."

Of greater long-term significance, the prospect of mandatory closure of our national parks rallied the American people to their defense. The public's challenge to Congress to seek creative methods that promised a measure of financial solvency within the national park system inspired more effective solutions toward that end. A multiyear program that began in 1996 to increase entrance fees in the parks with the explicit design of returning 80 percent of all collections toward capital improvements and routine maintenance was clearly the bill's most beneficial influence.[26]

In the final analysis, Hansen's Park Closure Commission was a bad idea that galvanized public opinion against the entire piece of legislation. In presuming that only 54 of 368 units administered by the NPS were worthy of recognition, Hansen effectively declared "open season" on all urban parks, military battlefields, national recreation areas, national seashores, and national memorials. If passed, Hansen's bill would have resulted in the preservation of a generic national park system with no regard for regional or ethnic distinctions—in effect, a social and political regression to pre-civil-rights America. More disturbing, it appears that the congressman's insistence that park closures would produce a surplus of money to be spent on the needs of the premier parks could not be substantiated. Secretary Babbitt questioned how Congress, on the one hand, could seriously consider closing national parks to raise money when it had just that month appropriated upward of $50 million for line-item construction projects not assigned a high priority in the NPS's fiscal year 1996 fiscal plan.

With the defeat of H.R. 260 it appeared to its detractors and to the American public that the NPS had weathered the storm.[27] The reprieve, however welcome, proved short-lived. Scarcely two months had elapsed since the defeat of H.R. 260 when the Symington-Arnberger confrontation at the Grand Canyon took place, showcasing again the persisting feud over federal versus state right to control.

In the aftermath of H.R. 260, the Grand Canyon incident, and the federal government's reorganization, the National Park Service has been obliged to take a hard, introspective look to determine its place in the future management of our national patrimony. As noted earlier, the congressional admonishment that the land-management agency critically examine its standards for the establishment of a national park was not wholly unwarranted. In his widely acclaimed book *Preserving Nature in the National Parks,* NPS historian Richard Sellars presents an unflinching critique of his own agency. Sellars takes the park service to task for focusing too much on recreation while neglecting to push science to the forefront of park management. "Historically," Sellars concludes through his exhaustive examination of federal records, "nature has lost out to recreation." He cites the Glen Canyon and Lake Mead National Recreation Areas as examples where the NPS, a leader in preservation, became too eager to "get into bed with the Bureau of Reclamation and the Army Corps of Engineers," the principal architects of recreational tourism in the postwar West. The NPS decision in the early 1960s to enter the recreation business, according to Sellars, has left the Glen Canyon and Lake Mead areas so "totally impaired from their natural condition" that it produced a fundamental schism within the agency.[28]

If western land-management policies in recent decades have instilled doubts among the many skeptics of the National Park Service, the decimation of forested lands and private residences in Los Alamos, New Mexico, in May 2000 evoked a greater loss of confidence in the agency's ability to manage the public domain. The result of an NPS-induced "prescribed" burn that flared into an uncontrolled wildfire, the Cerro Grande fire burned more than 42,000 acres and destroyed the homes of 385 families in its path. Even though the devastation of the Cerro Grande fire cannot be understated, the fact that the fire threatened to destroy one of the nation's most publicly renowned scientific laboratories outraged the state's congressional delegation as well as stunned the American public. Within hours of the conflagration, state and federal authorities rebuked the National Park Service's fire-management policies as wantonly irresponsible. In the words of one NPS observer, who later commented on the public relations aspect of the Los Alamos blaze, "To outsiders, it appeared as if we [NPS] did not care for the very resources we had been entrusted with."[29]

Placed in proper context, however, the Cerro Grande fire was one of only a handful of government-supervised prescribed burns authorized during the past five years to flare out of control. Of the 31,200 fires ignited by the principal federal land-management agencies—the National Park Service, the U.S. Forest Service, the U.S. Fish and Wildlife Service, the Bureau of Land Management, and the Bureau of Indian Affairs—only 0.5 percent have escaped immediate containment. Although unquestionably more devastating to personal property, the Cerro Grande fire was small when compared to the 1988 Yellowstone National Park fire, which destroyed nearly 800,000 acres. As one journalist summarized about the lessons learned from Yellowstone: "The Yellowstone fire is a reminder of the consequences of suppressing fires altogether." He continued: "After nearly a century of aggressively snuffing out every blaze, the fire fed on explosive conditions, burning an area about 20 times bigger than the Los Alamos fire." Ending his comments on a note of irony, the writer lamented, "As a result of the Yellowstone fires, the government [especially the NPS] more aggressively developed the kind of prescribed burns that were used in New Mexico."[30] We must not ignore that the forested regions of the West—whether under the protection of the NPS or its sister federal land-management agencies—are literally a tinderbox in dire need of aggressive ecosystem management. Those New Mexicans most critical of the park service—especially the state's congressional leaders—should be mindful that Cerro Grande was only one of a half-dozen uncontrolled wildfires that destroyed land and personal property throughout New Mexico during the month of May 2000.

Regardless of the outcome of the debates over the issues of state versus federal authority, multiple use versus preservation, or prescribed burning versus logging, the National Park Service has inherited a lingering "image" problem at the dawn of the twenty-first century. As the tourism industry becomes increasingly globalized, the Progressive Era ideals of preservation and public enjoyment congressionally mandated to the stewards of our national park system, nearly a century ago, have become consistently more incongruous. The National Park Service cannot serve two masters. The agency must impose restrictions on visitations, noise and air pollution, vehicular traffic, and recreational modalities if the cultural and natural treasures of this nation are to remain intact for future generations. Undoubtedly such impositions on the American taxpayer will receive mixed responses. Nevertheless, the National Park Service can ill afford to win visitor approval at the expense of management efficiency and competent stewardship. Only under such rigorous conditions will the so-called golden circle of national parks in the West—indeed the nation—remain unbroken.

Notes

1. Christopher Smith, "Constitutional Crisis at the Canyon," *Salt Lake Tribune,* 11 February 1996, 1.
2. Arthur R. Gómez, "Public Lands and Public Sentiment: A Comparative Look at National Parks," in *Land in the American West,* eds. William G. Robbins and James C. Foster (Seattle: University of Washington Press, 2000), 150–51. As part of the governmentwide 252,000 job reduction that the Clinton administration initiated, the NPS reorganization reduced most of the targeted 1,300 employees from its central office in Washington, D.C., ten regional offices, and two technical service centers. "NPS Reorganization Marks Most Significant Organizational Change in Agency's 79-Year History," U.S. Department of the Interior, National Park Service, news release, May 15, 1995; *Restructuring Plan for the National Park Service* (Washington, D.C.: U.S. Department of the Interior, National Park Service, 1994), 1–10.
3. Gómez, "Public Lands," 151; quote as cited in Christopher Smith, "White House Was Ready to Federalize Arizona Guard," *Salt Lake Tribune,* February 11, 1996, 3; [no author], "Report: Canyon Effort Courted National Crisis," *Scottsdale Progress Tribune,* February 11, 1996, 1–3.
4. Quote as cited in Arthur R. Gómez, *Quest for the Golden Circle: The Four Corners and the Metropolitan West, 1945–1970* (Albuquerque: University of New Mexico Press, 1994; Lawrence: University Press of Kansas, 2000), 191.
5. Quote as cited in Hal K. Rothman, *Devil's Bargains: Tourism in the Twentieth-Century American West* (Lawrence: University Press of Kansas, 1998), 10.
6. Figures for the years 1985–95 are as follows: Grand Canyon National Park, 2.7 to 4.5 million; Zion National Park, 1.5 to 2.4 million; Bryce Canyon National Park, 500,800 to 994,500; Arches National Park, 363,500 to 859,400; Capital Reef National Park, 320,500 to 648,900; and Navajo National Monument, 46,700 to 108,500. See U.S. Department of the Interior, National Park Service, Statistical Abstract, in *Community and Tourism on the Colorado Plateau* (Flagstaff, Ariz.: Colorado Plateau Forum, Northern Arizona University, 1997), 20; Art Gómez, telephone interview with Linda Towle, Chief of Interpretation, Mesa Verde National Park, May 22, 2000.
7. For statistical information on national park visitations during the past four decades, see Bill Conrad, "National Park Service Attendance and U.S. Population Growth: A Brief History and Projections" (paper presented at the George Wright Society Bi-annual Conference, Albuquerque, N.Mex., March 1997), 2–5; Dwight F. Rettie, *Our National Park System: Caring for America's Great Natural and Historic Treasures* (Urbana: University of Illinois Press, 1995), 253. At present, the national park system comprises 379 units.
8. Quote as cited in Bill Hedden, "Towns Angling for Tourism Should Beware of the Great White Shark," *High Country News,* 5 September 1994 (hereafter *HCN*), 1; for influences on other post–World War II western tourism industries, see Hal K. Rothman, "Selling the Meaning of Place: Entrepreneurship, Tourism, and Community Transformation in the Twentieth-Century American West," *Pacific Historical Review* 65 (November 1996): 544.
9. Tom Lewis, *Divided Highways: Building the Interstate Highways, Transforming American Life* (New York: Viking Press, 1997), 279–94; statement by Roger G. Kennedy, director, National Park Service, before the Subcommittee on National Parks, Historic Preservation and Recreation, Senate Committee on Energy and Natural Resources, 105th Cong., 1st sess., 1.
10. Jeff Phillips, "Can We Save Our National Parks?" *Sunset Magazine* 92 (June 1996): 1–4. Rettie,

Our National Park System, 222–23; Ed Marston, "Who Will Run the New Park Service?" HCN, 12 December 1994, 1.

11. Michael Milstein, "National Park Service Is Put on a Starvation Diet," HCN, 16 May 1994, 1; Ranger's quotes cited in Tom Wolf, "Shrink to Fit: National Park Service May Be Downsized and Reorganized," HCN, 12 December 1994, 3.

12. Kenneth W. King and S. T. Algermissen, Seismic and Vibration Hazard Investigations of Chaco Culture National Historical Park (Denver: DOI, USGS, 1985), 1–5, 6, 12; Art Gómez, interview with Linda Towle, 22 May 2000. See also Mark Lewis, "Bad Vibes: Road Change in the Works to Stall Damage to Ruins," Farmington Daily Times, 15 August 1994, 1; quote, Hedden, "Towns Angling for Tourism," HCN, 5 September 1994, 1.

13. Superintendent Dabney's quote as cited in Jim Stiles, "Canyonlands, Arches Are Invaded from Above," HCN, 21 March 1994, 1. Other western parks are grappling with the issue of overflights, "Proposed Rule Making for Overflights at Grand Canyon National Park," National Park Service, news release, July 1996, 1–4.

14. "Overflights of Units of the National Park System," Department of the Interior and Department of Transportation, National Park Service and Federal Aviation Administration, 36 CFR, parts 1 through 7, 8–15, in Taos Pueblo / Taos Airport Environmental Impact Statement Records, National Park Service, Intermountain Support Office–Santa Fe, box 2, file 43 (hereafter cited as TP, box, and file); National Park Service, Director's Bulletin Board, 23 January 1994; definition of natural quiet as cited in "Proposed Rulemaking for Overflights," 2.

15. The World Heritage Convention is an international agreement to preserve and protect properties considered to be of outstanding significance to world history and culture. Of the 150 signatories to the treaty, ratified in 1973, twenty-one nations make up the committee that meets annually to determine which sites are worthy of selection. As of 1997, a total of 552 sites have been designated to the World Heritage List.

16. Tony Reyna to Secretary of the Interior Manuel Lujan, Jr., 7 December 1992, National Park Service, Intermountain Region Support Office, Santa Fe, TP, box 1, file 6; "World Heritage List Briefing Paper," 11 December 1997, 1, ibid.; "Convention Concerning the Protection of the World Cultural and Natural Heritage: Nomination of Taos Pueblo, NM," 1987, 1, ibid.

17. Governor Reyna's remarks as cited in "Minutes: Taos Pueblo Military Overflights," 20 May 1994, TP, box 2, file 53; (a meeting at which the author was in attendance) "Military and General Aviation Overflights to Taos Pueblo Sensitive Land Areas," briefing paper, Office of the War Chief, Taos Pueblo; Vincent Lujan to Richard Cook, National Park Service, International Affairs Office, 10 May 1994, ibid., Colonel Thomas Runge to Jan Schmitt, Southwest Regional Office, September 12, 1994, ibid.

18. Quote from the Organic Act as cited in Richard West Sellars, "The Roots of National Park Management: Evolving Perceptions of the Park Service's Mandate," Journal of Forestry 90 (January 1992): 16–17; figures for "social crowding" as cited in Christopher Smith, "A Delicate Question: When Is an Arch Crowded?" HCN, 6 March 1995, 5.

19. "Operation Cost Recovery: Mesa Verde National Park," NPS briefing paper, 9 February 1999; interview with Linda Towle, 22 May 2000.

20. Until January 1997, 133 national parks charged admission fees. The Recreational Fee Demonstration Program, initiated in that year, has allowed not only 100 more "demonstration" parks to charge admission but also permits them to retain 80 percent of all revenues for use in park maintenance. The pilot program, which has enjoyed widespread support in Congress, is at present under consideration as a permanent feature of the national park system. See "Interior Department Announces Test Project to Fund Needed Improvements on Public Lands," DOI news release, 26 November 1996; Gómez, "Public Lands," 155–58.

21. Since September 1996, President Clinton's $1 billion "Lands Legacy Initiative" has resulted in federal set-asides of approximately 3 million acres of public lands near Kanab, Utah, Fredonia, Arizona, and Cortez, Colorado, all located on the Colorado Plateau. For details see Gómez, "Public Lands," 150–55; "President Clinton's Lands Legacy Initiative: Forging a Conservation Vision for the 21st Century," DOI, National Park Service news release, 12 January 1999; "Establishment of the Grand Canyon-Parashant National Monument by the President of the United States of America," DOI, Bureau of Land Management news release, 11 January 2000.

22. House Subcommittee on National Parks, *National Park System Reform Act of 1995: Hearings on H. R. 260*, 104th Cong., 1st sess.; Congressman Joel Hefley of Colorado speaking in favor of the National Park System Reform Act of 1995, *Congressional Record* (4 January 1995): 9084–86.

23. "Don't Close the Parks," *Salt Lake Tribune*, 6 May 1995, 1, 3; "America for Sale," *St. Louis Post-Dispatch*, 17 July 1995, 1; "Parks in Peril," *New York Times*, 4 July 1995, 2–3; "Congressional Budget Cuts and Anti-Government Attitudes Threaten America's Heritage," *Miami Herald*, 27 June 1995, 1, 3; Conrad, "National Park Service Attendance," 4–5.

24. "Parks in Peril," *New York Times*, 7 June 1995, 3; "GOP Readies Land Grab of Our Parks," *Las Vegas Sun*, 27 August 1995, 1; "National Parks Deserve Help to Protect Nation's Heritage," *Wichita Eagle*, 25 August 1995; Randal O'Toole, "The National Pork Service," *Forbes* (November 1995): 10–13.

25. Dissenting comments of Representative Bill Richardson in *Hearings on H.R. 260*; "Preserving America's Past," *St. Louis Post-Dispatch*, 14 August 1995, 1, 3.

26. Secretary Babbitt's comments as cited in "Statement on the Failure to Pass House Bill to Create a National Park Closure Commission," DOI, National Park Service news release, 19 September 1995; Phillips, "Can We Save Our National Parks?" 6–7. For the complete text of the Recreational Fee Demonstration Program, see Omnibus Consolidated Rescissions and Appropriations Act of 1996 (PL 104–208).

27. Secretary Babbitt's quote as cited in news release, 19 September 1995; "Commercial Tour Vehicles Fees to Increase under 3-Year Recreation Fee Demonstration Program," DOI, National Park Service news release, 14 January 1997.

28. Sellars's quotes as cited in Christopher Smith, "The Park Service Takes a Hard Look at Itself," *HCN*, 16 March 1998, 1; Richard West Sellars, *Preserving Nature in the National Parks: A History* (New Haven: Yale University Press, 1997), 2–4, 179–80, 206–7. For an in-depth analysis on the benefits and consequences of recreation management, see Russell Martin, *A Story That Stands Like a Dam: Glen Canyon and the Struggle for the Soul of the West* (New York: Henry Holt, 1989), especially 215–80.

29. *Cerro Grande Prescribed Burn: Investigation Report* (Santa Fe: DOI, National Park Service, 18 May 2000), 1–3; "Legislator Urges Fire Prosecution," *Albuquerque Journal North*, 20 June 2000, 1; William deBuys, "Los Alamos Fire Offers a Lesson in Humility," *HCN*, 3 July 2000, 16–17; quote as cited in "Prescribed Fire Talking Points," memorandum, Joe Zarki, National Park Service, Chief of Interpretation, Joshua Tree n.p., 3.

30. Scott Baldauf and Todd Wilkinson, "Across the West: A Burning Question," *Christian Science Monitor*, 15 May 2000, 1–2; Roger Kennedy, "Fires Illuminate Our Illusions in the Southwest," *HCN*, 3 July 2000, 17.

The Bureau of Reclamation and the West, 1945-2000

Donald J. Pisani

Visit the Bureau of Reclamation web site and you'll discover the following: The bureau is the nation's second-largest wholesale water supplier and the nation's second-largest producer of hydroelectric power, after the U.S. Army Corps of Engineers. It operates fifty-eight hydroelectric plants, 348 dams and reservoirs, and 308 recreation areas visited by 90 million people each year. It delivers water to more than 31 million municipal, rural, and industrial water users, including one in five western farmers, who cultivate 10 million acres. That's one-third of the irrigated land in the West. Those farms produce 60 percent of the nation's vegetables and 25 percent of its fruits and nuts.

But there is more. Although the Bureau of Reclamation has not constructed a major dam since the 1970s, it is not just the caretaker of a vast hydraulic museum. In recent years, the web site suggests, the bureau has transformed itself into a champion of the environment, dedicated to preserving wetlands, increasing migratory fish populations, and bringing "competing interests together to find consensus-based approaches in such areas as California's Sacramento Delta/San Francisco Bay to improve water quality." Its objectives now include "water conservation and environmental restoration," "water reclamation, recycling, and reuse," and support for the "self-determination efforts of Native American tribes." These are ambitious goals. Nevertheless, adjusted for inflation, the bureau's $850-million budget for fiscal year 2000 is but a small fraction of its construction budgets in the three decades following World War II.[1]

The Bureau of Reclamation has reinvented itself many times, particularly during the 1930s, after World War II, and in the 1980s and 1990s. The best-known history of water in the West, Marc Reisner's *Cadillac Desert,* suggests that following World War II, the Bureau of Reclamation and Corps of Engineers went on a dam-building "binge." The passion to manage nature, the assumption that Congress had a responsibility to subsidize the economic development of the West, and the desire of federal bureaus to protect their "turf" and expand their budgets all fueled the dam mania. Neither agency exhibited idealism, let alone vision. Wedded as they were to logrolling and pork barrel politics, the Bureau of Reclamation and the Corps of Engineers became a juggernaut beyond democratic control. It mattered little that most Americans found many of the projects they built wasteful and impractical. According to Reisner, the dam builders were stopped not by public opinion but by a simple geological fact: by the 1970s the West had run out of safe dam sites.[2]

There is truth to Reisner's interpretation, but it is only half the truth. In this essay, I will argue that the major impulse behind dam building in the 1950s and the 1960s was a postwar idealism that sought to revive and expand the New Deal of the 1930s and win the Cold War against the Soviet Union. Whatever the power of the dam builders in Congress, they did not lead the charmed life that Reisner suggests. They faced severe criticism, and not just from those dedicated to protecting parks and wilderness areas. That criticism mounted during the 1960s and 1970s, and eventually the public turned against the Bureau of Reclamation and Corps of Engineers. Some critics complained about the sheer cost of projects paid for from the general treasury. Some opposed the massive subsidies to agribusiness in the West. Some chastised the bureau for abandoning the goal of turning the West into a land of family farms. Still others deplored the damage that large water projects inflicted on the environment. In 1945, the great strength of the agency was its idealism. But that idealism proved hard to sustain, particularly in the face of congressional opposition to any form of "social planning." Furthermore, even though dams were icons of progress in the 1930s and 1940s, by the 1970s they represented an old and inflexible technology.

The Bureau of Reclamation—originally the Reclamation Service—was established in 1902 to irrigate desert land. Its mission was not just to create new family farms on the public domain but also to provide supplemental water to established farmers on private land. The objectives of the bureau were inconsistent from the start. Was its goal to stimulate regional economic development or to create a new society? Federal reclamation was not a welfare program. Farmers could claim government land within the projects for nothing, but they had to pay their pro-rata cost of constructing dams and canals in ten years, without interest. The bureau launched thirty water projects in the years from 1905 to 1917, but the agricultural depression of the 1920s and 1930s, added to many other problems, limited the land reclaimed to less than 3 million acres—far from the 100 million acres promised by the most optimistic proponents of the Reclamation Act in 1902. And most of the 3 million acres had been irrigated before 1902.[3]

In the 1920s, the bureau faced a host of seemingly insurmountable problems, including that the farmers it served were unwilling or unable to repay their debt to the government. There was talk of giving the Bureau of Reclamation's work to the Corps of Engineers. The 1930s provided the bureau with new opportunities when it built such high dams as Hoover, Grand Coulee, and Shasta. But most of those dams were authorized to put people to work rather than because their water and power were needed at the time. World War II made high dams look like good investments. By increasing the demand for power, the war gave the bureau a new source of revenue that could be used to subsidize agriculture and provide the agency with a new lease on life.

At the end of World War II, and for some years thereafter, the fear of a return to the depression played a prominent part in Reclamation Bureau planning. In 1944 Bernard DeVoto observed, "The fear is that, terrible as the war is, the coming peace will make these war years seem to have been a time of quiet, order, and optimism. That, ghastly as the problems of war are, the problems of peace will prove worse. That, whatever the war may have done to us, it has kept us comparatively united, comparatively of one purpose, comparatively effective as a society. That, once the external discipline of war is relaxed, there will be grave danger of our collapsing into disorder, disunity, civil and social strife. That whereas war has brought us hope, or at least courage, the coming peace may bring despair." Not the least of DeVoto's fears was that jobs would have to be found for 12 million former soldiers, sailors, and marines, along with countless workers from the defense industry. Public works became a vital part of reconversion to a peacetime economy.[4]

New Deal Democrats assumed that the West had sufficient potential water projects that they could be used as a *permanent* economic stimulus to prevent recessions, ensure full employment, and sustain economic growth. Not surprisingly, in April 1945, the bureau presented to Congress plans for 415 irrigation and multiple-purpose water projects in seventeen western states. State by state the number varied, from a modest five projects in Washington to ninety-six in Montana, and from 101,000 acres in Utah to 2.2 million acres in California. These projects were expected to add 11 million acres of new land to cultivation and provide supplemental water to nearly as many acres of old land, in all twice the amount of land irrigated in 1945.[5]

In 1945, Reclamation Bureau officials regarded the West as an undeveloped region: it contained only 20 percent of the nation's population, a fourth of its farms, and an even smaller share of its industry. If the West did not continue the process of industrialization begun during the war, its economy would stagnate. But industrialization could advance only if the federal government provided the West with new dams for power and irrigation. A second assumption followed from the first: in the future almost all major water projects would be built by the federal government, not by private companies, municipalities, or the states. Save for California and Texas, the cost of such multiple-purpose projects lay beyond the means of the western states. Third, hydroelectricity was not just the cheapest and most reliable form of power available to westerners, its use would help to conserve other natural resources, including oil, coal, and natural gas. In this way, the Reclamation Bureau would strengthen the nation's defenses. Fourth, the crop surpluses of the 1930s were a thing of the past, if only because the United States would have to feed large parts of Europe and Asia for decades after the war was over. There was no danger of bringing too much land into production too fast.

World War II solved many chronic farm problems. Farm income more than doubled between 1939 and 1945, and the amount invested in machinery more than tripled. The need for food and fiber wiped out the surpluses of the 1930s, the demand for soldiers and war workers drained off the surplus farm population, and high wartime crop prices restored agriculture to a prosperity that lasted into the 1950s. Farmers on government irrigation projects doubled their production between Pearl Harbor and the end of the war, and the value of their crops increased by more than 250 percent from 1941 to 1945. Postwar demands for food and fiber in Europe, and generous price supports from the Department of Agriculture, sustained prosperity after the war. Reclamation Bureau officials believed, as they had always believed, in a direct correlation between the rate of population increase and the expansion of irrigation. In the decade from 1940 to 1950, the population of the seventeen western states rose by nearly 25 percent, and the number of people in California, Washington, and Oregon soared by 48 percent. The population of the entire nation increased by 15 percent during the same decade.[6]

Hundreds of thousands of war workers moved west during World War II, and the hydroelectric power produced at dams like Grand Coulee and Hoover contributed to the relocation of much of the defense industry, particularly aircraft and shipbuilding. Half the military airplanes produced in the United States during World War II were built with the power from one dam, Grand Coulee. When the war ended, or so it was widely assumed, cheap and abundant hydroelectric power would expand the region's industrial base and give the West the balanced or diversified economy it had long lacked.[7]

In the years between 1945 and 1948, the cold war against the Soviet Union dominated every aspect of American life. It proved a mixed blessing for the Bureau of Reclamation. The bureau provided much of the power and food needed to defend the free world against communism. Nevertheless, the struggle against Russia also helped to undermine the New Deal, or the Fair Deal as it was called in the Truman administration. It shifted attention from domestic to international concerns and killed the idealism that sustained political reform. And by draining money from the civilian economy, it threatened to undermine the standard of living that distinguished the United States from the Soviet Union. "Indeed," as Secretary of the Interior Oscar Chapman observed in 1951, "the final test of victory will lie in the answer to this simple question: Is America richer, stronger, better able to provide her people with a good life and to assume her position of world leadership than she was before the challenge [of the cold war] was first raised?" Chapman feared that if the United States returned to a wartime economy, "we shall find that the old economic freedoms which give American life so much of its richness have disappeared. We shall be supporting an enormous budget, with a huge proportion for defense, and yet find ourselves poor as church mice where our great basic [social] programs are involved." The United States must, Chapman warned, avoid the "pinched, Spartan existence which is inevitable under a straight military economy."[8]

Nevertheless, there was a great deal of idealism within the Reclamation Bureau after World War II. That idealism is often overlooked by historians who think of the bureau as a pack of engineers bent on building as many dams as possible as rapidly as possible. For example, arid land reclamation was quickly perceived as an instrument of international diplomacy, and the Reclamation Bureau developed close ties to the State Department. The Cold War gave the Bureau of Reclamation a new mission as the defender of freedom and democracy around the world. In 1945, on his return from the Yalta Conference, President Franklin D. Roosevelt asked to fly over the Arabian Desert, and that experience suggested that a major dam project in the Middle East would relieve poverty and the danger of revolution. "When I get through being President of the United States and this damn war is over," FDR remarked to his secretary of labor, Frances Perkins, "I think Eleanor and I will go to the Near East and see if we can manage to put over an operation like the Tennessee Valley system that will really make something of that country. I would love to do it." In 1944 John L. Savage, the Reclamation Bureau's chief design engineer, a man who had played a large part in planning the Grand Coulee, Shasta, and Boulder dams, went to China at the request of the Chinese government. There he made preliminary surveys for a gigantic power, irrigation, and flood control project on the Yangtze River. He also spent several months inspecting likely water projects in India. At the end of the war, thirty-eight engineers from fifteen foreign countries visited Reclamation Bureau projects and offices, and the bureau launched a program to teach its methods to foreign engineers. Nineteen engineers from China began training with the bureau in the summer of 1945.[9]

As the cold war deepened, dam building became a major diplomatic weapon. The widespread human suffering in Asia, Africa, and the Middle East, it was widely believed, offered fertile ground to the spread of communism. Yet the so-called underdeveloped world was full of potential water projects that could eliminate or mitigate poverty, just as the Tennessee Valley Authority had improved the lives of poor residents of Tennessee and Alabama during the 1930s. Some projects were staggering in size. For example, the Yangtze River project would have impounded twice the water captured by Boulder Dam and generated twice the electricity produced by the Grand Coulee, Boulder, and Shasta dams combined. In fiscal year 1952, the bureau sent ninety-two employees to twenty-two different countries on thirty-three separate missions. The countries included Costa Rica, Ethiopia, India, Iran, Iraq, Jordan, Lebanon, Liberia, Libya, Northern Rhodesia, and Thailand. The bureau also arranged international water conferences, including the first "International Reclamation Conference," held in Yakima, Washington, in June 1952. It was attended by representatives from twenty nations.[10]

At home, New Deal and Cold War idealism could be seen in the Reclamation Bureau's abortive attempts to revive homemaking after the war. In many parts of the West, the average farm size increased dramatically during the agricultural depression that extended from 1920 to 1940. Average farm size in Montana leaped from 480 acres to 821 acres and in Wyoming from 749 to 1,866 acres. Tenancy had also increased. In 1946, Commissioner of Reclamation Michael Straus predicted that within five years the bureau would have opened more than 45,000 family-sized farms on 4 million acres.[11] The bureau's magazine, *Reclamation Era,* promised that federal reclamation would provide as many homes to returning veterans and their families as it had created during the four decades prior to World War II. The first farms would be on the Klamath, Yakima, Minidoka, and Shoshone projects, but the single-largest project would be in the Columbia River basin, where the bureau hoped to have at least 400,000 acres ready for settlement by 1950 or 1951. "The ultimate objective of the Bureau of Reclamation and its staff," *Reclamation Era* reported, "is to develop the West through the creation of permanent family farms on Federal Reclamation projects."[12]

The irrigable public domain was long gone by the 1930s. Therefore postwar government projects would reclaim private land or land purchased by the federal government. As early as 1906, Congress had prohibited the bureau from laying out model towns, building roads, schools, and sanitation systems, or selling electricity directly to consumers for purposes other than pumping water for irrigation. In anticipation of the end of the war, however, in 1943 Congress authorized the bureau to buy up more than 1 million acres of privately owned, dry-farmed land north of Pasco, Washington, subdivide it, and lay out 10,000 to 20,000 farms. At the time, the irrigable lands of the Columbia River basin were inhabited by struggling ranchers and wheat farmers. By regulating land sales and enforcing the 160-acre limitation on water each farmer could receive, the bureau hoped to prevent the chronic land speculation that had undermined the effectiveness of both private and public irrigation projects in the past. Project towns and farms were expected to provide homes for more than 300,000 people. Central Washington, it was hoped, would become a model for future government reclamation projects within the Colorado and Missouri basins.[13]

The Columbia River project was as close to planned settlement as the bureau ever got, but it failed to live up to expectations. Congress required the bureau to cooperate with the state of Washington and local irrigation districts in planning the project, but there was constant tension among federal, state, and local officials. There were also problems with drainage and alkali. Project land proved incapable of producing high-value crops, and government farmers resisted planning and direction—as farmers always had on government projects. By 1958 the project was still only half complete, and it was home to fewer than 2,300 families rather than the 10,000 to 15,000 anticipated at the end of the war.

The Columbia Basin Project did not result in the resettlement of farmers from marginal lands on the Great Plains, nor did it become a land of small subsistence farms. Most settlers came from Washington or Utah. They were not young men looking for a fresh start–the median age was forty. Nor were they poor–over half had family assets of more than $20,000. They did not relish building homes on the land, and one-third lived in towns or cities, usually within twenty or thirty miles of their farms. Worse still, 25 percent of those who owned Columbia Basin Project land received 75 percent of the government benefits. In 1968, the bureau turned the project over to three irrigation districts, tacit acknowledgment that the federal government would never complete it. Had the bureau finished the project, the results would have been even worse. "It would be a collection of family farms ranging from forty to eighty acres," the leading historian of the Columbia Basin Project has concluded, "none of them capable of supplying their owners with a satisfactory living. The area would be a rural slum. It is for the best that this aspect of the project failed."[14]

In the years immediately following the war, the Reclamation Bureau received as many as a thousand queries a month from returning veterans who wanted land, but in 1947 the government could offer only 245 farms covering 20,000 acres. By 1952, less than 4 percent of the veterans who had applied to the Reclamation Bureau for a government farm had received one, compared to 13 percent after World War I. Secretary of the Interior Julius Krug blamed "large land companies and their adherents" for thwarting the bureau's plans. But within the bureau there was also opposition to the creation of family farms for settlers with limited means. In the 1930s, the bureau had shifted its focus to the urban West. The bureau's history from 1902 to 1940, some of its leaders feared, suggested that only those who were prosperous when they took up government farms would succeed. A return to homemaking would invite a "welfare class" onto the projects, a class destined to fail no matter how much federal aid it received. Therefore the bureau required a family to have $7,500 in savings before it could move onto the Columbia Basin Project, and it expected them to have several times this amount in assets. The dream of turning the West into a democratic Eden or "planned promise land" through the resettlement of veterans on government water projects disappeared in the 1960s.[15]

The Reclamation Bureau had other reasons to fear large-scale planning, including its distrust of autonomous river basin authorities. During and after the war, a handful of western Democrats pushed legislation to transplant the Tennessee Valley Authority model to the West, legislation nominally favored by presidents Franklin D. Roosevelt and Harry S Truman. New Deal planners hoped that river basin authorities would result in the marriage of national and local government, limiting state authority over water. But the Reclamation Bureau feared that such authorities would restrict its ability to survey, plan, select, and build western water projects, particularly within the Columbia, Missouri, and Colorado river basins.[16]

The bureau never entirely rejected the idea of regional governments. Such authorities could lay the foundation for public power, and for a time the bureau advocated building its own transmission lines and steam power plants to supplement the hydroelectricity generated by its dams. In that way, it could become the West's major source of power. President Truman favored expanding the bureau's role in electrifying the West, but Congress rejected it, even after the Democrats regained control of Congress in 1948. Opposition to direct sales of power to consumers, and to community planning, became so intense that in 1948

Congress refused to appropriate money to pay the salary of any reclamation commissioner who was not an engineer. In the early 1950s, the fear of "creeping socialism" and opposition to the "Sovietization" of the West undermined what remained of the idealism that had been so strong in 1945.[17]

Marc Reisner characterizes the postwar period as the "Go-Go Years." He can be faulted for ignoring the powerful impact of the New Deal and Cold War on postwar planning, but some water projects that appeared in the 1950s and 1960s *were* incredible. The Pacific Southwest Water Plan, proposed in 1964, included a thousand-mile aqueduct to carry a water supply half the size of the average flow of the Colorado River from the Columbia River, past a string of irrigation projects in Oregon and Nevada, to southern California. It was rejected not because it was impractical or too expensive but because Senator Henry "Scoop" Jackson of Washington opposed it. Another scheme, released by the bureau in 1971, proposed pumping water uphill from the Mississippi River to the High Plains of West Texas and New Mexico, where groundwater depletion threatened a collapse of the local economy. The electrical power needed to defy gravity would have exceeded all the energy used in the entire state of Texas at that time.[18]

A project nearly as questionable won the approval of Congress in 1968, in no small part because of Senator Carl Hayden of Arizona. This was the Central Arizona Project, the single largest public works appropriation ever made by Congress. When asked why the project had been authorized, Floyd Dominy, the commissioner of the Reclamation Bureau in the 1960s, responded: "Well—number one—Senator Hayden was a man that I loved." More important, Senator Hayden was a powerful member of the Senate Appropriations Committee, and no water project, east or west, could be approved without his support. Everyone in Congress deferred to Carl Hayden.

The legislation passed in 1968 was designed to pacify both upstream and downstream interests on the Colorado River. Upstream, a series of new dams would be built, and downstream, an aqueduct from Lake Mead, the reservoir behind Hoover Dam, to Las Vegas and a 300-mile-long aqueduct across Arizona that would pass by Phoenix on its way to Tucson. This aqueduct carried more water each year than the annual supplies of Cleveland, Detroit, and Chicago combined, and it included a massive pump system to lift the water more than 1,000 feet as well as a series of reservoirs to store it. The increasing political clout of the southwestern United States was demonstrated in 1984. As the Central Arizona Aqueduct neared completion, only one of the five projects slated for Colorado was under construction.[19]

Dams often threatened the boundaries of national parks and wilderness areas, and they tested the vigilance of conservation groups in the 1950s and the 1960s.[20] The struggle to protect Echo Park, which many historians credit for creating the modern environmental movement, is well known. The debate centered on whether public works projects should take precedence over the sanctity of national parks and whether economic growth should take priority over the rights of future generations.[21] There was far more to these battles than protecting extraordinary scenery in remote parts of the West. Gradually, as Samuel P. Hays has shown, middle-class Americans came to see wilderness in very personal terms—as part of their own backyard and as an antidote to a highly regimented society rather than as an obstacle to progress. Americans no longer feared unemployment or a return to the Great Depression, and their attitudes toward nature were changing.[22]

More and more Americans thought that rivers ought to be preserved in their existing state for future generations, not managed to the last drop. Just as Congress enacted legislation to protect wilderness areas in 1964, it protected wild, scenic, and recreational rivers in 1965. The "wild" rivers, like the wilderness areas, were "living museums" of nature. They constituted less than 2 percent of the waterways in the United States, but putting them off-limits sharply reduced the remaining dam sites available to the Bureau of Reclamation and the Army Corps of Engineers. Even within cities, rivers once seen as sewers were now regarded as amenities. Riverfronts became parks complete with bicycle and jogging paths. The recreational value of rivers–for urban dwellers as well as for those who rafted through the Grand Canyon–symbolized a new kind of consumer economy in which experiencing nature was as important as purchasing factory goods.[23]

Yet it was not just a greater appreciation for nature that undermined public faith in dams and canals. As the West's population grew in the decades after World War II and as California eclipsed New York as the most populous state in the Union, easterners became more and more concerned as their residents, as well as their tax dollars, moved west. In the late nineteenth century, western politicians complained that their region did not get its fair share of the money Congress spent on river and harbor improvements. But from 1950 to 1976, the Northeast received only 6 percent of the funds spent by the Corps of Engineers and the Bureau of Reclamation. The West received about half the money spent and the South 28 percent. By the time Jimmy Carter became president in 1977, residents of northeastern cities complained that they were subsidizing the growth of southwestern cities at their expense. The "Rust Belt" took a stand against the "Sun Belt."[24]

Equally important, criticism of massive Bureau of Reclamation subsidies to western farmers mounted. Taxpayers paid twice for irrigation projects, first for the direct subsidy and then for the crop price-support programs required, partly because of overproduction on subsidized lands in the West.[25] In an age of crop surpluses, it made little sense to cultivate subsidized cotton in the San Joaquin Valley and pay farmers not to grow cotton in the South. The Bureau of Reclamation irrigated land while the U.S. Department of Agriculture attempted to hold down agricultural production through its Soil Bank Program, its Cropland Conversion Program, the Commodity Diversion Program, and the Cropland Adjustment Program, all of which were designed to convert cropped land into fields of trees and grass. More than 50 million acres of land had been idled by government farm programs, and more than one-third of all available farmland was unused. Why expand irrigation in the West when the production of food and fiber on already cultivated land could be increased by 40 or 50 percent simply through the use of new insecticides and farm machinery?[26]

At the end of World War II, 95 percent of the money spent on federal reclamation was reimbursable; only 5 percent of project construction costs were excused in the name of navigation improvement or flood control. The Reclamation Project Act of 1939 permitted the bureau to write off the cost of these benefits as well as fish and wildlife protection. After the war, the bureau wanted to add to that list recreation, salinity abatement, sediment control, public health, the promotion of the national defense, and international treaty obligations.[27] In 1978, agricultural economist Philip LeVeen estimated that western farmers repaid only 3 percent of the cost of land reclaimed by the federal government. Proceeds from the sale of electricity paid for 57 percent of the cost, but another 40 percent came from general tax revenues. On the Westlands Irrigation District in the San Joaquin Valley, farmers repaid only 10 percent of the cost of constructing their irrigation works, and 70 percent of their profit came from federal subsidies.[28]

Aside from the subsidies, critics of the Reclamation Bureau raised doubts whether dams represented the best technology for generating electrical power. In the dark days of the Cold War, military strategists worried that centralizing the production of power at huge dams would make the United States more vulnerable to attack from Soviet missiles. If the Soviet Union targeted the West's massive dams, it could cripple the region's economy—including much of the defense industry. Then, too, there had always been questions about whether hydroelectric power was as reliable as steam-generated power. Few high dams produced a flow of water consistent enough to generate the same amount of power all year long, and the cost of steam-powered plants had declined markedly during the 1920s, 1930s, and 1940s. Increasingly, hydroelectric power was used to supplement steam-generated electricity, rather than the reverse.

The promise of atomic energy also raised doubts about the wisdom of building more high dams. In the 1940s, David Brower suggested that this form of power would make dams obsolete long before they began to silt up. "If we learn to use it [atomic energy] properly . . . we won't need to harness all the rivers of the land. . . . At least we might wait a little while and see what happens before we drown out our greatest canyons and destroy forever so much natural beauty." One dream of the post–World War II era was to use the atom to desalinize water from the oceans, rendering unnecessary dams and canals to serve the cities of the Pacific Coast. By the 1960s, General Electric produced reactors that could generate more power than the largest existing or planned bureau dams, at half the installation cost. Atomic plants also had the advantage that they could be situated closer to cities and more accessible to transportation and raw materials. Eventually, nuclear power would be seen as even more of a threat to the environment than dams, but that was not true in the 1950s and 1960s.[29]

By the early 1970s, study after study revealed that dams damaged or threatened the environment, including the Ralph Nader study group's *Damming the West,* published in 1973.[30] R. L. Coughlin of the Federal Water Quality Administration observed, "The Bureau of Reclamation is the prime source of water pollution in the far West. They manage their damn reservoirs as if they had blinders on." Critics also pointed to massive fish kills in the Snake and the Columbia rivers. Bureau dams did not just interfere with the spawning of salmon, they altered the temperature and oxygen level in water far below the dams. Dams also increased the impact of municipal and industrial wastes by reducing the capacity of rivers to dilute sewage and chemicals. The result was the prolific growth of algae and eutrophication.[31]

Equally important, by the 1970s the West was running out of safe, let alone cost-effective, dam sites. As Marc Reisner put it, "Fontenelle [on the Green River in southwestern Wyoming] was an inferior site compared with Flaming Gorge, as Glen Canyon was inferior to Hoover, as Auburn was vastly inferior to Shasta. . . . The Bureau was now being forced to build on sites it had rejected forty, fifty, or sixty years earlier. It was building on them because while the ideal damsites had rapidly disappeared, the demand for new projects had not."[32]

The collapse of the Teton Dam provided a prime example. Finished during the winter of 1975, the dam stood 300 feet above the bed of the Teton River—a tributary of the Snake—and stretched nearly 3,000 feet across the canyon. Unfortunately, it was erected in what geologists call a "fill valley" created by earthquake faults. Three grout curtains were used to prevent seepage under and around the dam, but the first leak appeared on June 3, 1976, and two days later the north end of the dam gave way, sending a ten-foot tidal wave down the valley, killing eleven people, leaving 15,000 homeless, drowning 13,000 cattle, and stripping the topsoil from 100,000 acres of prime farmland. In all, the failure of the Teton Dam cost a billion dollars in property damages. An independent study of the disaster concluded that the dam had not been properly designed for its location.[33]

The Teton Dam disaster had little impact on public works spending for fiscal year 1977. But it came in the wake of other bad news for the Bureau of Reclamation. In August 1975, an earthquake of 5.9 magnitude hit Oroville, California, on a seismic fault thought to be inactive. The quake raised doubts about the safety of the proposed Auburn Dam above Sacramento, which was also on or near a supposedly "inactive" fault. Bureau of Reclamation studies required by the state of California revealed that a complete failure of the Auburn Dam would render 750,000 people homeless, put five military bases out of commission, and destroy the state capital. More than $200 million had been invested in the project when work was halted. The dam was not financially feasible, anyway. The water it stored would cost more than seven times the price of water from Shasta Dam and over three times the cost of water from Oroville Dam. Auburn Dam would cost ten times the amount originally authorized by Congress, more than all the money the bureau had spent in California since the 1930s.[34]

Much has been made of Jimmy Carter's "hit list," his abortive attempt to reduce pork barrel spending on federal water projects. Carter was a "New Democrat" who came to Washington in the post-Watergate era. It was a time characterized by public hostility toward the "Old Politics" and "stagflation." The American economy was in the doldrums, afflicted by double-digit inflation. In

April 1977, Carter deleted eighteen water projects from the proposed fiscal year 1978 budget, which had been prepared by the Ford administration. A firestorm of criticism exploded in the West, which persuaded the president to backtrack and cut the number in half. This concession did not placate those who thought that Congress, not the president, should control the purse strings, but environmentalists now considered the president as inconstant, inconsistent, and undependable. Carter, who owned a family peanut farm in Georgia, supported California governor Jerry Brown's demand that the 160-acre limitation on the amount of water each farmer could receive from the Bureau of Reclamation be raised to 1,260 acres, and he supported cheap water for one of the West's most heavily subsidized irrigation projects, the Westlands Irrigation District in the San Joaquin Valley. He opposed many new water projects, but he had little interest in challenging agribusiness.[35]

Jimmy Carter learned his lesson too late. Yet from the perspective of the Bureau of Reclamation, this was much ado about very little. Most projects cut by Carter were Corps of Engineers schemes. The bureau continued to build water projects into the 1980s, but the last major authorization for a *new* project came in 1968. Long before the collapse of Teton Dam, and long before Jimmy Carter became president, irrigation had begun to move to the center of the country, where dam sites were few and farmers relied heavily on underground water. Underground water was less subject to litigation than surface water, and the supply was more dependable. The Great Plains covered vast pools of water, such as the Ogallala Aquifer, and a new generation of powerful gasoline pumps pulled the water to the surface. Often center-pivot irrigation systems distributed that water. By the 1960s and 1970s, most new land opened to irrigation was in Texas, Nebraska, Colorado, Kansas, and the Dakotas, not in the Far West. During the 1970s, irrigated land in California increased less than 2 percent per year as opposed to 9 percent on the Great Plains. Put another way, the High Plains accounted for 40 percent of the new acreage irrigated in the West between 1945 and 1974.[36]

In a time of scarcity and constraints, officials in the Bureau of Reclamation recognized that the age of the high dam had passed. It made little sense to invest billions of dollars in new dams and canals when a small fraction of that amount spent on conservation could expand the water supply at far less cost. Lining ditches with concrete, using sprinkler and drip irrigation, and carrying water to crops through underground pipes rather than furrows made sense. In any event, when Ronald Reagan, James Watt, and David Stockman came to Washington in 1981, they demanded that those who benefited from water projects—whether the projects involved navigation, flood control, or irrigation—pay more of the cost. The result was a stalemate, and in the West no major dams were authorized in the 1980s or 1990s. Cost sharing was a very old idea, an idea that the Bureau of Reclamation had first suggested before World War I, but it never had much support in the West. Although the future of the Bureau of Reclamation was uncertain, the boom years of dam building were clearly over.[37]

Conclusion

Historians often attribute far more power and foresight to the Bureau of Reclamation than it exercised. For example, the bureau faced a rapidly changing economy in which agricultural productivity increased far faster than the nation's population. The per-acre yield of wheat more than doubled between 1940 and 1970, and the per-acre yield of potatoes tripled. Put another way, in 1940 one farm-worker fed eleven people; twenty years later he fed twenty-six. Meanwhile the number of farms declined across the United States, from 6.1 million in 1940 to 3.7 million in 1960, and the average farm size increased from 174 to 302 acres. In 1935, the farm population was 25 percent of the nation's total; by 1980, less than 3 percent. Rural life was not attractive to most Americans, and for good reason. By 1970 the proportion of rural residents living below the poverty line was twice that of urban dwellers, and in many parts of the nation the family farm had become synonymous with rural slums. There was less and less justification for reclaiming arid land.[38]

Federal reclamation had been launched with ambiguous goals, but subsistence agriculture and regional economic development often clashed. By the 1930s, and increasingly during and after World War II, building up the West meant building up the region's cities. Indeed, Bureau of Reclamation water policies gave rural residents plenty of excuses to flee their alfalfa farms for the defense plants of Seattle, Oakland, Portland, or Los Angeles.

This inconsistency in objectives contributed to changing public attitudes toward dams from the 1940s to the 1970s. A 1948 article in *Fortune* magazine proclaimed, "When men of future centuries come to examine the artifacts of this age, the great dams will stand as monuments to whatever civilization we have had the wisdom to produce, still delivering their legacies of power to new generations under the sun. . . . The great dams, more than armies, are a big part of the real power of the West."[39] From the 1930s to the 1970s, the vision of the Reclamation Bureau shifted from the rural to the urban West, from the land to be reclaimed to the dams themselves, and from homemaking to technology. As dams grew in size, as they became capable of generating ever-larger numbers of jobs and greater amounts of power revenue, their story eclipsed the older saga of the transformation of the land. In the 1930s and the 1940s, dams commemorated the human desire to transcend nature and to escape the unpredictable and the transitory in life. By the 1970s, however, they were concrete anchors to the past, reminders of an age of rigid, inflexible, and simple technology, relics of an age vexed by very different problems from those Americans faced in the 1970s and after. A few, such as Hoover Dam, still inspired awe, but their very size also prompted deep misgivings and dismay. Were these monuments to human ingenuity or to human folly?

It was not just the dams that came into question; so too did the men who built them. By the late 1960s, engineers were no longer the statesmen of progress they had been in 1902 or 1950. The war in Vietnam had undermined faith in "the experts," and engineers were the quintessential experts. Although Americans exhibited a naive faith in technology and the ability of technology to solve human problems, no amount of technology seemed able to win the Vietnam War, and no amount of technology seemed able to provide the West with an unlimited supply of water. In the 1970s, a growing sense of scarcity and limits afflicted Americans, ranging from long lines at gasoline pumps during the Arab oil embargo to tight money in Congress. Big water projects were one of the casualties of retrenchment.

The political context also changed. Congress generally lumped water projects together in omnibus bills, making it difficult for representatives and senators to oppose bad projects because a vote against one was a vote against all. And when a bill landed on the president's desk, he had the same choice: take all or none. The success of such legislation depended on the strength of the "iron triangles" that drafted it. Iron triangles are, of course, alliances among federal bureaus, local interest groups, and congressional committees that permit the triumph of public works projects that enjoy little widespread support. This explanation suggests that ideology and differences between the two major political parties played little part in the Reclamation Bureau's history. A powerful combination of real estate speculators, private construction companies, industrialists, and agribusiness interests pushed water projects through Congress.

The iron triangle is at best a partial explanation of why the Bureau of Reclamation built so many water projects after World War II. Prior to the New Deal, the West's population was small, and the midwestern farm bloc successfully resisted any substantial expansion of federal reclamation. Between the 1920s and 1950s, however, the power of the old agricultural states in Congress declined dramatically, as did the power of the Department of Agriculture to resist the expanding authority of the Department of Interior, which was home to the Bureau of Reclamation. The declining importance of agriculture in the American economy, as well as the growing wealth of the United States after World War II, counted for more than iron triangles.

Seniority in Congress, the flamboyant personalities of such bureau leaders as Michael Straus and Floyd Dominy, and a new generation of presidents who practiced the politics of fiscal constraint also mattered. The West, like the South, returned many of its politicians to office term after term, giving them seniority on key congressional committees. As mentioned earlier, Carl Hayden was particularly powerful as chair of the Senate Appropriations Committee. And both Straus and Dominy were larger than life. "I became Reclamation," Dominy once observed, "and I'm proud as hell of the fact that for 13 years I ran the damn place. And I was running it long before that, but they wouldn't admit it." Dominy was not an engineer, but he was a politician—one with great personal magnetism and incredible boldness. Finally, in the 1970s, 1980s, and 1990s presidents tripped the balance against new water projects despite considerable support for those projects within Congress. Presidents do matter, and no president since the mid-1970s has been a fan of water projects.[40]

Who knows what the future holds for the Bureau of Reclamation? Will we enter an era of "green pork," as the bureau attempts to carry out its new conservation agenda? Will cleaning up selenium and other dangerous by-products of irrigation give the bureau a new mission? Or building new dams to replace unsafe ones? Or tearing down dams? Will the bureau be able to live in harmony with western environmental groups? Who knows? But one thing is certain: water will remain the most important public policy issue in the West. The trends seem inexorable. Phoenix and Las Vegas model their futures on Los Angeles, and more and more the region is characterized by what Gerald Nash once called "urban oases."[41] The Bureau of Reclamation was created to decentralize America, but the West contains most of the nation's fastest-growing cities. The bureau no longer commands the power it exercised in 1950 or 1960, but its legacy is still enormous.

Notes

1. "Bureau of Reclamation Fact Sheet," dated 23 August 2000, On the same web site, see the bureau's annual report for 1998. The most complete statistical compilation of Bureau of Reclamation activities is the Department of the Interior's *1992 Summary Statistics: Water, Land, and Related Data* (Denver: U.S. Department of the Interior, n.d.). My thanks to Brit Storey, senior historian of the Bureau of Reclamation, who kindly provided additional data on the bureau's recent activities.

2. Marc Reisner, *Cadillac Desert: The American West and Its Disappearing Water* (New York: Viking, 1986). Other histories of water in the West include Donald Worster's *Rivers of Empire: Water, Aridity & the Growth of the American West* (New York: Pantheon Books, 1985) and Daniel McCool's *Command of the Waters: Iron Triangles, Federal Water Development, and Indian Water* (Berkeley: University of California Press, 1987).

3. The most dispassionate and reliable survey of federal reclamation is still Paul Wallace Gates's "Reclamation of the Arid Lands," in his *History of Public Land Law Development* (New York: Arno Press, 1979), 635–98.

4. Bernard DeVoto, "The Easy Chair," *Harper's Magazine* 188 (March 1944): 345; "Basis for Postwar Planning: One-Fifth of a Nation Government Owned," *Business Week* 720 (June 19, 1943): 57–58; Stuart Chase, "Big Government," *Survey Graphic* 33 (December 1944): 487.

5. *Annual Report of the Secretary of the Interior for the Fiscal Year Ended June 30, 1945* (Washington, D.C.: GPO, 1945), xii–xiii; *Annual Report of the Secretary of the Interior, Fiscal Year Ended June 30, 1948* (Washington, D.C.: GPO, 1948), 3–4, 14.

6. Gilbert C. Fite, *American Farmers: The New Minority* (Bloomington: Indiana University Press, 1981), 80; Donald E. Green, *Land of the Underground Rain: Irrigation on the Texas High Plains, 1910–1970* (Austin: University of Texas Press, 1973), 146; *Annual Report of the Secretary of the Interior for the Fiscal Year Ended June 30, 1944* (Washington, D.C.: GPO, 1944), 10; *Annual Report of the Secretary of the Interior for the Fiscal Year Ended June 30, 1945* (Washington, D.C.: GPO, 1945), 7.

7. Wayne Whittaker, "Power for Our Western Empire," *Popular Mechanics* 82 (September 1944): 18–25.

8. Reisner, *Cadillac Desert*, 169–70; *Annual Report of the Secretary of the Interior, Fiscal Year Ended June 30, 1948* (Washington, D.C.: GPO, 1948), 52; *Annual Report of the Secretary of the Interior, Fiscal Year Ended June 30, 1951* (Washington, D.C.: GPO, 1951), iv–vi.

9. Willard R. Espy, "Dams for the Floods of War," *New York Times Magazine*, October 27, 1946, 12–13, 56–58; *Annual Report of the Secretary of the Interior, Fiscal Year Ended June 30, 1945* (Washington, D.C.: GPO, 1945), 36–37.

10. *Annual Report of the Secretary of the Interior, Fiscal Year Ended June 30, 1951* (Washington, D.C.: GPO, 1951), xxxix; *Annual Report of the Secretary of the Interior, Fiscal Year Ended June 30, 1952* (Washington, D.C.: GPO, 1952), 15, 22–23.

11. *Annual Report of the Secretary of the Interior, Fiscal Year Ended June 30, 1946* (Washington, D.C.: GPO, 1946), 57.

12. Goodrich W. Lineweaver, "The Human Side," *Reclamation Era* 32 (May 1946): 110; John R. Murdock, "Veterans—Here's Your Farm," ibid., 95–96; "Return of the Homesteader," ibid., 32 (July 1946): 149–50.

13. The Public Works Administration had constructed Grand Coulee Dam during the 1930s, but in that decade there was no demand for irrigated land in the Pacific Northwest, and markets for hydroelectric power were limited.

14. Paul C. Pitzer, *Grand Coulee: Harnessing a Dream* (Pullman: Washington State University Press, 1994), 176–87, 287–88, 298–99, 315, 327, 329, 365–67. The quote appears on p. 367. See also Alfred R. Golze, *Reclamation in the United States* (New York: McGraw-Hill Book Co., 1952), 176–87. On postwar enthusiasm for the Columbia Basin Project, see "Columbia Basin Reclamation," *New Republic* 113 (13 August 1945): 145, and Rafe Gibbs, "Million-Acre Boom," *Collier's* 119 (1 March 1947): 14–15, 58.

15. *Annual Report of the Secretary of the Interior, Fiscal Year Ended June 30, 1946* (Washington, D.C.: GPO, 1946), 4–5; Golze, *Reclamation in the United States,* 369–72; Pitzer, *Grand Coulee,* 308.

16. On river basin authorities after the war, see Donald J. Pisani, "Federal Water Policy and the Rural West," in *The Rural West Since World War II,* ed. R. Douglas Hurt (Lawrence: University Press of Kansas, 1998), 120–27. See also Elmo Richardson, *Dams, Parks and Politics: Resource Development and Preservation in the Truman-Eisenhower Era* (Lexington: University Press of Kentucky, 1973); Henry Hart, *The Dark Missouri* (Madison: University of Wisconsin Press, 1957); and Marian E. Ridgeway, *The Missouri Basin's Pick-Sloan Plan* (Urbana: University of Illinois Press, 1955).

17. Charles Coate, "'The New School of Thought': Reclamation and the Fair Deal, 1945–1953," *Journal of the West* 22 (April 1983): 58–63; Clayton R. Koppes, "Public Water, Private Land: Origins of the Acreage Limitation Controversy, 1933–1953," *Pacific Historical Review* 47 (November 1978): 607–36; Joseph Kinsey Howard, "Golden River: What's to Be Done About the Missouri?" *Harper's Magazine* 190 (May 1945): 522.

18. Reisner, *Cadillac Desert,* 13, 284–88.

19. Reisner, *Cadillac Desert,* 300–16; Dennis Hanson, "Pumping Billions into the Desert," *Audubon Magazine* 79 (May 1977): 133–45.

20. See, for example, the following articles in *Living Wilderness:* Laurette S. Collier, "Congress and Jackson Hole Monument" 10 (February 1945): 28–31; Bernard Frank, "The Wilderness: A Major Water Resource" 11 (June 1946): 5–16; "The Lake Solitude Case" 13 (spring 1948): 15–25; and "News Items of Interest" 13 (summer 1948): 24–29. See also Bernard DeVoto, "Shall We Let Them Ruin Our National Parks?" *Saturday Evening Post* 223 (22 July 1950): 17–19, 42–48.

21. Mark W. T. Harvey, *A Symbol of Wilderness: Echo Park and the American Conservation Movement* (Albuquerque: University of New Mexico Press, 1994).

22. Samuel P. Hays, *Beauty, Health, and Permanence: Environmental Politics in the United States, 1955–1985* (New York: Cambridge University Press, 1987), and Hays, "Three Decades of Environmental Politics: The Historical Context," in *Government and Environmental Politics: Essays on Historical Developments Since World War II,* ed. Michael J. Lacey (Baltimore: Johns Hopkins University Press, 1989), 19–79.

23. Tim Palmer, *Endangered Rivers and the Conservation Movement* (Berkeley: University of California Press, 1986), 138, 147.

24. Ibid., 182–83.

25. Kenneth D. Frederick, "Irrigation and the Future of American Agriculture," in *The Future of American Agriculture as a Strategic Resource,* eds. Sandra S. Batie and Robert G. Healy (Washington, D.C.: The Conservation Foundation, 1980), 165, 187.

26. Richard L. Berkman and W. Kip Viscusi, *Damming the West* (New York: Grossman Publishers, 1973), 15.

27. Ibid., 79; *Annual Report of the Secretary of the Interior for the Fiscal Year Ended June 30, 1944* (Washington, D.C.: GPO, 1944), 4; *Annual Report of the Secretary of the Interior, Fiscal Year Ended June 30, 1949* (Washington, D.C.: GPO, 1949); "Time to Modernize," *Reclamation Era* 32 (December 1946), 279–80.

28. Worster, *Rivers of Empire,* 292–94; Reisner, *Cadillac Desert,* 501–2.

29. "Dams," *Sierra Club Bulletin* 33 (June 1948): 4; David Brower, "To Dam or Not to Dam," *Sierra Club Bulletin* 33 (September-October 1948), 3–4; Ginny Wood Hill, "Rampart–Foolish Dam," *Living Wilderness* 29 (spring 1965): 3–7.

30. Palmer, *Endangered Rivers,* 132. For a good summary of the environmental problems caused or exacerbated by water projects, see Worster, *Rivers of Empire,* 317–26.

31. Berkman and Viscusi, *Damming the West,* 29, 31.

32. Reisner, *Cadillac Desert,* 396–97.

33. Dorothy Gallagher, "The Collapse of the Great Teton Dam," *New York Times Magazine,* 19 September 1976, 16, 95–103; George Laycock, "A Dam Is Not Difficult to Build Unless It Is in the Wrong Place," *Audubon Magazine* 78 (November 1976): 132–35; *Business Week,* 24 January 1977, 21–22.

34. Palmer, *Endangered Rivers,* 116.

35. In 1982, the 160-acre restriction was raised to 960 acres and allowed the landowner to lease any amount of land if he or she paid interest on the per-acre charge for construction. See Worster, *Rivers of Empire,* 300–302.

36. Gates, *History of Public Land Law Development,* 698; John Opie, *The Law of the Land: Two Hundred Years of American Farmland Policy* (Lincoln: University of Nebraska Press, 1987), 119; Kenneth D. Frederick, "Irrigation and the Future of American Agriculture," in *The Future of American Agriculture as a Strategic Resource,* eds. Sandra S. Batie and Robert G. Healy (Washington, D.C.: The Conservation Foundation, 1980), 160–61, 170.

37. Daniel McCool, "Water Welfare and the New Politics of Water: The Era of Water Welfare," *Halcyon* 14 (1992): 98–99.

38. Willard W. Cochrane, *The Development of American Agriculture: A Historical Analysis* (Minneapolis: University of Minnesota Press, 1979), 128; Fite, *American Farmers,* 101, 115, 234; Earl O. Heady et al., *Roots of the Farm Problem: Changing Technology, Changing Capital Use, Changing Labor Needs* (Ames: Iowa State University Press, 1965), 10, 20–21; Stanley Andrews, *The Farmer's Dilemma* (Washington, D.C.: Public Affairs Press, 1961), 9, 158.

39. "Power of the West," *Fortune* 37 (January 1948): 98.

40. Hanson, "Pumping Billions into the Desert," 136.

41. Gerald D. Nash, *The American West in the Twentieth Century: A Short History of an Urban Oasis* (Englewood Cliffs, N.J.: Prentice Hall, 1973).

Activist Women in the West and Their Fight for Political Equity, 1960-2000

Marjorie Bell Chambers

As the year 1999 came to a close and the year 2000 began, the United States' activist women of the last third of the twentieth century arranged to meet in Baltimore at the end of March to reflect upon the most exciting time of their lives. There they would plan their strategy for completing the revolution they had started in the 1960s. Few people outside this group of movers and shakers recognized the importance of the revolution that these women had launched. Perhaps by the year 3000, if not by 2100, people will look back and recognize their impact on transforming the patterns of human lives and acknowledge that this revolution ranks with the earlier agricultural and industrial revolutions.

This chapter concentrates on the United States' western, middle-class, largely white, activist women. It will discuss their contribution to the national women's movement in their states on only two notable women's issues that have encompassed the women's movement. These issues are ratification of the Equal Rights Amendment and the election of western women to their state legislatures and to the federal Congress.

The thirteen states included in the western region are Alaska, Arizona, California, Colorado, Hawaii, Idaho, Montana, Nevada, New Mexico, Oregon, Utah, Washington, and Wyoming. These states are multiethnic and multiracial. Alaska has its indigenous people, as does Hawaii. California and Hawaii have many Asian-Pacific racial groups within their midst. New Mexico, southern Colorado, Arizona, and southern California all have major populations with Spanish and/or Mexican origins. The intermountain states all have large Native American populations. The major cities of these western states have significant black populations. This western region is perhaps the nation's most populous multiracial region. In a single chapter it is impossible to do justice to all the women of these many peoples and their cultures that enrich the West. As an Anglo-American historian, I have chosen to write about those activist women I know best.

Scholarly literature on western women active in the late twentieth century's phase of the women's movement is quite limited. Available sources offer little comparability. Revealingly, most of the data used came from political science, not history. These books are primarily collections of individual papers by different authors, usually including a chapter by the editor. The University of New Mexico Press has published two such books relevant for the overall topic but not for the limitations of this chapter. They are *Politics and Public Policy in the Contemporary American West*, edited by Clive S. Thomas, and *New Mexico Women: Intercultural Perspectives*, edited by Joan M. Jensen and Darlis A. Miller. In addition, three books on the western region essential for general background are *The American West: A New Interpretive History*, by Robert V. Hine and John Mack Faragher, and Gerald Nash's studies, *The American West in the Twentieth Century* and *Creating the West*. Gerald Nash and Richard Etulain's recent works of historical interpretations, *The Twentieth-Century West* and *Researching Western History*, both of which include a chapter on western women, are essential reading. Ethel Klein's *Gender Politics* also contains valuable information. Among the political science studies, the most helpful were Jane Jaquette's *Women in Politics*, Lois Lovelace Duke's *Women in Politics, Outsiders or Insiders*, and Sue Thomas and Clyde Wilson's *Women and Elected Office*.

Few regional studies, however, concentrate primarily on the West. Most regional studies pertain to the South, New England, Middle Atlantic, or Midwest. On the other hand, the autobiographies of Colorado's first lady Dottie Lamm and Congresswoman Pat Schroeder provide interesting data on their state and their own political experiences. The most useful data, and that which many others have used, come from the Internet site of the Center for American Women and Politics at Rutgers University. These data are primarily national in scope but fortunately are presented by states. I extracted that data that pertained to the western thirteen states.

The West, as a region, is the farthest from the nation's capital. Correspondingly, a sizable number of rugged, individualistic westerners have had little affection for the federal government. Issues of land, water, natural resources, cattle grazing, sheep, and coyotes frequently put western ranchers, miners, farmers, and lumbermen at odds with each other and especially with federal officials. Other current arguments are about private militias, environmental issues, such as the Mexican spotted owl's habitat and the silvery minnow's survival in the Rio Grande, and wildfires that blaze out of control in the western national forests. Many westerners prefer to keep federal officials as far away as possible, except when they need federal funds to deal with emergencies.

Western women have displayed their own brand of independence and individualism when faced with the rigors of life in the West. Over the course of the nineteenth and early twentieth century they established their homesteads, sometimes on their own without a male partner, and adapted to the strenuous life of the mountains, high plateau country, deserts, and great river valleys of the West. In more recent times, these activist, strong women were often professionals: lawyers, doctors, dentists, university professors, teachers, and ministers. Many others were full-time homemakers and/or full partners with their ranching husbands or sons. A good number of these women became active in politics. They fought the battles for suffrage. Their daughters and granddaughters led the fight for women's equality with men in the 1970s in the vast West that stretches from New Mexico to Alaska and from Montana to Hawaii.

To combat their isolation from each other on the large ranches of the West, rural women organized themselves into a variety of women's organizations. They sought companionship, cultural and intellectual life, social entertainment, and answers to community problems that they and their children faced. In the post–World War II era, these organizations were often chapters or branches of the same national organizations found in the small western cities and the few metropolitan areas of the West. These were the American Association of University Women (AAUW), organized in 1881 to help women obtain a university education equal to men's and subsequent lifelong learning and equity for women and girls; the League of Women Voters (LWV), which grew out of the suffrage movement and after the ratification of the suffrage amendment educated voters on political issues; and the General Federation of Women's Clubs, the most eclectic in its program of all the women's groups. Urban women joined several of these groups and/or the National Federation of Business and Professional Women (BPW), organized in 1919 to achieve equity for all working women. In the metropolitan areas, the Young Women's Christian Association (YWCA) offered single women a safe place to reside, educational workshops, a place to socialize with other women, and use of their recreational facilities.

In these organizations women learned the leadership and organizational skills they put to work in politics. They appeared before local school boards, city or county governments, and state legislatures to solve the problems of their lives, the lives of their children, and sometimes to address concerns of their ranches, businesses, and husbands' interests, which they had made their own. These western, organized women also wrote letters to their congressional representatives and U.S. senators to make known their views on their organizations' national legislative agendas. Thus when the Equal Rights Amendment came before their state legislatures for ratification, they were ready to play strong leadership roles in that process.

In 1869 the western territory of Wyoming, later "the Equality State," passed legislation granting women the right to vote. Myth attributes the passage to Wyoming males, who wanted to entice single, eastern women to immigrate to the territory because of the great shortage of women residents for wives. This reason might well have been why some male legislators, twelve of twenty, voted for the suffrage bill in the Wyoming legislature. However, historian Eleanor Flexner gives more credit to the efforts of six-foot Esther Morris with her "craggy, granite-like face." Originally from New York, Morris had heard Susan B. Anthony, the great suffrage leader, speak in Illinois on her way west. Morris proceeded to invite a number of community leaders and legislators from the then largest community in the Wyoming Territory, South Pass City, to her home. She made an appeal for votes for women, stating many of the points that she had heard Anthony make. All those present "pledged their support." At the first territorial election, one of Morris's guests, William H. Bright, became president of the territorial council, the upper house of the legislature. Bright was also married to a strong suffragist. Some have said the bill was "a joke on the Governor." Nonetheless the women's suffrage bill passed in the lower house six to four with one abstention, and six to two in the upper house, again with one abstention. The antisuffrage forces quickly put tremendous pressure on the governor to veto the bill. They did not know that he had attended an early women's rights convention in Salem, Ohio, sitting quietly in a back row and listening to the women and watching the "amazing spectacle of women conducting such a gathering for and by themselves." The memory probably caused him to sign the suffrage bill.[1] Women's suffrage was incorporated into Wyoming's state constitution when Wyoming was admitted to the Union in 1890.

In 1870, the Territory of Utah gave women the right to vote. However, twelve years later a congressional bill, the Edmunds Act, took the right to vote away from polygamist women and their menfolk. Five years after, in 1887, the Edmunds-Tucker Act denied all Utah women the right to vote. The women objected to the injustice of applying the penalty to all women, even those not in plural marriages. Why, they asked, should such women be penalized when men in plural marriages could still vote? The women of Utah were not able to vote again until the Church of Jesus Christ of Latter-day Saints denounced plural marriage. Utah was then admitted to the Union on January 4, 1896, with a constitution that guaranteed women's equal rights.[2]

In 1893 Colorado had allowed women to vote, and in 1896 Idaho adopted a state constitutional amendment that gave women the franchise. Other western states soon followed: Washington State in 1910, California in 1911, and Oregon and Arizona in 1912. All these western states acted before a single state east of the Mississippi granted women the right to vote. Then in 1913 Illinois finally gave women the right to vote. The same year the Alaskan Territory did likewise. In 1914 Montana joined the western parade to enfranchise women. Of the western states only New Mexico and Nevada failed to take action before the federal amendment was ratified in 1920.

Montana was the first state to send a woman to Congress. She was Jeannette Rankin, a pacifist, who was first elected on November 9, 1916, even before the Suffrage Amendment was ratified. But Montana women had won the right to vote two years prior to Rankin's run for Congress. Rankin only lasted for one term because she put principle ahead of pragmatism, voting against President Woodrow Wilson's request in 1917 for a declaration of war. For twenty years she stayed out of the spotlight. Then in 1940, as war raged in Europe, Rankin decided to run for reelection to Congress. She did and won, running on a pacifist platform attracting the isolationist vote. After Pearl Harbor, when President Franklin Roosevelt asked Congress to declare war, Rankin once again was faced with same question of principle. She again voted her conscience, "No." Although forty-nine other representatives had voted with her in 1917, this time she cast the sole negative vote. Once again she served only one term in Congress, for most of the isolationists, who had abhorred going to war, had agreed with President Roosevelt that the Japanese attack had been "a day of infamy."[3]

Wyoming also produced the first woman governor, Nellie Tayloe Ross, who was elected in 1925 to fulfill the unexpired term of her deceased husband, William Bradford Ross. She served almost two full years before being narrowly defeated when she ran for reelection in 1926. Thereafter she served as vice chair of the 1928 National Democratic Convention. She seconded the nomination of Al Smith, who became the presidential nominee. She also organized women for the Democratic Party and directed women's activities in 1932 for Franklin Roosevelt's campaign. On his election he rewarded Ross by making her the first female director of the U.S. Mint in 1933. She served in that capacity until President Eisenhower replaced her with a Republican in 1953.[4]

In more recent times, the West has seen one of its daughters appointed as the first woman to serve on the U.S. Supreme Court, Sandra Day O'Connor. Although born in El Paso, Texas, Justice O'Connor went to Stanford University in California for her undergraduate and law degrees. After graduation from law school, no private law firm would hire O'Connor despite her magna cum laude degree and her service on the *Stanford Law Review*. Discrimination against women lawyers was the rule of the day in the 1950s. She found work in public service instead. First she served as deputy county attorney for San Mateo, California. Then O'Connor moved to Arizona to become assistant state attorney general for Arizona. In 1969 she was appointed to the state senate to fill an unexpired term and then won election to the seat the following year. There Sandra O'Connor became the first woman senate majority leader in any state. She supported ratification of the Equal Rights Amendment and worked to revise the Arizona statutes that discriminated against women. In 1974 she returned to the legal profession as a judge on the Superior Court of Maricopa County. Four years later, Governor Bruce Babbitt promoted Judge O'Connor to the Arizona Court of Appeals. President Ronald Reagan appointed O'Connor to the U.S. Supreme Court in 1981.[5]

Interestingly, in 1965 Arizona also produced the first woman in the nation to serve as chief justice of a state supreme court, Justice Lorna Lockwood. In 1998 Arizona voters elected the first all-female slate of state officers in the United States: Governor Jane Hull, Secretary of State Betsey Bayless, Attorney General Janet Napolitano, Treasurer Carol Springer, and Superintendent of Public Instruction Lisa Graham Keegan. Arizona does not have an office of lieutenant governor. Hull, Bayless, and Keegan were incumbents, whereas Napolitano and Springer replaced men who had not sought reelection.[6]

Wyoming, Montana, and Arizona have not only led the West in contributing distinguished daughters to be the first women to serve in major positions of government, they have also led the nation. The "glass ceiling" for women in elected office remains only for the positions of president and vice president of the United States. Women have run for those positions. Geraldine Ferraro, a New Yorker, made it through the nominating process as a Democratic candidate for the vice presidency, but she and presidential candidate Walter Mondale lost the general election in 1984.[7] Twenty years earlier, in 1964, Senator Margaret Chase Smith of Maine sought the Republican Party's nomination for president. Shirley Chisholm, another New Yorker, campaigned for the Democratic Party's nomination in 1972. Republican Elizabeth Dole of Kansas ran for the Republican Party's nomination for president in 2000. Since none of these women from the East and the Midwest were successful, there is still a chance that a westerner may be the first successful woman to hold either of these positions.

Equal Rights Amendment

The crucial first section of the proposed Equal Rights Amendment reads: "Equality of rights under the law shall not be denied or abridged by the United States or by any State on account of sex." One would think that this simple, straightforward statement would raise little opposition as the nation's two hundredth anniversary approached. While some admirers in the twentieth century labeled the United States "the greatest democracy on earth," others noted that less than 50 percent of the population had full citizenship and civil rights.

The House of Representatives finally passed the Equal Rights Amendment in 1971 and the Senate in 1972, after which it was sent to the states for their ratification. To become a part of the U.S. Constitution, thirty-eight states had to ratify it, three-fourths of the fifty states. The importance of the ERA to women and their movement was best stated by eastern activist Bella Abzug: "ERA became the heart and soul of the contemporary women's peaceful revolution, with its quest for equality and economic justice. It was the legal bedrock on which all other changes were to be inscribed."[8]

State legislators reflected many of the same mind-sets as their counterparts in Congress. They either supported the ratification of the amendment, or they sounded like they belonged in the nineteenth, if not the eighteenth, century. The opposing legislators charged that the ERA would break up the family, require women to go to work, dictate homosexual marriage laws, and deny the right to privacy. Some even complained that the ERA would make rest rooms unisex. Evidently legislators did not fly in airplanes, where toilets were already unisex. For some opponents, the amendment seemed to speak to people's worst sexual nightmares. Proponents of the amendment declared it "a matter of simple justice." By the end of 1973, thirty-one states had ratified the amendment.

Here again the West demonstrated its unique talent for being first. The first state to ratify the ERA was Hawaii. On March 12, 1972, since that state was six hours behind Washington, it was easy to convince the legislators to remain in session to ratify the Equal Rights Amendment. An airplane sat on the tarmac at Washington's National Airport, waiting for a courier from Congress carrying the official copy of the amendment and the letter requesting the state's ratification. As soon as the pouch with the documents was on board, the plane took off for Hawaii. When the documents arrived on the speaker's desk in Honolulu, he announced that the ratification was before the House. In the Senate the lieu-tenant governor did likewise. With a minimum of debate, the vote took place, and by an overwhelming majority the amendment was ratified. Colorado's Congresswoman Pat Schroeder in her book, *24 Years of House Work . . . and the Place Is Still a Mess,* made a caustic aside to the Hawaiian story, noting, "Little did it know no other state was vying for the privilege."[9] Four other western states (Idaho, Alaska, Colorado, and California) ratified in 1972. The next year four more western states ratified: Wyoming, Oregon, New Mexico, and Washington. In 1974 Montana ratified the ERA. Thus within the first three years of the ratification process, ten western states had ratified the ERA.[10]

Reason seemed to overcome emotional fears in all but three western states—Utah, Nevada, and Arizona, each with large conservative Mormon populations who opposed the amendment. The other states in the nation that did not ratify the amendment were primarily in the South. They were home to considerable num-bers of conservative Southern Baptists, from Virginia to Louisiana. Interestingly, the Civil War border states of West Virginia, Kentucky, and Tennessee all ratified the amendment. The rest of the states that opposed the ERA lay in the Midwest, most along or near to the Mississippi River: Arkansas, Oklahoma, Missouri, and Illinois. In all the opposing state legislatures except perhaps for Illinois, organized religion played a predominant role on issues of marriage and the traditional roles of men and women. In the eyes of many people, God intended man to be supe-rior to woman. The United States might be a nation "under God," but it seemed that its government was not to be a full and equal democracy. In Illinois a politi-cal bargain was reached that if the ERA was not brought up for vote, the abortion issue would not be brought forward and vice versa. Thus the Illinois legislature was deadlocked on the two major women's issues. Eventually Catholic bishops saw the ERA as reinforcing the Supreme Court decision made in *Roe v. Wade,* making abor-tion legal, which the bishops opposed. Thus the Catholic Church threw its weight against the amendment.[11] Still, it must be said that Idaho, also a largely Mormon state, ratified the ERA but rescinded its ratification in 1977. Three eastern states also rescinded their ratification, but the governor of one vetoed the rescinding![12]

Sixteen state constitutions grant women equal rights with men. In two of those states, Wyoming and Utah, the equal rights were granted as part of their state constitutions when they were admitted to statehood, in 1890 and 1896 respec-tively. The other fourteen include the western states of Alaska, Colorado, and Hawaii, which gained their state ERAs at the same time these states' legislatures ratified the federal amendment. Washington State adopted its state amendment in 1972, a year before it ratified the federal amendment in 1973. Montana and New Mexico adopted their states' equal rights amendments in the latter year. The remaining western states that ratified the federal amendment did not adopt a state ERA. They were California, Idaho, and Oregon. Thus eight of the thir-teen western states made up half of the sixteen states nationwide with state ERAs.[13] The West led the nation's other regions in making its women equal cit-izens with men.

In several western states that had adopted state equal rights amendments, a cohesive and determined opposition wanted to rescind not only their state's ratification of the federal amendment but also their state's amendment. All of the states were able defeat these attempts by the opposition. Colorado's former first lady Dottie Lamm tells the story of how Colorado was able to save its ERA in her book, *Second Banana*. In 1976, the year of Colorado's centennial and the country's bicentennial, a small group of "intense" women organized themselves as the League of Housewives (LOH) to "escalate" a drive to rescind the state ERA from the Colorado constitution. Another small "but equally determined group" of women was led by the National Organization for Women (NOW), a sixties organization founded by Betty Friedan, whose book *The Feminine Mystique* had launched this phase of the woman's movement. The National Organization for Women appealed to younger women who wanted action NOW. Its organization of the states and the cities had been developing slowly. In the West, NOW was most successful in the bigger cities. The Colorado NOW "vowed" to save their ERA "at all costs." The Colorado legislature placed the measure for repeal as Amendment 8 on the November 1976 ballot. Suddenly, another new women's organization appeared on the scene, the Homemakers for ERA. These women did not have NOW's strident voice. Instead these women, many of whom belonged to one or more of the traditional women's organizations, had soft but strong voices. These were voices with whom rural, suburban, and even urban woman could easily identify. In addition these homemakers were older and had more political skills. Lamm accompanied these women as they went door-to-door, seeking support for the state's ERA. She writes of how the Homemakers for ERA talked

confidently of equality for women and parity for homemakers, bearing testimony to the fact that one need not be a career woman to be a feminist. Most of the women they approached opened their doors, their minds, and their hearts. In turn they communicated their enthusiasm . . . to the men with whom they resided. On Election Day, the Colorado ERA was retained by a two-to-one margin.[14]

As the women's movement intensified, reaching for the last three states needed for ratification of the federal amendment, NOW established a boycott in all the unratified states, asking groups not to hold conventions in those states. Further, AAUW established an ERA task force to work with the national coalition of women's organizations and to provide technical assistance to AAUW state organizations when the ERA was up for ratification in their state. The task force mobilized its members. The AAUW president wrote letters to more than 140,000 state division and local branch members and to presidents of other women's groups. The task force tried to help local women with their research needs and strategy and offer political advice. Ethel Klein reveals in her book *Gender Politics* that she saw the AAUW task force as overseeing the states' lobbying effort. However, task force members did their best not to ruffle the feathers of their sisters in the other organizations or their own members. They saw the task force's job as stiffening backbones and providing information to the local groups. The task force members knew that state legislatures did not welcome outsiders telling them what to do.[15]

When this author, a member of the task force and AAUW's former vice president from the Rocky Mountain Region, spoke at Weber State University for the Utah AAUW Division's state convention, she found the front row of seats in the auditorium filled with elderly men of the Church of Jesus Christ of Latter-day Saints, all dressed alike in black suits. They sat with their arms crossed over their chests, signifying their rejection of the speaker. Their facial expressions left no doubt of their opinion of the ERA or its messenger. The AAUW's national visitor was not intimidated. Five-and-a-half feet tall and wearing her three-inch heels, she looked over the heads of these black-suited men and addressed the colorfully dressed AAUW delegates. She probably gave her best speech of the ten-year campaign for the ratification of the Equal Rights Amendment.

After her talk at Weber State University, she returned to Salt Lake City to be interviewed on Salt Lake's Public Broadcasting System's TV station. The interviewer, a supporter of the amendment, led a strong, positive interview. When the AAUW task force leader entered her hotel's dining room alone that evening, suddenly there was absolute silence. She was convinced that everyone in the dining room had seen the interview and had recognized her, for she had not taken the time to change her clothes. The evil, disgusted glances sent her way, she considered worthy of those cast upon the witches of Salem 300 years earlier. Later some Mormon women organized "Mormons for ERA." They wrote songs of their plight, even one about excommunication, for one of their group had indeed been excommunicated by the church.[16] Unfortunately, these actions did not change the outcome in Utah's vote on ratification, but it did build a friendly, supportive sisterhood across religious and state lines.

In Carson City, Nevada's capital, the AAUW's regional leader for the ratification cause found not only many association members openly supporting the ERA, but also a large coalition group including members of BPW and LWV. This coalition had been working well together. Hopes were high that Nevada would ratify. In fact, as early as 1918, before the ratification of the Suffrage Amendment, the Nevada legislature had had a woman assembly member, in 1918. Later, in 1943, Josie Alma Woods and Mary Sharp had both been elected to the assembly in 1943 in the midst of World War II. Two of their state's many distinguished, outspoken suffragists were Eliza Cook, the first woman doctor in Carson Valley, and Felice Cohn, a Carson City lawyer. There was also Jeanne Elizabeth Weir, who called the first meeting of the Nevada Equal Franchise Society and was a professor of history and the founder of the Nevada Historical Society.[17] With these and many more prominent activist women in the previous fight for ratification of the Susan B. Anthony suffrage amendment, the activist women of the 1970s could not imagine failure. Perhaps they had forgotten that although Nevada had granted women suffrage in 1914, the state had not ratified the federal amendment in 1920.[18] Once again Nevada declined to ratify a federal amendment by defeating the state's ratification of the ERA.

Interestingly, legislators with only daughters usually voted for the amendment, whereas those with only sons voted against it. Those with both daughters and sons proved a toss-up. Part of the research done by the national AAUW task force for the local women was to develop a state legislator file, including the governor and lieutenant governor. This "Farley File" was named for Franklin Roosevelt's presidential campaign manager, James Farley, who made such a file for Roosevelt. Three-by-five index cards, one for each legislator, contained the name of the legislator, the spouse's name, the children's names, usually an address and phone number, place of employment, party registration, education, and any useful facts that might be helpful to the lobbyist to impress and persuade the legislator. Just as President Roosevelt had studied his Farley cards before he went on a trip, so the women lobbying their state legislatures for the ERA used their state's cards.

When the United Nations proclaimed 1975 "International Women's Year" and later expanded the year to a decade for women, U.S. president Gerald Ford established a national commission on the observance of the year. The commission called for a national conference to be held in Houston, Texas, in 1977. For that conference each state had its own conference to discuss the World Plan of Action that had been adopted at the United Nations' Mexico City Conference on Women in 1975. They also were to determine what part of that plan needed attention in a U.S. Plan of Action to be adopted in Houston. In addition the state conferences were to elect delegates to the national conference. Each of the western states had a delegation in Houston. However, most of the state conferences were held in the spring of 1977. By early summer a strong opposition had developed. This was largely organized by Phyllis Schlafly through her Eagle Forum and STOP ERA organizations. Others participating in the opposition were American Women Against ERA (AWARE), Females Opposed to Equality (FOE), Happiness of Motherhood Eternal (HOME), and Women Who Want to Be Women (WWWW).[19] These groups began showing up at the remaining state conferences, held in late spring and early summer. They managed to get a good number of their members elected delegates to the Houston conference.

These happenings warned those supporting the ERA that ratification was in trouble. Sensing these problems, the coalition of pro-ERA organizations began to think of asking Congress for an extension of time in which the states could ratify the ERA. The time limit that Congress had set for ratification was seven years, from 1972 to 1979. Since not all amendments have had time limits, these pro-ERA women hoped that Congress in its wisdom might extend the time for ratification of the ERA. In 1978 more than 100,000 women descended on Washington to march down Pennsylvania Avenue to the nation's Capitol Building and call upon Congress to extend the deadline for ratification. After the march each marcher then visited her own representative and senators. This writer, by then the national president of AAUW, marched in the parade and visited one of her senators, Jack Schmitt, who was opposed to the extension of time. Her other senator and her representative were supporting the ERA. Senator Schmitt's staff was predominantly made up of women, and they were happy to see her when she walked in and asked to speak with the senator. They got him to come out from behind his closed door and speak with the lobbying AAUW woman. The senator and the lobbyist knew each other well, for they had been on the campaign trail together. She asked him why he was not supporting the extension. His reply was that he did not want to set a precedent, for no other amendment had received a time extension. Her reply to the former astronaut was, "If you had been in Neil Armstrong's boots, would you have refused to step out on the moon for fear of setting a precedent?" He stared at her and then roared with laughter and said, "I guess you have me." All his staff had been standing around the edge of the room and burst out in applause and cheered their feminist "sister."[20]

Congress had held hearings and finally voted to extend the time limit three years, to 1982. That year came and went without a single additional state ratifying the federal amendment during the extension of time. The last state to ratify was Indiana in 1977, two years before the extension began. In an article asking the question, "What killed Equal Rights?" Anastasia Toufexis wrote, "The feminists relied too much on moral fervor and impassioned rhetoric, and displayed little of the political savvy needed to wage an effective state-by-state ratification drive." For example, Eleanor Smeal, NOW's president, had caught the eye of the media, who mistakenly identified her as the single leader of the movement. This dismayed the Business and Professional Women, who had supported the ERA since 1923, when Alice Paul, chair of the National Women's Party, had convinced some Republican congressmen to introduce the Equal Rights Amendment. The older women's organizations exhibited plenty of political skills and experience, but they were viewed as "old fogies" by the younger, media-oriented generation. Toufexis described Smeal thus: "Symbolically perhaps, Smeal showed great tenacity and faith but revealed little taste or talent for politicians or politics."[21]

Several books describe why the ERA failed. The reasons given are as varied as the authors. However, one book offered a suggestion for the future: the U.S. Supreme Court might declare women equal citizens with men under the Fourteenth Amendment. This position incidentally was one of Phyllis Schlafly's reasons for there being no need for the ERA. The opponents of the federal ERA were upset over the second section of the proposed amendment, which states: "Congress shall have the power to enforce, by appropriate legislation, the provisions of this article." To those who feared the ERA, this section was seen as an open-ended invitation to any legislation without citizen approval. Jane J. Mansbridge, in her book *Why We Lost the ERA,* suggests that "equal rights advocates . . . consider urging Congress to pass an Equal Rights Act." Such legislation might be considered under Section 5 of the Fourteenth Amendment, which has the same wording as Section 2 of the Equal Rights Amendment. Under such a law, according to Mansbridge, "Congress might be able to invalidate all state and local public policies that discriminate on the basis of sex." She implies further that such an act "could also spell out just what it would do in specific areas, reassuring the wary." Such a bill would of course require only a majority vote in Congress and the president's signature.[22] A change in congressional ideology would be necessary before such a bill would stand a chance of passage, but it might be worth a try.

On one occasion, Chief Justice of the Supreme Court Warren Burger appeared to support the concept when he was approached by the president of the AAUW at a reception to honor him with an award. She asked, "Mr. Chief Justice, when will the Supreme Court declare women equal with men under the law?" He responded, "Why, you already have the precedent in *Reed v. Reed,*" an Idaho case challenging a state law that would not allow a woman to serve as executor of a will. Reed was a widow who had been named executor in her husband's will. The Court had ruled in her favor based on the Fourteenth Amendment.[23]

Election of Women to State Legislatures and Congress

Noting the difference in the way that men and women state legislators had voted on the ratification of the Equal Rights Amendment, Bella Abzug wrote, "It is obvious that the ultimate success of ERA depends on electing much larger numbers of women as state legislators." The Center for the American Woman and Politics at Rutgers University did a survey of how state legislators had voted on ratification and found that

> more than three fourths of women legislators (77 percent) favored ERA, but only 49 percent of the men did. In states that have not ratified, the disparity was even wider, with 76 percent of women legislators and only 36 percent of the men pro-ERA. However, . . . men compose 86.7 percent of state legislators.[24]

Once the ERA failed to pass by June 30, 1982, the end of the extension period, the women's movement put greater focus on electing women to their state legislatures and to Congress. The National Women's Political Caucus (NWPC), founded on July 10, 1971, for that purpose, changed gears. The caucus members raised more money to support women candidates, encouraged any bright star they had seen in the ratification process to run, and put this goal at the head of their agenda. The caucus is nonpartisan although predominantly Democratic. Each party has its own caucus within the national caucus. If the caucus leaders thought a woman's campaign was well organized and stood a chance of winning, she was supported regardless of party. However, there were two requirements that the candidate had to meet. She had to be pro-ERA and pro-choice on abortion. The year following the NWPC's founding, Pat Schroeder of Colorado sought the organization's help in her run for Congress, but members tried to discourage her, telling her to run for school board first! Still, she won without the NWPC's help, becoming her state's first congresswoman.[25] The National Organization for Women also provided funds for women candidates with the same proviso. These two causes, the Equal Rights Amendment and pro-choice in women's reproductive lives, had come to define whether a woman was a feminist and really supported the movement. Still, Ethel Klein notes that although the NWPC provided technical assistance, an excellent campaign management book, and funds, it was not the primary base from which the women candidates came. In "the mid-70s . . . the women candidates were much more likely to come out of the League [of Women Voters] than out of NOW or NWPC."[26]

The cost of campaigning seemed to climb dramatically with each succeeding election. Additional moneys were needed to cover the ever-rising costs of media ads, campaign staff, and travel. Thus women in each of the predominant parties, Democrat and Republican, also created political action committees to raise funds. The Democrat committee is known as Emily's List, whereas the Republican one is called the Wish List. Although these funds have helped the women candidates to compete with their male opponents, women candidates have had to be successful fund-raisers themselves.

Women's representation in western state legislatures has grown steadily since 1964. At that time women made up 4.5 percent of the total legislators serving in the thirteen western states. Ten years later it was 7.5 percent. In 1984 the western states average was 14.2 percent, and a decade later it was 25.8 percent, or an increase in thirty years of 21.3 percent. In Alaska the number of women legislators went from three in 1964 to twenty-three thirty years later, whereas Arizona went from eight to thirty-three women in the 1993–94 legislature. However, Arizona lost three of those women legislators in the 1994 election. Surprisingly, much more heavily populated California went from only one woman in 1964 to twenty-four women in its 1993–94 legislature. California also lost three women in the 1994 election. Colorado went from seven to thirty-five, whereas Hawaii went from four to twenty-five women. In the same thirty-year period, Idaho went from one to thirty and Montana went from two to twenty female legislators. These states, with the exception of Montana, at the low end of the group, were above the regional average. Nevada also was below the average for women members of the western region's legislatures, going from six to twenty. Amazingly, with the next election, in 1994, Nevada jumped to thirty-five female legislators! This of course was due to the Gingrich-led Republican surge of that year. New Mexico grew from one woman legislator in 1964 to twenty-six in the 1993–94 legislature, but as a Democrat state the election in 1994 showed a loss of five women, the opposite of Nevada, a Republican state. Oregon followed Nevada's pattern with ten women legislators in 1964, the largest number in the West at that time but growing to only seventeen by 1994. However, the election of 1994 put twenty-nine women in the next legislature. Utah had the lowest pattern of growth of all thirteen western states, beginning with six in 1964 and growing to only fourteen women in 1994. The star of the western region was Washington State, which went from seven women in 1964 to forty women thirty years later.[27] These figures suggest that if the Equal Rights

Amendment were to come before these legislatures in the early years of the new millennium, the outcome might be different. Of the three states that refused to ratify—Utah, Nevada, and Arizona—Arizona and Nevada might join the "yes" column. Idaho, which had voted to rescind its ratification, might well remain in the "yes" column. Only Utah still appears to believe strongly that woman's place is in the home, not in the house of the legislature.

In 2000 the total number of women legislators across the country was 1,670, or 20 percent of all legislators. It seems for now that Mansbridge's recommendation for equal rights legislation under Section 5 of the Fourteenth Amendment would be best. Although the West can be proud of leading the nation's state legislatures in their percentage of women, the West consists of only thirteen states, and it takes thirty-eight to ratify a constitutional amendment. The top four states in the percentage of women legislators today are all western states, as is the seventh. The first four are Washington State, with 40.8 percent; Nevada, with 36.5; Arizona, with 35.6; and Colorado, with 34 percent. Oregon ranks seventh in the nation, with 30 percent women. Once more western states lead the nation, this time in their percentages of women legislators.[28]

If the Equal Rights Amendment were brought before Congress for a vote in the near future, an increase in the number of congresswomen, especially Democrat women, will be needed to overcome the current far-right, religious ideology of many in the Republican Party leadership and membership and in the Congress. Otherwise the amendment will not get beyond Congress to the states for ratification. Nor would Mansbridge's idea for equal rights legislation likely pass. Meanwhile the gender gap at this time favors the Democrat Party, with far more women voting Democrat than Republican out of fear of a change on the Supreme Court that might overturn *Roe v. Wade,* the court case that made abortion legal.

The current numbers and percentages of women in Congress are minimal. In 2000, women held sixty-five seats, or 12.1 percent of the total 535 seats in Congress. In the Senate, with 100 seats, only nine seats, or 9 percent, were held by women in 2000, and four of those consisted of two pairs of women from the states of California in the West and Maine in the Northeast. The election of 2000 added another pair of women U.S. senators for the West when Washington State's Maria Cantrell joined Patty Murray in the U.S. Senate in January 2001. Surprisingly, the western states once again lead the nation as the region with two states, California and Washington, represented in the U.S. Senate by two females. Of the 435 seats in the House of Representatives, fifty-six, or 12.9 percent, were held by women in 2000. In the numbers of women holding office, Congress appears to be where the state legislatures were thirty-six years ago, in 1964.[29]

By 1992 things seemed to be improving for the West. Of the thirteen western states, California, the largest in population with nearly 30 million people, has produced the most women congressional representatives since 1965, twenty-one. The earliest congresswoman in this period was Yvonne Brathwaite Burke, who was elected in 1972 and served three terms. Another was Barbara Boxer, who served five terms in the House, 1983–93, and then moved on to the Senate to join Diane Feinstein, elected one year earlier in a special election. In the pattern of most earlier elections of women to Congress, four women during this period were elected to take their deceased husbands' seats: Sala Burton in 1983, Shirley Neil Pettis in 1987, Representative Mary Bono in 1998 (perhaps the best known), and Lois Capps, also elected to follow her husband the same year as Mary Bono.

Four western states have had one woman representative elected since 1964 or boast one still in the Congress from an earlier election. They are Arizona, Idaho, New Mexico, and Wyoming. Two other states have had two female representatives. Colorado has had the colorful Pat Schroeder, who served on the Armed Forces Committee from 1973 to 1997, and the current representative, Diana DeGette. Hawaii has had two Japanese American women representatives. One was Patsy Mink, who first served from 1965 to 1977. She resigned to run for the Senate and lost. Then in a special election in 1990, she was again elected to the House. The second was Pat Saiki, who served from 1987 to 91. In 1990 she too ran for the Senate and lost. President George H. W. Bush then appointed her to direct the Small Business Administration.

From 1965 to 2000, Oregon had three women representatives and one female senator. The senator was Maurine Brown Neuberger, who served from 1960 to 1967, taking her deceased husband's place. The best known of the three Oregon representatives was Edith Green, who served twenty years after her 1955 election. A former teacher, she made education her primary task in the House. She worked her way up to be the second-ranking member of the House Education and Labor Committee and chair of the Special Subcommittee on Post-Secondary Education. She was also the author of the 1963 Equal Pay Act. That act, in addition to the *Kennedy Commission on the Status of Women Report* and Betty Friedan's *The Feminine Mystique,* which also came on the scene in 1963, have been considered to be the instigators of the second wave of the women's movement. The first wave was the long fight for suffrage.

Since 1965 Washington State has had five female representatives and one senator, Senator Patty Murray. With the election of 2000, Washington gained its second female senator. The best known of the five representatives is most likely Jennifer Dunn, who began her service in 1993 and whom the Republican Party often showcases. Alaska has never sent a woman to Congress, and Montana has not sent anyone since Jeannette Rankin.[30]

Behind these statistics and the data earlier in the chapter is an amazing thread. It runs from Wyoming's grant of suffrage to women in 1869 to Washington State's 40 percent female legislature in 2000. This heritage is remarkable when one considers that male voters made much of this possible, for in 1869 women did not yet have the vote. Yet in 2000 men and women together elected these greater numbers of women to the western state legislatures, among which Washington ranked first in the nation, Nevada second, Arizona third, and Colorado fourth. These activist women of the West have clearly demonstrated that they too possess the pioneer spirit of independence and individualism based on the need for self-reliance. These women have taken charge of their lives as they have led the nation in women's political advancement toward the new millennium goal of equal justice and equal citizenship with men. Together with feminists around the world, they are transforming global society.

Notes

1. Eleanor Flexner, *The Century of Struggle* (Cambridge, Mass.: Bellknap Press of Harvard University, 1959), 159–61.
2. Ibid., 163.
3. Christine A. Lunardini, *Women's Rights* (Phoenix: Oryx Press, 1996), 104–5.
4. Notes prepared by students of LBCC 791 [college course], College Library and Information Services, "Wyoming," available from www.umd.edu (University of Maryland, College Park).
5. Jeffrey D. Schultz and Laura van Assenfelft, eds., *Encyclopedia of Women in American Politics* (Phoenix: Oryx Press, 1999), 164.
6. *Boulder Daily Camera,* 5 January 1999, 5A.
7. Geraldine A. Ferraro with Linda Bird Francke, *Ferraro: My Story* (Boston: G. K. Hall, 1986), 1–4, 470–84.
8. Bella Abzug with Mim Kelber, *Gender Gap* (Boston: Houghton Mifflin, 1984), 18.
9. Pat Schroeder, *24 Years of House Work . . . and the Place Is Still a Mess: My Life in Politics* (Kansas City, Mo.: Andrews McMeel Publishing, 1999), 25.
10. Janet K. Boles, *The Politics of the Equal Rights Amendment* (New York: Longman, 1979), 2–3.
11. Riane Eisler and Allie C. Hixson, *The ERA, Facts and Action Guide* (Washington: National Women's Conference Committee, 1986), 44.
12. Boles, *The Politics of the Equal Rights Amendment,* 3.
13. Eisler and Hixson, *The ERA, Facts and Action Guide,* 75.
14. Dottie Lamm, *Second Banana* (Boulder: Johnson Books, 1983), 9.
15. Ethel Klein, *Gender Politics: From Consciousness to Mass Politics* (Cambridge, Mass.: Harvard University Press, 1984), 26, and minutes of the ERA task force in Chambers's personal files.
16. Notes by task force member Marjorie Bell Chambers in her AAUW president's file.
17. "75th Anniversary of Women's Suffrage Amendment," (Nevada Women's Lobby, 1995). A flyer, listing Nevada distinguished women, in Chambers's personal files.
18. Flexner, *The Century of Struggle,* 268.
19. Klein, *Gender Politics,* 27.
20. Marjorie Bell Chambers, "Extension of Time for Ratification of ERA," manuscript in her personal files.
21. Anastasia Toufexis, "What Killed Equal Rights?" *Time,* 12 July 1982, 32–33.
22. Jane J. Mansbridge, *Why We Lost the ERA* (Chicago: University of Chicago Press, 1986), 197–98.
23. Notes by Marjorie Bell Chambers in her AAUW president's file.
24. Abzug, *Gender Gap,* 104.
25. Schroeder, *24 Years of House Work,* 14.
26. Klein, *Gender Politics,* 31.
27. Barbara Norrander and Clyde Wilcox, "The Geography of Gender Power: Women in State Legislatures," in *Women and Elective Office: Past, Present and Future,* eds. Sue Thomas and Clyde Wilcox (New York: Oxford University Press, 1998), 103–15. Norrander and Cox use the date of the second year of the legislature for the number of women then serving as legislators. Those are the same years in which elections occur in November, but technically those who win for the first time are not legislators until sworn in the following January.
28. Center for American Women and Politics, Eagleton Institute of Politics, Rutgers University, "Women in Elective Office 2000," pp. 1, 2, and 4, available from www.cawp.rutgers.edu/facts/cawpfs.html.
29. Ibid.
30. CAWP, Rutgers, "Women in Elective Office—State by State Historical Summary," pp. 1, 2 for each state, available from www.cawp.rutgers.edu/facts/stby/st/az.html.

The Cultural Life of Boise, Idaho, 1950-2000

Carol Lynn MacGregor

At the turn of the millennium Boise, Idaho, is enjoying a cultural renaissance. Although outsiders often misunderstand Idaho, Boise, a cultural center in isolation, is overcoming its bad press and darker experiences while its high standard of living and cultural life flourish. Symbolic of its evolution was NBC's choice of Boise to represent the mountain time zone in showcasing one location for each time zone as clocks struck January 1, 2000. Boise was the smallest, the youngest, and the most isolated of the four cities: New York, St. Paul, Boise, and Los Angeles. At midnight, the air jets from sixty hot air balloons flashed their brilliant colors along Capitol Boulevard from the mission-style "The Depot" on a hill (formerly a train station) down a mile to Idaho's state capitol, in the center of town, where fireworks brightened the winter night.

Even in the history of the American West, Boise's past seems recent. Boise began in 1863, as a support community for mining at nearby Boise Basin. The town burgeoned when promises of irrigation development and railroad transportation brought workers, merchants, hoteliers, bankers, and other community builders to the cottonwood-lined Boise River valley between the higher desert to the south and the mountains rising to the north.[1] Topography, climate, and geography continue to attract people to the area, now called "the Treasure Valley." On the same latitude as Marseilles, France, and Florence, Italy, Boise's mild climate still surprises people who expect six feet of snow at the time when crocuses and daffodils are blooming. Although winters are mild downtown, skiers enjoy the snowpack of Bogus Basin, just eighteen miles north of, and several thousand feet higher, than the city's center.

Contrary to widespread misconception, Boise lies nowhere near Columbus, Ohio, Des Moines, Iowa, or other midwestern cities that begin with an *I* but lie about 2,000 miles distant from Idaho. In fact, Boise lies almost directly north of San Diego, California, and west of Montana, a state everyone knows is "west." This essay will survey the major cultural changes in Boise from 1950 to 2000, showing how prosperity in isolation continues to define the community. Many individuals who have prospered in the area have historically reinvested in cultural amenities that have enhanced life in the state's capital. Boiseans continue to assert their leadership to steer the community toward a favorable future by giving their time and money to improve it.

Images of the Area

The area's image has changed through time. Many have pictured Idaho as the land of mountains, a "primitive area" hosting wild rivers and wild animals, an exotic and unknown "throwback" to the Old West at a time when most of the West harbored large urban settlements. In the middle of the twentieth century, Averill Harriman chose Baldy Mountain as the best site for the Union Pacific Railroad's fabulous ski resort development. That changed Idaho's image. Movie stars, who discovered that it took only six weeks of residence to get a divorce in Idaho, soon appeared. Many remained to build second homes. The state became known for glamorous Sun Valley, a place much different from the rest of Idaho. Then in the 1970s Governor Cecil Andrus conducted a successful public relations campaign from the state's Department of Commerce to advertise Idaho's chief crop: potatoes. Idaho and its capital city then became synonymous with "spuds," although that vegetable grows mainly in eastern Idaho, particularly from Twin Falls east to Idaho Falls. Even the state's license plate proclaims "Famous Potatoes," aiding potato producers like the J. R. Simplot Company, the largest supplier of McDonald's french fries in the 1980s.

Outsiders' misconceptions about Boise's weather, geographic location, or agricultural areas do not concern most residents. However, images of Idaho as a bastion of racism upset thoughtful Boiseans. When Richard Butler, an aerospace engineer from California who started the Aryan Nations movement, retired to beautiful Hayden Lake in north Idaho in the 1980s, and Mark Fuhrman, infamous officer of the Los Angeles Police Department, in the 1990s also moved to north Idaho, those events captured the attention of the international news media. Violence rocked the region. Bombings in Boise occurred at the beautiful historic Temple Beth Israel and at the home of a priest who spoke out against the Aryan Nation, both in the 1970s. In 1992, a shoot-out at Ruby Ridge took the lives of Vicky and Samuel Weaver and U.S. Marshal William Degan. These events helped the media paint all of traditionally conservative Idaho as reactionary.[2]

The 1950s in Boise depicted the area's nadir of diversity. The large Chinese population that migrated from the Boise Basin to establish large farms to supply Boiseans with fresh produce throughout the first half of the twentieth century had dwindled to a few. The postwar era blended Jewish, Basque, and African American citizens with other cultural and religious communities toward the dominant Anglo-Saxon, fifties ideal of a hardworking, clean-cut, optimistic citizenry. Conservative politics and isolation forced conformity even more than that trend described the nation in the 1950s. When a scandal broke about "the boys of Boise" during the McCarthy era, it turned into a homosexual witch-hunt, ruining the lives of some innocent young men. Meanwhile courts found several older men guilty among those who had not already fled town.[3]

Despite these negative incidents, Boise enjoys a cultural renaissance at the turn of the millennium deserving of a changed and better image. During the past half century, Boise has grown in size, diversity, and cultural activity. The trends discussed here will help readers to understand how a relatively small city in an isolated location enjoys more than its share of the arts and the humanities. The foundation for this began with settlement of the valley, when pioneers established progressive social institutions. New schools, hospitals, churches, and charitable foundations continue to thrive in Boise. Although not immune from national social problems, Boise's isolation has allowed citizens to turn inward to "take charge" of their problems and return part of their good fortune to their community.

The Fifties: Homogeneity, Safety, and Familiarity

Boise mimicked most American towns in the town layout of square city blocks from its beginnings through the sixties. Additions followed a block pattern until subdivisions later began using a cul-de-sac pattern. Small neighborhoods like Hyde Park thrived through the fifties with mom-and-pop stores like Riebe's Shoe Shop, Mrs. Brewer's hand-dipped chocolate shop, Mrs. Alexander's beverage store, a barbershop announced by a spiraled post, and Dan Johnson's Drug Store.[4] But the center of activity lay downtown.

In the "nifty fifties" Boiseans joined service clubs and fraternal societies, attended church, and enjoyed what oldies refer to as "good clean fun." The latter included private cocktail parties or dancing at public lounges like Joe's Les Bois Club and the Tradewinds or at private ballroom events at the Miramar, the Elk's Ballroom, Hillcrest Country Club, and the Basque Center. When many people danced in the fifties and sixties, the Arthur Murray Dance Studio advertised "free trial lessons."[5] Boise had a few notable restaurants like Dixon's, which advertised seafood all the time; the Royal, which featured "Fish-a-rama" every Friday; and The Lampost, in Hotel Boise, which promised good steaks and potatoes. Boise's youth cruised from Howdy Partners on Fairview Avenue down to Murray's Drive-In off Capitol Boulevard and up "the bench" above the Boise River to Pete's Pizza on Vista Avenue, only to see the same faces they had just seen at the previous point of the triangle. The Youth Center near Gowen Field, a military base south of town, offered dancing to the great swing music of Gib Hockstrasser's band, which also played at the Newport Jazz Festival in the fifties. These dances brought weekly excitement for Boise's teenagers.

The "beat generation" did not happen in Boise in the fifties. Instead, sports, churches, the military, and clean-cut deportment reflected local values and the *Leave It to Beaver* mind-set that much of the nation shared. Boise High School, the only public high school in the 1950s, rivaled the teams of Nampa High School, about twenty miles away. The Reserve Officers Training Center held classes for boys in high school and enjoyed enthusiastic support as a way to train "tomorrow's soldiers." Each company of cadets chose a girl to be its "Sponsor," and she, in a bright red-and-white uniform and four-inch-high heels, inspected the troops with the youth officers and the sergeant instructor each Friday. St. Theresa's Academy offered Catholic parochial high school education in Boise. One of its alumni, Adelia Garro Simplot, remembers, "Nuns sailed through town in pairs in their black robes, stiff white collars and beads clanking at their sides. They tried to make us ladies and gentlemen at St. Theresa's."[6] A narrowly based consensus facilitated that possibility for most parents and teachers.

Respect for law and order was reflected in the neatly clipped green lawns, in club meetings conducted with strict parliamentary procedure, in the neatly coifed or nicely hatted ladies ungloving themselves while eating and playing bridge, and in the few white males who ran the government and the businesses of Boise. Policemen often knew young people's parents and could use that knowledge to ensure better behavior. This conformity and consensus in a relatively small population, however, also bred friendliness, openness, and safety. Walking downtown, one felt as though one knew almost everybody. Standing in line at theaters while waiting to see movies, patrons could always talk to friends. Previews had newsreels of faraway events like President Dwight Eisenhower's bolstering America's troops in Korea. Local people walked to movies, to school, to work. Most families in Boise had only one car. A graduate of Boise High's class of 1950 remembers that only one girl in all the school drove to school in her car.[7]

Boiseans wanted to feel safe after the bombs that ended World War II. This desire surfaced in the construction of a bomb shelter (later converted into a teacher resource center) north of town at the entrance of "The Highlands," a subdivision on the crests of foothills overlooking the growing town. (The Highlands was becoming a popular location for the homes of managers of the national and multinational corporations headquartered in Boise.) Meanwhile elementary school teachers conducted periodic civil defense drills in which students scrambled under their desks, actions that might have mitigated the impact of a heavy foreign projectile but could not have affected radiation exposure.

To escape the homogeneity of Boise's green haven in arid Idaho, the well-to-do often traveled to San Francisco to shop and attend theater shows, especially the popular musicals of the era. Some Boiseans never traveled elsewhere in Idaho, save to McCall or Sun Valley. The rest of Idaho featured small rural towns dependant on mining, timber, and agriculture. Three hundred miles separate Boise from the next town of its own or greater size. To overcome this cultural isolation, Boiseans looked inward to create their society and far outward to expand their experiences. From their travels, they brought home new ideas to improve the city's life.

The myopic view that many Boiseans held concerning their own state exacerbated the frustration that the rest of the state felt toward the capital city. Dr. Robert Sims, professor emeritus at Boise State University, stated that he does not know of another place in our nation where citizens from other areas of the state resent the capital as much as Idahoans outside the Treasure Valley take offense to

Boise's perceived advantages.[8] The state geographically splits into three areas: eastern Idaho, with Salt Lake as its center; northern Idaho, with Spokane as its center; and southern Idaho, with Boise as its center. Nevertheless, all sections must join in the state legislature. Although most of the state has been historically Republican, there is tension between the rural and urban interests in Idaho's legislature. To this day, the three universities in the state system hire lobbyists at the taxpayers' expense to compete for funding for their institutions: Idaho State University at Pocatello in eastern Idaho, the University of Idaho at Moscow in the north, and Boise State University at Boise, the largest with more than 16,000 students a semester since 1998.

In the fifties, Boise's political power base seemed narrow. From 1955 to 1967, Robert E. Smylie of Boise served as governor for the longest continuous service in that office in the state's history. A liberal Republican, Smylie removed legal gambling, improved the state's infrastructure, and implemented the first sales tax. In 1959, the Smylies entertained their friend Nelson Rockefeller at the Governor's Mansion in the North End of Boise. Nine Russians of at least gubernatorial status also visited Boise at Smylie's invitation in 1960. Usually about 300 to 400 people received invitations to these receptions. In those days, such invitations emanated from the membership lists of the Arid Club, the Hillcrest Country Club, and the Junior League of Boise (this group, called "Old Boise," typically appeared on all of the above lists), with additional names of people elected or appointed to the state's political offices.[9]

Homegrown talent provided entertainment. In 1918, Music Week started in Boise and served as a model for cities throughout the nation.[10] By the 1950s, almost every schoolchild participated in the program during the first week of May. The Boise Little Theater, begun in 1948, built its new facility at the Veterans grounds in 1957 and celebrated its fifty-second continuous year of operation in 2000. The Boise Little Theater prides itself on having never sought government funding and on always appealing to the public for talent in open auditions.[11] The Boise Master Chorale has also used local talent for annual performances, although the audition requirements have become more demanding with time. In the fifties, Boise Junior College held occasional concerts of faculty, students, or artists visiting the area. For instance, the fifth year of their "Bach to Boogie" show occurred in 1951.[12] Occasionally a truly renowned artist visited the city, as when Artur Rubenstein performed at the Boise High auditorium on Saturday, January 8, 1951.[13]

In the fifties, Boise reflected the national trends as women quit war production jobs to embrace the roles of housewives and mothers, even though few Boise women had worked in factories during World War II. In the fifties, women did not compete with men. Instead they served as "auxiliarians." In 1952, the local newspaper reported that thirteen Red Cross volunteers, the "Symbol of Mercy," gave 20,000 hours to the Red Cross.[14] Gender separation characterized other organizations. The Idaho Press Association (male) was separate from the Idaho Press Women. The Arid Club did not admit women for forty years (1991). In 1951, "The Inquiring Reporter," a daily feature of the area's newspaper, asked, "Would you be in favor of women on the city council?" To their credit, all of the seven people pictured answered that they did not know why women would not be able to serve in that position.[15] Reviewing the periodicals of the time, one realizes the societal value of "beauty" for women. Frequent contests of Miss Boise, Miss Idaho, Miss Wool, Miss Flame, Miss Rodeo, *ad infinitum,* apprised females of society's expectations for them in the fifties.

Corporate Headquarters Spawn Cultural Growth in the Sixties

The influx of well-educated people to work in the offices of major corporations headquartered in Boise in the late fifties and early sixties started to change the community. For example, Morrison-Knudsen, a construction company formed in Idaho, operated worldwide by that time. Albertson's food chain and the J. R. Simplot Company (first potatoes and fertilizer, then mining, ranching, and other businesses) expanded well beyond their Idaho origins. Boise Cascade Corporation changed its focus under the leadership of Robert Hansberger, who was educated at the Harvard Business School. Alice Hennessey, recruited from that school to become his administrative assistant, found Boise in 1958 "a small, sun-baked western town without a blade of grass downtown . . . an isolated place, but more sophisticated than I expected." In contrast, Boise today is "on the crest of the wave. . . . It has the best in educational resources, climate, medical resources, and cultural resources. . . . Boise is the finest small city in America."[16]

When Hennessey arrived, Boise's cultural life needed improvement. The Boise Art Museum consisted of a WPA building with two rooms and a lobby. Its annual fund-raiser featured a clothesline pinned with art for sale. Hansberger put Hennessey to work writing grant proposals after Governor Smylie appointed him as the first president of the newly created Idaho Arts Commission. Hansberger had also served on the board of the Aspen Institute for Humanistic Studies. After a speaker from that group visited Boise, auxiliarians formed and staffed the Beaux Arts Society to support the Boise Art Museum. The institution changed its name to the Boise Gallery of Art and hired its first professional director. Bradford Paine Shaw, a Boise architect on its board, designed a new entrance and facade for a larger gallery building to "invite people into the space beyond."[17] After its opening, attendance skyrocketed. Lectures and classes connected to traveling exhibits on display took place in a large multipurpose room.

In the sixties, Boise Cascade's Hansberger also brought the Joffrey Ballet Association to Idaho to perform in Lewiston, Boise, and Pocatello. Hennessey rallied an appropriate audience, and Bob and Clara Hansberger hosted a dinner at their home prior to the event to ensure its success. The Joffrey portrayed a modernistic piece with "people undulating onstage," quite a different kind of program for Boise's traditional tastes in the early sixties, but the response nevertheless brought the Joffrey back the following year.[18]

At the same time, the Boise Philharmonic Orchestra hired violinists from Portland to complement local talent. In the late fifties, Alyce Rosenheim became the first woman president of that board. Moving from Colorado and Hawaii, she found Boise in 1952 "a dumpy little town . . . with nowhere to eat out."[19] But she learned how to play golf and volunteered to help build the orchestra. Rosenheim attended a national workshop to network with other philharmonic boards. This led to the professionalization of the orchestra and the hiring of a permanent conductor and a half-time manager.

Not everyone in the Treasure Valley participated in the expansion of the arts. More people seemed interested in enjoying the amenable climate while hunting, fishing, boating, skiing, hiking, or horseback riding. Lucky Peak Dam, only twenty-five minutes from downtown Boise, was constructed in the 1950s just above the site of the canyon home of artist Mary Hallock Foote and her engineering husband, A. D. Foote, who had come to develop the New York Canal in 1882. Lucky Peak Dam offered waterskiing from its Spring Shores dock. Also in the fifties, snow-skiing enthusiasts Fentris Kuhn, Bill Everts, Bob Loughrey, and Peter Johnson promoted the establishment of Bogus Basin Ski Resort, only eighteen miles from the heart of town. It took fearless drivers only thirty minutes to wind their ways up the curvy road adjacent to steep drop-offs. At Peter Johnson's request, Romaine Hon raised money for a new lodge from "Mothers of Skiers." She couldn't tell them the funds' purpose until all financing had been secured and the opening of the ski area had been announced.[20]

New people poured into Boise during the late sixties and early seventies. Not all of them came to join corporations. Dr. Gustav Rosenheim, who was born in Boise and practiced gynecology in his hometown for about forty-five years, served on the Boise Chamber of Commerce in the early sixties. He remembered that in 1952 St. Alphonsus Hospital had no full-time pathologist and St. Luke's Hospital had only a half-time pathologist. By the end of the sixties, both large regional hospitals had expanded in services, expertise, and infrastructure. There seemed to be a medical "brain drain" toward Boise in the sixties.[21] Today the medical facilities in Boise serve all of southern Idaho and eastern Oregon with up-to-date equipment and hundreds of well-qualified medical professionals. During the sixties, seventies, and eighties, medical auxiliaries of wives of doctors and dentists formed a core of volunteers to serve patients at the local hospitals and later to raise money for capital improvements.[22] In the seventies, hospital management formed foundation boards to help raise big sums of money for large expansions. Newcomers found that they could become agents of change in Boise if they so desired.

In the sixties and seventies, new corporations to the region augmented the already strong corporate life of the area. Ore-Ida, a division of Heinz Corporation, brought Paul Cordorry, who stayed twenty years instead of the six months that he and his employer intended. His modern tastes made a difference in the art world of Boise. When the author served on a fund development committee under real estate developer Larry Leasure to appeal to corporations to sponsor exhibits, Cordorry pledged Ore-Ida's sponsorship for art exhibits. Corporations, banks, and utility companies expanded in the seventies and joined in sponsoring regional arts and humanities.

The Seventies Expand Arts and Humanities
while the Urban Center Disintegrates

In the early seventies, Governor Cecil Andrus worked hard to lure Hewlett-Packard Company to Boise. The majority of its computer printers have been produced in Boise ever since. This forward-looking business succeeded in recruiting a wide diversity of people to Boise. Practicing flexible employment schedules and generous benefits, HP has donated generous funds and leadership to community projects. It answered the quest that Merle Wells, noted Idaho historian, said Boise has pursued for decades. Not being on the main line of the railroad until 1925, Boise lay over 300 miles from any major city. It needed a lightweight product to ship long distances.[23] Boise never had factories except a few smaller manufacturers of agricultural equipment, mobile homes, and other implements. That helped the city preserve an upper- and middle-class citizenry, employed mainly in various commercial, professional, and educational concerns as well as city, county, and state governmental agencies. Unlike the rest of Idaho, Boise became less tied to the extractive industries of agriculture, timber, and mining.

From its inception until the seventies, Boise had largely ignored its central topographical asset, the river. Over the years, the Boise River had been used only for irrigation and industrial purposes. It looked dirty; nobody swam or tubed in it. The salmon that the Boise Shoshoni band and the Bannock tribe enjoyed for centuries, and that pioneers wrote about, had long since disappeared. In about 1962, the Boise City Council and the Boise Chamber of Commerce created "the Atkinson Report" to study how to better treat, protect, and enjoy the river. Boisean Brad Shaw went to San Francisco at his own expense to learn how to best link the three city parks along its shores (Municipal, Julia Davis, and Anne Morrison). He created a slide show for the Ada County commissioners and the city council. Those groups dedicated $10,000 and commissioned Arlan Nelson to devise a plan. Mayor Jay Amyx and the city council formed the Greenbelt Committee. It threw aside the San Antonio commercial model and opted for a nature path. Ken Pursley, an Idahoan who returned from Chicago to practice law in Boise, formed The Citizens Alliance. This advocacy group met at the YWCA to raise consciousness about pollution and waste in the river and the possibilities of executing a plan for a city-imposed setback to keep building away from the river. The committee did not get the 100-foot right-of-way that it desired. The equestrian component was lost. But the seventy-foot setback they achieved proved a major victory. Good tax incentives helped owners donate land that could be used for federal matching funds that made cleanup and construction of the Greenbelt feasible. Today a natural path along the river's banks stretches nearly thirty miles from the canyon to the east at Lucky Peak Dam downriver to Eagle Island. Along it, one encounters people biking, walking their dogs, roller blading, or strolling with friends under native cottonwoods unobtrusively fenced with mesh wire to stop the beaver from chewing them down. From June to October, tubers float down the river. Eagles, osprey, and other birds fly over it, and a number of attractive Boise State University buildings and corporate head-quarters in the Park Center area overlook it.

Volunteers continued to add to Boise's cultural possibilities. The Fortnightly Club kept up its cultural discussions over elegant luncheons at the homes of its lady members through the seventies.[24] Members of the Junior League of Boise worked during the sixties in Boise's schools, taking marionettes to perform plays for elementary school children. They also presented one of several framed prints of classical artworks to each elementary school to teach students how to look at them. Later Junior League projects included cleaning up the Boise City Zoo, planting forsythia along Boise's traditional streets, educating schoolchildren about the ills of alcohol, and building a brilliant Discovery Center to teach people, espe-cially children, about science. The Junior League trained its provisional members to approach volunteerism professionally. During the first year, they attended city council meetings and learned management techniques that honed brainstorm-ing sessions into specific goals with timelines. At each step, the volunteer com-mittees required consensus and commitment of their members. After organizing its projects, the League turned them over to the community. Now, however, the majority of women work for pay outside their homes, so volunteerism suffers.

Some Boise women used their training as volunteers to form employment opportunities. For example, Sally Adams used her expertise in encouraging Idaho artists to form Artists Unlimited ("as opposed to Ducks Unlimited," she says). For twenty years, over fifty Idaho corporations have hired her to place the work of over 250 Idaho artists in their office buildings. One of her most famous con-tacts has been with John Takehara, a Japanese potter who was born in Korea and has lived in Boise for decades. With money from the international sale of his own fine work, Takehara brought artists from Russia, Europe, and the British Isles to inspire his students at BSU.[25]

Another of many outstanding Boise volunteers was Bev Harad, who came to Boise in 1976 with her husband, George, now president of Boise Cascade Corporation. The couple had lived in New York, Philadelphia, Boston, and San Francisco. When they first came to Boise, they found it "a rude awakening." Then they decided to work for change. Bev headed the committee for the Beaux Arts Christmas Sale in the late seventies. Her committee brought the sale back to the museum from the Train Depot, decorating around various furniture vendors' dis-plays with numerous crafts and arts to benefit the Boise Gallery of Art. Sales quadrupled. Likewise, for several years, Harad headed the committee for "Art in the Park," an annual fund-raiser for the BGA. Her committee orchestrated a plan to invite over 200 artists to participate while demanding high-quality art.[26] Today the event encompasses Julia Davis Park for several days in September, providing entertainment for residents of the Treasure Valley. The BGA, renamed the Boise Art Museum, again expanded its function, remodeling and enlarging its facili-ties, thereby reaching a larger audience.

New programs in the humanities paralleled the influx of educated outsiders to Boise in the early seventies. The Committee on Foreign Relations formed out of the Boise Valley World Affairs Committee, an organization that discussed foreign affairs once a month at Boise Junior College. It began as a men's-only group. Newspaper editor Alice Dieter became its first woman member when her husband, Les, ran the forum for thirteen years. Dieter later accompanied Don Mitchell, a Boise attorney, and several others to Washington, D.C., to start the Idaho Association for Humanities. Today it is called the Idaho Humanities Council, a nonprofit association that administers grants from corporate, individual, and charitable sources to further knowledge of the humanities throughout Idaho.[27] Housed in a renovated home on East State Street, IHC recently sponsored the Scholars-in-the-School program. Funded by the Albertson Foundation, a multi-million-dollar charity that benefits Idaho education from kindergarten through high school, this program pays scholars, asked by teachers of any school in Idaho, to speak on areas of their expertise.

In spite of improvement in the arts, humanities, and sports, the seventies witnessed the decline and near death of downtown Boise. Idaho native L. J. Davis wrote in the November 1974 issue of *Harper's:*

Boise stands an excellent chance of becoming the first American city to have deliberately eradicated itself.... Downtown Boise gives the impression that it has recently been visited by an exceedingly tidy bombing raid conducted by planes that cleaned up after themselves. Main Street is virtually deserted. A few eerily patronless stores still stand on the north side, the offices above them empty, while across the street a small inland sea of parking lots stretches as far south as the railroad tracks two blocks away.... On a recent warm bright Tuesday morning—perfect shoppers weather—a cannonball, if fired the length of the sidewalk, would have struck exactly nineteen people.[28]

The Boise Redevelopment Agency (BRA), formed in 1966, had tried unsuccessfully to modernize Boise's downtown. By 1974, the agency had gone through three developers, all of whom supported a similar idea of an air-conditioned megastructure containing 800,000 square feet of shopping mall under one roof, a hotel of 250 rooms, parking structures with 2,444 spaces, and 300,000 square feet of office space. To accomplish this goal, the BRA needed to clear eight blocks in the city's heart and portions of three adjacent blocks. The fortresslike building that they planned would have looked inward to itself, containing all features necessary for survival except a moat. The area around it could just wither, as did the entire downtown for nearly two decades even though the shopping mall was never built there.

Lack of planning produced both sprawl and the destruction of Victorian-era buildings, conditions typical of western towns. When Boise had only 40,000 inhabitants, it took up a space equal to that of Munich or Paris. To build modern buildings, reformers with no appreciation of the city's history began to destroy important old buildings. The elegant city hall on Eighth and Idaho Streets fell to the wrecker's ball in the forties. The DeLamar House, depicted in the *San Francisco Chronicle* as an excellent example of the mansard roof style in the 1870s, fell in the early 1970s. The Hip Sing Building at the center of Boise's Chinatown was leveled to make way for urban renewal. The elegant old St. Alphonsus Hospital and the Eastman Building ended in arson flames during controversies over their fates. Meanwhile many businesses had placed aluminum facades on the fronts of older buildings to modernize them. Alan Minskoff, who moved from New York to Boise and created *Boise Magazine,* wrote in *Harper's* in 1975 that aluminum facades were like "putting moustaches on Modigliani's" (paintings). False fronts hid the lovely brick and stone that were original to old buildings of integrated design, buildings that could be redesigned on the inside to serve updated uses.[29]

Such destruction spawned reaction. Several concerned citizens formed The Idaho Historic Preservation Council to discuss the value of old buildings, the lack of support for a downtown mall, and the alternative of recycling what already existed. Out of this private group came the "Orchids and Onions" award, which praised outstanding restoration efforts and identified poor choices for Boise's appearance. Joan Carley, one of its founders, bought and restored the large Pioneer Tent and Awning Building at Sixth and Main, dividing it into a number of smaller business spaces that still charm customers. At the same time, the White Savage Associates formed to buy and renovate old buildings. Calvin Jensen, a Boise native, invited Alan Minskoff to come to Boise to work with him and Ray Allen in this effort. They renovated the Patterson Apartments, Belgravia, the Idan-ha Hotel, and the Miner's Exchange in nearby Idaho City. The trio put into practice what they believed: that old buildings defined a place's past and could also serve modern needs. They and others started the "Friends of Old Buildings." Arthur Hart, director of the Idaho State Historical Society, Romaine Hon, a civic worker, Ron Thurber, an architect, John Bertram, a Canadian VISTA volunteer in Boise who had trained as a city planner, and others joined them. Because these and other citizens raised the consciousness of Boiseans about their historical buildings, the Ada (originally and again, the Egyptian) Theater, the Union Block, the Mode Building, the Boise City National Bank Building, the Idan-ha Hotel, the Alexander Building, the Bouquet bar, and others still remain today. Not only do they house thriving businesses, they also remind people of Boise's past. Boise, Idaho, became the last capital city of fifty states to build a mall, this one well outside the heart of town, about nine miles to the west. Today a highway connector to that area whisks traffic to Boise Towne Square mall and a series of chain stores auxiliary to it, a stunningly successful commercial area that draws shoppers from southern Idaho, northern Nevada, and eastern Oregon.

To further the goals of downtown, the "Boise Now" group formed in the early eighties. Advocating public and private uses of downtown, its members included Betty Lou Donnelley, Ken Pursley, and Larry Leasure. Meanwhile Jane Lloyd and Sue Reents worked on the Downtown Boise Plan. These organizations supported the mixed use of public and private concerns. They also sought an environment with planted trees, flowers, and open space, amenities to enhance historic buildings that Boiseans already enjoyed.[30] As talk continued about Boise's future, Joe Albertson (founder of Albertson's food chain) invited hundreds of leaders to a lunch that he did not attend himself. He sent a spokesman to say that he was "tired of looking at this damned mess." That proclamation helped to push the effort to revitalize downtown Boise.[31] Today downtown is hopping with activities like "First Thursdays," when galleries stay open late, and "Alive after Five," a happening every Wednesday during warm weather when vendors sell food, soft drinks, and beer. Various musical acts invite people to "the Grove," a bricked open space on Main Street next to The Grove Hotel, which has 250 rooms, a ballroom, and viewing rooms for sports events held in a multievent center that seats 5,500 for Boise's ice hockey team, the Steelheads, and other venues.[32] Adjacent to the Grove sits the twenty-story U.S. Bancorp Plaza branch and, on the block's northwest corner, the new Wells Fargo Bank building.

New appreciation for its history helped Boise to fund the Historical Museum. Begun on the eve of Pearl Harbor, construction of the building stalled until the fifties. In 1970, when Martha and Norman Noonan moved to Boise, after researching climates and environments of midsized towns in the West, they found the museum "a dark little building with a two-headed calf and the bar from the old Overland Hotel."[33] Arthur Hart, hired in 1969 to direct the museum, stated that Jack Simplot paid Jerry Swinney's salary the first year to make sure that the museum would have a director. When Hart came, the previous director had fired the society's auxiliary. Hart reinstated them to help in acquisitions of artifacts and in running a volunteer oral history project until he convinced the legislature to fund it in the mid-1970s. He educated the public about Boise's architectural past, Hart's heart's project.[34]

Important buildings to save included the old penitentiary (after a large, new modern one was built on the desert south of Boise), the Chinese Joss House on Capitol Boulevard, with its ancient collection of Chinese herbs, and the Bishop's House, which was moved to the old prison as part of a historic area at the end of a grassy boulevard under Table Rock. Hart had spoken to over fifty organizations in the area to explain the potential uses of the old prison. A relic in penology, the site later became a museum. Its grounds now host events such as "Jai Aldi," an international Basque celebration held in Boise every five years. Romaine Hon helped Hart form a nonprofit corporation called "Friends of the Bishop House" and spearheaded the effort to save that structure. Once moved down Warm Springs Avenue in the mid-1970s, the 220-ton house employed the talents of many, including "Teenagers at Risk," who ripped out old plaster and lathe. Today it hosts many wedding receptions.

The energy crisis of the late seventies saved Boise's unique geothermal development. When aged wooden pipes spouted leaks, pessimists believed that the existing user cooperative could not afford to install a new system. Then oil prices escalated to affect projected electrical costs, changing their perception of cost. Thus Boise's 1890 geothermal system, the world's first commercial use of this resource, continues to function 108 years later. The new system serves the surrounding neighborhood and state and university buildings, with over 300 connections.

Amidst the destruction and renovation period of the late seventies, the

Shakespeare Theater began in an outdoor amphitheater on a downtown lawn. Doug Copsey, a theater graduate from the University of Nevada, Reno, formed a small group to stage Shakespearean plays. Soon the White Savage Associates donated a lawn at the Plantation Golf Course, which they had just purchased. The Idaho Shakespeare Festival completed its capital campaign to build a grand outdoor theater on the Boise River east of the city. It opened for the 1998 season. The group stands as another Boise hallmark.

In the late seventies, nightlife in downtown Boise took an upward turn when Gene Harris, a talented African American jazz pianist from the Midwest, began playing in the newly renovated Idan-ha bar in the historic marble-floored lobby. On Tuesday nights, Harris invited aspiring musicians to join his trio. The jam sessions drew legion crowds, spilling way over seating capacity. He encouraged many jazz musicians. Among them appeared Phillip Batt, popular Republican legislator and successful onion farmer from Canyon County, who became governor of Idaho in the nineties. The Baldwin Piano Company furnished Gene Harris with a grand piano. Fans swear that no one else could play a left hand as powerfully as he did. After marrying Janie Hewitt, the daughter of a Boise banker, the two traveled internationally for Harris's performances. They returned to their home in Boise every year to play for outdoor concerts at the St. Chapelle Winery on the Snake River at Sunny Slope. Before his death of diabetes in January 2000 at sixty-seven, Harris established an endowment at Boise State University to encourage music students. The Gene Harris Jazz Festival will happen each spring in his memory.

The Eighties See Growth of Technology, Education, and Cultural Facilities

Another unique educational facility exists on the desert south of Boise at The Birds of Prey Center. Thousands of schoolchildren and other visitors travel there each year to see birds and learn the story of the successful breeding facilities paid for by the Peregrine Fund, a group that moved to Boise in 1982. Tom Cade, a professor at Cornell University, noticed the disappearance of peregrines and attempted a breeding program in New York that did not succeed. After trying again at Colorado Springs, the program moved to Boise for the high desert country and the leadership of peregrine specialist Morley Nelson. Because of the success of the Boise program, the peregrine falcon came off the endangered species list in 1999, the first species ever to do so. Other birds currently in the program include the Mauritius kestrel, the aplomado falcon, the California condor, the Madagascar serpent eagle, and the harpy eagle. Idahoans serving on the board include Morley Nelson, Harry Bettis, Ron Yanke, Tom Nicholson, Velma Morrison, Jim Nelson, Rob Comstock, Wayne Griffin, and its founder, Tom Cade, who is now a Boisean. They provide another example of Boise area businesspeople who give time and money to civic concerns that improve the region.

Idaho's largest private employer at the turn of the millennium, Micron

Technology, began with the homegrown talent of Idahoan Ward Parkinson, a graduate from the Stanford School of Engineering and former employee of several Silicon Valley companies before moving to Boise. He invented the dynamic random access memory chip, one much smaller (a fifth of a square inch in size) than those of the Japanese competitors then dominating the market. Over the next few years, Ward and his twin brother, Joe, an attorney, rallied the support of Jack Simplot, Allen Noble, Ron Yanke, and Tom Nicholson to raise the capital that financed Micron. It opened its first fabrication plant in 1981 and the company went public in 1984.[35] Micron has brought great rewards to investors unafraid of financial roller-coaster rides, although it has left a few of the faint-hearted "in the dust." The company increased its production, employment, and contributions to the area over the past two decades. In the November 1998 issue of *Newsweek,* six cities appeared on the cover as "The Hottest Tech Cities"— Seattle, Austin, Salt Lake City, Washington, D.C., Boise, and Boston. The first page and only color photograph in the story features a young woman at the corner of Eighth and Idaho Streets, sitting at an outdoor café under a blue sky. The article states that "because of the Internet, technoids in places as distant as Tel Aviv and Boise, Idaho, are actually as close to each other as to their compatriots across town."[36] That puts a whole new slant on Boise's isolation.

A Micron gift from Jack Simplot further enhanced Boise State University, which had grown from a small junior college to a four-year state school. By the eighties it had become a large, urban university. The new Simplot Micron Center, a multimedia center, supports faculty and students alike with the latest audio, video, and computer equipment in nearly every classroom. In the eighties, BSU built The Pavilion, a huge facility for sporting events or rock concerts. The School of Technology, which offers degrees in various practical fields like catering, mechanics, and nursing, recently split to form the new School of Engineering. Warren McCain, after retiring as CEO of Albertson's in the early nineties, matched community contributions for a huge library addition that amplified teaching of the arts and humanities. As a ten-year foundation board member, Donald James Nelson noted, "It costs less to go to B.S.U. than most car payments, but it offers a great education. . . . The endowment of $66 million continues to grow."[37] Many foundations, including the Laura Moore Cunningham Foundation, various corporations, and private individuals contribute to scholarships for the university.

Another major cultural institution came to Boise when Velma Vivian Morrison, head of the Harry Morrison Foundation, gave Boiseans a world-class auditorium. Situated on the Boise River at BSU, the facility is now called the Velma V. Morrison Center for the Performing Arts. The story of this gift is intriguing. In 1975, the bond election failed for lack of only sixty-five votes. After the second bond election failed the next year, Velma asked Fred Norman to take her to the airport. She had sold the family home in McCall but retained one in Boise. At the airport, newscasters asked her how she felt. She replied that building the Morrison Center did not appear urgent to Boiseans, but "it was too right to be wrong." Fred Norman, who had taught music at Boise State, had worked for years to promote the center with various musical productions that he directed. In Morrison's absence, he kept together the "family" of supporters. Norman got acquainted with the university's new president, John Kaiser, and then produced two new shows to promote building the Morrison Center on that campus. Velma returned to Boise to play Sophie Tucker in Norman's rendition of an original musical, *Vaudeville Revisited*. The crowd went wild, and Velma took sixteen bows. The momentum for the facility rose, and the effort to raise $9.5 million succeeded, spearheaded by First Security Bank president Ralph Comstock.[38]

The performing arts center opened on April 7, 1984, just as the trees outside had burst into blossom. At an early breakfast that morning, Velma Morrison learned from Governor Cecil Andrus that long-term senator Frank Church had died, which she announced to the crowd that opening night. She also pledged that night to match every contribution to the facility's endowment, plus a fund to secure future operating expenses, so as to avoid the sad fate of many other performing arts centers throughout the nation.

The acoustics of the Morrison Center for the Performing Arts are second to none. Thus said Itzhak Perlman, who performed there seven times; Kenny G, who sang "What a Wonderful World" (written by George Weisman, husband to former Boisean Clair Nicholson, for Louis Armstrong); and Judy Collins, who sang "Amazing Grace" a cappella. In 1987, Harry Belafonte noted, "Who in the world had the vision to build an edifice of this magnificence in such a small town? I've traveled the world and I've not seen its like." Marilyn Horne asked patrons after her performance, "Do you know what you have here?"[39] In February of 2000, the audience had grown large enough for the center to host the traveling troop of *Miss Saigon* for ten performances.

Another woman, Esther Simplot, who married potato magnate Jack Simplot, also greatly changed Boise's cultural life. She reflected, "Imagine a movie with no music! Music permeates our lives in politics, in art, in everyday life. Arts are great for children's psyches, their development. You don't have time to get in trouble if you are working on your talent."[40] She should know. She had been working on her own ever since her high school band director had complimented her voice. Starting Opera Idaho with a group of other aficionados in 1972, soon after she moved to Boise, Esther understands what starving artists go through. She had moved from Wisconsin to a music school in southern Illinois and then to New York to further her talent. When Esther came to Boise, the Philharmonic Orchestra performed at Capital High School.

Ballet did not move to Boise until the late eighties. When the American Festival Ballet suffered management disputes and confusion about rehearsal space, patrons asked Esther to take it over. The professional company became a shared one: "Ballet Idaho" when performing in Boise and "Eugene Ballet" when performing in Oregon. The opera and the ballet needed a place to learn, practice, and advance their arts.

In 1992, the Esther Simplot Performing Arts Academy opened. It provided a home for the ballet, the opera, and the symphony orchestra. During the building's renovation, Esther's cancer had stopped construction. Recovered, she ordered that plans proceed. Today the ballet school enlists about 500 students and the opera classes involve two age groups of children of about 100 students and offer three educational grants in addition to a program for older adults. Reflecting on the academy, Simplot said, "My husband has had a million good ideas; this is my one good idea."[41] She expects to generate a 2 percent audience from the greater Boise area of 389,000 people (in Canyon and Ada counties in 1997), or nearly 6,000 people. Therefore she plans soon for two performances of each production. A recent performance of *Carmina Burana* combined the talents of the Boise Opera, Ballet Idaho, the Boise Philharmonic Orchestra, and the Boise Master Chorale. Simplot mused, "People expect more and demand more. They want action while they hear symphony; they want ballet with symphony."

Another distinct ballet company, The Idaho Dance Theatre, resides at BSU. A quasi-professional organization directed by Marla Hansen, this company encourages and trains young dancers for later professional opportunities.

Boise's old warehouse district now harbors a new cultural area in Boise. In 1987, Jack Simplot bought the old Hendren Furniture Building to house the Esther Simplot Performing Arts Academy. It is situated northwest of the newly expanded Boise Public Library, which had moved into the old Salt Lake Hardware building near the Boise River. The library is across Capitol Boulevard from the Boise Art Museum and the Idaho Historical Museum. South of the river from the museums sits the Velma V. Morrison Center for Performing Arts on the BSU campus. This cultural cluster spills into downtown, just blocks south of The Grove.

Diversity Increases with Excellence in the Arts during the Nineties

In the nineties, the development of the Boise Symphony Orchestra has been "astonishing," asserts Ninth Circuit judge Steve Trott, who hoped and plotted for years to be able to move to Boise and have a good job. Trott thinks that Jim Ogle, a transplant from Scotland, conducts a symphony orchestra as good as those he attends in Pasadena, Portland, or Seattle.[43] The Langroise Trio helps keep the standards high. It was fully endowed by Gladys Langroise, another Boise patron of the arts, the recently deceased widow of Bill Langroise, partner of Langroise & Sullivan law firm and president of Continental Life and Accident Company. The Langroise Trio includes a first violin, cellist, and violist. The endowment requires that the three performers participate in the orchestra and teach at Albertson College, a private four-year college in nearby Caldwell.

On the river's north bank next to the library, one sees a quaint log cabin that was used by the Forest Service for many years. Today it houses the Log Cabin Literary Center to promote writing and stage readings and to encourage writers. In September 1999, its first Bookfest to benefit programs attracted 1,300 people. In comparison, Salt Lake, a city four times the size of Boise, rallied only 1,000 people to its first similar event.

Behind the Log Cabin, the new Anne Frank Center will be built to commemorate the Holocaust. Greg Carr, an Idaho native who retired in his thirties after he sold the Internet company Prodigy, offered a challenge grant of $500,000 for its construction. Speaking at Boise's City Club in April 2000, Carr said that Boiseans need to continue discussions about diversity. For instance, public television must offer a range of issues, and the BSU lectures and seminars that occurred for nearly a month after Martin Luther King Day in 2000 must continue. Paradoxically, the negative image surrounding Idaho may actually help it. Unlike states where similar ignorance of diversity exists but less attention has been called to it, Idaho now has a mandate to improve. Carr admonished Idahoans to be vigilant to lessen any attraction for racists to move to Idaho.[44] Marilyn Shuler, former director of Human Rights in Idaho, agreed and added, "The response to the Anne Frank Memorial exceeded all hopes: she stands for all persecuted people. From January to March this year and the past few years in Boise, one could attend a fine event nearly every day—speeches, fora, panels, and activities—on human rights."[45]

The Boise Peace Quilt Project currently works on a design for a human rights quilt to hang in Boise's city hall. Formed in 1981, when thirty-five women made a quilt for Russia and presented it to the Soviet embassy, this group has been stitching for peace ever since. They have sent a quilt to Hiroshima to a *hibabshu* for people suffering from radiation sickness. They sent the National Peace Quilt to Washington, D.C., requesting that all 100 U.S. senators sleep under it. They have honored Frank Church, Norman Cousins, Pete Seeger, Mister Rogers, César Chávez, Rosa Parks, Habitat for Humanity, and Boise's own Community House and Booth Memorial Home (for unwed mothers) as well as many other worthy honorees.[46]

The heightened diversity from recent corporation recruitment and new students at Boise State has stimulated another look at Boise's ethnic roots. Unique celebrations of ethnicity from the city's past reverberate the new appreciation that people have for multiethnicity. Adelia Garro Simplot (daughter-in-law of Jack Simplot) bought the old Jacobs house at 607 Grove Street, formerly a boardinghouse, to save it from destruction. Then she settled on the idea of celebrating her own Basque culture.[47] In 1986, the Basque Museum and Cultural Center was incorporated to honor the cultural heritage of many people who emigrated from the Pyrenees Mountains between France and Spain to the Boise area at the turn of the last century through the post–World War II period. The center offers Basque language classes, a display of various family artifacts from the old Basque church on Idaho Street, photographs and family oral histories in the archives, a gift shop, and a library containing 8,000 volumes given by the University of Idaho. It is the only Basque museum in the United States. The museum sits next to the Basque Center, where men play cards, couples celebrate marriages, and the Oinkari Dancers have been performing more intricate dances than "La Jota" and "La Porresilda," which almost every Basque child in Boise learns even today. The Idaho Hispanic Cultural Center will respond to the needs of Idaho's largest minority, the Mexican population (18.6 percent of Canyon County, 4.5 percent of Ada County, 7.9 percent of Idaho). This center will use the old rodeo grounds of the Snake River Stampede in Nampa to stage cultural events. A board of Anglos and Hispanics from Nampa and Boise held a *quinceañera* party in May 2000 to kick off their endowment campaign.

Other unique ethnic celebrations exist. The new Black History Museum resides in the old St. Paul's Baptist Church building that was recently moved to the Julia Davis Park. It is the only museum of its kind in the Northwest. Cherie Buckner-Webb's grandmother persuaded her to preserve the old church after the congregation had expanded and moved to a larger building. Completion of the museum and its opening in 1999 made this dream come true.[48] Each June the Greek Festival occurs in Boise, and each January the campus of BSU hosts what has become the largest celebration of "Bobby Burns's Birthday" in the United States to honor Scotland's poet laureate and the numerous residents of Scottish heritage.

Although growth and celebration describe the nineties in Boise, problems remain. Increasing population has brought traffic stalemates, homelessness, and a growing incidence of poverty, particularly among children. Responding to the homeless in Boise, Michael Hoffman, a BSU theater major who now directs Hollywood films and still lives in Boise, spearheaded the plan to provide shelter. In 1994, he enlisted various individuals and foundations to build Community House. In 1998, the operation extended 58,990 bed nights of service to 1,500 people. Its Child Development Center houses all residents under six while their parents seek jobs, counsel, or work. This facility will soon be doubled. Most of the residents come from "the urban working poor," said Linda Grossman, director of Community House. Some came to the area because Boise has been booming; some came from Boise itself. Residents cannot meet the expenses of food, clothing, housing, and transportation, especially those who have small children. One must earn far more than minimum wage to accomplish those ends.[49] Even though the homelessness rate is less than 1 percent of the area, it affects 100 percent of those concerned.

Another indicator of growing poverty among children shows in the numbers qualifying for free or reduced-rate lunches at public school. Last year, this figure rose to 40.6 percent. Demographic projections of this trend demand vigilance. Good programs exist in Boise, such as the Women's and Children's Alliance (offering shelter from abuse for mothers and children and rape crisis treatment), the Lutheran Social Services, and the Children's Home Society of Idaho, which subsidizes counseling for troubled children and their families. Boise's wealth must spread to citizens who need it most. With growth come challenges. Boise's population grew 20.6 percent between 1990 and 1996.[50]

Failure to plan for growth should be a lesson Boiseans learned from the seventies. In the nineties, Boise faces the threat that the historic Warm Springs Avenue and Harrison Boulevard districts will collapse with traffic, pollution, dirt, and lower property values, as did Meridian Avenue in Indianapolis and Connecticut Avenue in Washington, D.C. Unless traffic is diverted around historic homes and streets, unplanned growth will surely destroy them.

Conclusions

Despite challenges and problems, Boise is still prosperous, friendly, and generous. It is in the midst of a wonderful cultural renaissance. People can and do make a difference because easy access to the sources of power still exists. Some have called it "the Paris of the West."[51] Civic volunteer Lois Lenzi described the Boise area as "a big land punctuated by mountains with a small city of tight social connections,"[52] and John Bertram pointed out that Boise is "a more liberal, livable city in a very conservative state."[53] As Boise grows and embraces cultural diversity and its cultural activities expand, so do its cultural values. The spirit of giving back to the community has set the foundation for historic Boise. It remains the best hope for Boise's future as well.

In the past fifty years, Boise has echoed its past of strong individual investment toward community improvement in the arts, humanities, education, and the newest technology. It still features unusual prosperity in a relatively isolated geographic place. Attainment of higher standards of cultural amenities occurs as its population expands and its leadership in technology supplants extractive industries. As Boise becomes closer to the shrinking world and its human diversity expands, its cultural advantages will only become better known in the twenty-first century.

Notes

1. Carol Lynn MacGregor, "Founding Community in Boise, Idaho, 1882–1910" (unpublished Ph.D. diss., University of New Mexico, 1999).
2. Interview with Marilyn Shuler, former director, Idaho Human Rights Commission, under Governor Cecil Andrus, Boise, 28 February 2000.
3. John Gerassi, *The Boys of Boise* (New York: Macmillan Company, 1966).
4. Interview with Dan and Carmelyn Johnson, continuous residents for seven decades, Boise, 20 March 2000.
5. *The Idaho Statesman,* 5 March 1950, 5, cols. 2–4.
6. Interview with Adelia Garro Simplot, founder of the Basque Museum, Boise, 6 April 2000.
7. Interview with Bradford Paine Shaw, architect and ballet aficionado, 28 February 2000. Memories of the author and of Don and Emily Riley, interviewed in Boise, 1 April 2000.
8. Interview with Dr. Robert Sims, professor emeritus at Boise State University, 29 February 2000.
9. Interview with Governor Robert and Lucille Smylie, Boise, 23 March 2000.
10. *Idaho Daily Statesman,* 7 May 1950, "Society and Features," 1, all columns.
11. *The Arbiter,* Boise State University, 15 March 2000, 16, all columns.
12. *Idaho Daily Statesman,* 4 March 1951, Society & Features, 1, all columns.
13. Ibid., 16, cols. 7–8.
14. Ibid., 16 March 1952, "Society and Features," 1, all columns.
15. Ibid., 11 November 1951, 7, cols. 2–3.
16. Interview with Alice Hennessey, director of the Idaho Community Foundation, Boise, 30 March 2000.
17. Bradford Paine Shaw, interview.
18. Alice Hennessey, interview.
19. Interview with Alyce Rosenheim, community volunteer, Boise, 22 March 2000.
20. Interview with Romaine Gailey Hon, civic worker and writer, 10 March 2000.

21. Interview with Dr. Gustav Rosenheim, retired gynecologist, Boise, 22 March 2000.
22. Interviews with Jean Wilson, owner of The Book Store, Boise, 15 March 2000, and Lois Lenzi, civic volunteer, Boise, 8 March 2000.
23. Interview with Dr. Merle Wells, Idaho historian, Boise, 23 March 2000.
24. Interview with Jean Sullivan, lifelong resident and descendant of Boise pioneers, Boise, 28 March 2000.
25. Interview with Sally Adams, Artists Unlimited, Boise, 8 April 2000.
26. Interview with Bev Harad, school board member who serves on many community boards, Boise, 15 March 2000.
27. Interview with Alice Dieter, journalist, Boise, 13 March 2000.
28. L. J. Davis, "Tearing Down Boise," Harper's 249 (November 1974): 32, 34.
29. Interview with Alan Minskoff, journalist and publicist, Boise, 10 April 2000.
30. Interview with Betty Lou Donnelley, civic activist, Boise, 11 April 2000.
31. Interview with Adelia Simplot, founder of the Basque Museum and Cultural Center, 6 April 2000.
32. Interview with Jim White, developer of The Grove Hotel, Boise, 10 May 2000.
33. Interview with Martha and Norman Noonan, architect for the state and calligrapher, Boise, 1 April 2000.
34. Interview with Arthur Hart, lecturer and former director of the Idaho State Historical Society, 3 April 2000.
35. "Micron Mastermind: How Ward Parkinson Went from Founding Micron to Fighting Crime," Boise Weekly 7, no. 28 (21–27 January 2000): 12–15.
36. "The Hottest Tech Cities," Newsweek, 9 November 1998, 50.
37. Interview with Donald James Nelson, businessman and philanthropist, Boise, 18 March 2000.
38. Interview with Velma V. Morrison, philanthropist, Boise, 26 April 2000.
39. Interview with Fred Norman, playwright and musician, 26 April 2000.
40. Interview with Esther Simplot, founder of the Esther Simplot Performing Arts Center, Boise, 28 March 2000.
41. Ibid.
42. Ibid.
43. Interview with Steven Trott, Ninth Circuit judge, Boise, 31 March 2000.
44. Paraphrase of Carr's talk at Boise City Club by member Sue Reents, former state legislator; interview in Boise, 2 April 2000.
45. Marilyn Shuler, interview.
46. Lyn McCullom, unpublished writings for the Boise Peace Quilt Project.
47. Adelia Garro Simplot, interview.
48. Interview with Cherie Buckner-Webb, founder of Black History Museum, Boise, 6 May 2000.
49. Interview with Linda Grossman, director of Community House, Boise, 13 April 2000.
50. Statistical Abstract of the U.S. 1998, U.S. Dept Commerce, Bureau of the Census, October 1998, 47.
51. Jean Wilson, interview.
52. Lois Lenzi, interview.
53. Interview with John Bertram, preservationist, Boise, 12 April 2000.

"Squeezing Out the Profits":[1]
Mining and the Environment in the U.S. West,

1945-2000

Christopher J. Huggard

The mining industry collided head-on with a new environmentalism during the last quarter of the twentieth century. For the first time in American history, the nation's citizens valued the environment and its resources for their own sake rather than just as commodities in a global economy. A new ecological consciousness, although based in science like the technocratic worldview, called for an end to the modernist belief in "industrial progress" that threatened the earth's biospheres. For environmentalists, the mining industry was the logical villain. Critics emerged to demonize corporate mining companies as "rapists" of the earth, despoilers of air and water, and paternalistic exploiters of miners and their families.

In his classic study *Mining America* (1987), historian Duane Smith explains that by the 1960s, "Americans . . . discovered the threat to the environment, and they moved with a vengeance to remove it [mining]. . . . The country felt a collective guilt and sought repentance for its past sins."[2] The industry's "pollute today, worry about it tomorrow" attitude came home to roost even though the industry felt betrayed by the public, which had for more than a century supported the technological assault on the environment. The return of this assault was the material well-being of an affluent society. Moreover, as Smith contends, "Without mining–from coal to iron to gold–the United States could not have emerged as a world power by the turn of the century [1900], nor could it have successfully launched its international career of the twentieth century."[3] Mining bolstered the fledgling nation, placing it atop the international power structure in a world dominated by nationalist sentiment. Industry leaders were shocked that the American public had abandoned them after many generations of applause for their patriotic work. Without mining, the industry lamented during the rise of the new environmentalism, there would not have been a people of plenty and a democracy secure from aggressive forces from outside the nation's borders.

Mining, in fact, has been a key cog in the machinery of what I call the "nationalist imperative,"[4] an all-encompassing economic and political affirmation of western culture and its imperialist tendencies. Multinational mining corporations, such as the United States' Phelps Dodge, Canada's Barrick Gold, and South Africa's DeBeers, operate under the guise of western capitalist imperialism. Mining in the American West from 1945 to 2000 has been directly linked to this European-based worldview and especially to the preservation of the liberal tradition–marked by democratic government, capitalist imperialism, and the general "pursuit of happiness," ideals ingrained in the minds of the American public since the late eighteenth century. This industrial idealization has led to influential roles for multinational mining corporations as well—the 1973 fall of the Allende government in Chile and recent rebel violence in West Africa being just two examples.[5] The industry also fueled the development of the most sophisticated national defense systems in history in the United States and other developed nations. Without a doubt, mineral exploitation–from the blasting of hard-rock ores deep in the earth's bowels to the refining of metals and on to the manufacturing of military and consumer goods–elevated the United States to world preeminence and an unprecedented superpower status. From the California gold rush of 1849 to the rise of the "copper century" before World War II to the federally grub-staked uranium boom and the resulting atomic age, mining was celebrated as a national imperative. As a result, prior to the 1960s, the industry and its adoring public rarely considered "beyond progress and profit, why the environment–land, water, and air– received such shabby treatment."[6]

For environmentalists, the industry's rude awakening was poetic justice. Since the late nineteenth century, when the federal government first began to curb frontier abuses, the mining industry has protested each attempt to reform its ecologically unsound practices. Chief Forester Gifford Pinchot in the early part of the twentieth century, for example, naively believed that miners would wholeheartedly support conservation of timber, water, and other resources in the newly established national forests. But prospectors and independent miners, in particular, felt targeted by the far-off federal government in Washington, D.C. And despite sustained-yield policies, miners chose to operate under the Mining Law of 1872, which gave them the authority to extract ores underground and to exploit, at little cost, the natural resources aboveground on the public lands. The results were deforested lands pocked with glory holes and deep mines and the concomitant waste dumps that served as giant funnels for floodwaters that washed through many a mining town. The independent-minded frontiersmen viewed conservation as a threat to democratic exploitation of the seemingly "free" lands and their natural abundance in the American West. They were not about to change their practices.[7]

Ironically, the twentieth-century emergence of the large mining corporations, such as AMAX, ASARCO, Barrick, Kennecott, and Phelps Dodge, translated into an acceptance of conservation practices. Whereas small-time, financially strapped miners could not afford to develop efficient, conservation-minded operations, corporations had the capital and know-how to implement conservation into their business systems. As conservationists they demanded efficiency, in spending and in conserving water, timber, and other natural resources, so that they could extract as much of the precious ores, whether gold and silver or copper and molybdenum, to maximize profits and feed the expanding American economy and its emergent military-industrial complex. Open-pit mining, for instance, which overtook lode mining as the principal technique for extracting copper ores by the 1930s, was designed to efficiently extract very low-grade ores and facilitate the change to "wise use" of water, coal, natural gas, oil, and other natural resources used in the extracting, refining, and manufacturing processes.

The industry may have conserved some natural resources, but it also worked to exhaust the West's mineral resources. In fact, mining was so successful in the first half of the twentieth century that by the time of World War II, Congress had already passed stockpiling acts to ensure that mining corporations did not export the nation's strategic minerals, such as copper and, later, uranium. In short, mining industry conservation practices were not linked to preservation of ecosystems and the biota therein, but were part of a structured operations system designed to maximize use of the natural resources and to capitalize on mineral resources for profits, to drive the consumer economy, and as materiel for the cold war military-industrial complex. As justification, industrialists viewed their conservation practices as their patriotic duty to serve the nationalist imperative, not as a system for protecting the fragile biospheres of the American West or elsewhere on the globe. The industry's rude awakening during the rise of the new environmentalism in the 1960s, then, should come as no surprise.

The year 1970 was the watershed. In the previous year, Congress had passed the National Environmental Protection Act, resulting in the establishment of the Environmental Protection Agency (EPA) on January 1, 1970. Later, on April 22, the first Earth Day further galvanized the American public under the environmentalist umbrella. Similarly, Congress passed an amendment in 1970 to the Clean Air Act, which in its previous forms of 1955 and 1967 had literally been written by industry "experts" but now had teeth to enforce compliance with minimum standards for emissions from smokestacks. Congress followed suit with the Mineral Policy Act of 1970, the Water Pollution Control Act of 1972, the Endangered Species Act of 1973, the Federal Land Policy and Management Act of 1976, the Mining Regulation Act of 1976, which established an abandoned mine reclamation fund, another Clean Air Act Amendment in 1977, the Comprehensive Environment Response Act (Superfund) in 1980, and many other "environmental" laws.[8] The idealism and protests of the 1960s, which resulted in congressional passage of the Wilderness Act of 1964, translated into broader federal initiatives that forced the mining industry and other industrial behemoths to consider a new viewpoint, a philosophical ideology that I call "nature's imperative."

Nature's imperative is a shift within the modernist paradigm. From the *longue durée* perspective, it cannot be argued that the new environmentalism forms an original way of thinking; instead it provides a reformulation of a long-standing worldview. The Cartesian world system gave rise to the industrial revolution and a faith that science could ameliorate all of western society's ills. Ironically, however, that absolutist, rationalist system left little room to question the "machine in the garden" attitude, a vision of technological domination of nature that has pervaded western thinking at least since the eighteenth century. When Albert Einstein himself in the early twentieth century shocked the scientific world with his theory of relativity, some of the traditional viewpoints of the modernists came into question. Among those absolutist views was a belief that science, as the source for technological achievements, would serve as the lone blueprint for future western society. Twentieth-century biological scientists, however, have countered technocratic science with an ecological application to force a rethinking of industrial practices. And like Einstein's theory, which revealed that the universe is not a perfectly run machine but rather a dynamic and rapidly changing entity unbound by a system, ecological theory eventually argued that the earth's ecosystems are also dynamic, albeit vulnerable to the effects of unbridled technological exploitation. And like the delayed acceptance of Nicolaus Copernicus's 1543 theory that the sun is the center of our solar system, it took time before the general public accepted the principles of ecology. Once understood (at least in a rudimentary way), ecological thinkers such as Aldo Leopold and Rachel Carson influenced a broader American public to act on this new earth science. That action translated into the popularization of environmentalism during the 1960s, when grassroots activism exploded from a few thousand participants at the beginning of the decade to millions by its close.[9] Hence the birth of nature's imperative fueled the rise of the new environmentalism, with the older, technology-driven science caught in the middle of the passionate new international movement.

What follows are vignettes—historical and contemporary—that illuminate the clashes and continuities between the "nationalist" and "nature's" imperatives. These stories offer insight into the mining-environment dichotomy as it played out in the last thirty years of the twentieth century. These narratives also present avenues for future, more in-depth studies of mining and the environment in the postwar period. I begin with the clean air battle in the American Southwest in the 1970s and 1980s. Then I tell the contemporary story of Libby, Montana, to reveal the complexity of modern issues related to mining and the environment and the inconsistencies of industrialists in applying cleaner technology to their processes and in accepting responsibility for their past actions. And I close with a discussion of the Nevada gold rush from the 1960s to the 1990s to show how that event illustrates the exploitation of public lands, the Mining Law of 1872, globalization, and the long-term environmental consequences.

Story 1: "I Am for Industry. And I Am for Clean Air."

When John Bartlit, longtime president of the New Mexico Citizens for Clean Air & Water (NMCCA&W), made the above comment in a December 14, 1993, interview, I was intrigued that he was combining new and old ways of thinking into his brand of environmentalism. My initial thought was that he was selling out the environmental movement in favor of a technocratic solution, or "techno-fix." But after additional research and interviews, I began to understand his logic.[10] He hoped, beginning in the early 1970s, to convince the mining industry, which was not going away anytime soon, to implement environmental technology, some features that had been available since the 1950s, to clean up smelter stack emissions at the Kennecott smelter in Hurley, New Mexico. Once one copper corporation came into compliance with new federal standards, he strategized, other companies would fall in line.

Bartlit is a pragmatic man of science. A retired chemical engineer from Los Alamos National Laboratory, the nation's atomic research headquarters, he holds a deep faith in the efficacy of science. He is a modernist. His training and worldview mesh well for an activist eager to convince the mining industry to use the "best" environmentally friendly technology. He understands science and the role it plays in the development of industrial technology and realized, with some preliminary homework in the 1970s, that the copper-mining corporations—namely Kennecott and Phelps Dodge—were not using the cleanest technology obtainable on the international market. Bartlit's response was to mobilize, at the grassroots level, to force the industry to clean up its toxic emissions. For this scientist, nature's imperative translated into convincing the industry to implement environmental technology at the southwestern smelters to reduce sulfur dioxide, arsenic, and particulate levels. The health and scenic vistas of southwesterners were at stake.

For most of the twentieth century, the mining industry had been putting off implementation of clean air technology. As early as 1906, in fact, copper companies began paying for the right to pollute the air. That year, Utah farmers won a settlement of $60,000 against the American Smelting & Refining Company (ASARCO) and other mining companies for despoiling crops and poisoning livestock with sulfur fumes and arsenic dust. This precedent-setting case established the "polluter pays" principle but, unfortunately, postponed the formulation of environmental standards that could have reduced or even eliminated air pollution. Although the industry sporadically adopted the use of bag houses and zinc oxide to reduce emissions, they had little overall effect.[11]

Until the 1920s, industry leaders and emissions experts paid little attention to smelter pollution. During that decade, farmers from Washington State filed a lawsuit against the Trail Smelter in British Columbia, Canada, bringing an international flavor to legal and scientific questions about industrial air pollution. Ironically, however, biological scientists and engineers at the U.S. Department of the Interior did such a poor job of presenting the Americans' case before the international arbitration commission that their new scientific theory—the so-called invisible injury argument (the belief that microscopic toxins in the air can kill plants and animals)—gained little acceptance with the tribunal and was dismissed summarily. The case, which pitted the Canadian government, the U.S. Bureau of Mines, and American and Canadian mining corporations against the U.S. Department of the Interior (the parent agency of the Bureau of Mines) and the complainants, reiterated the polluter-pays principle, which remained the industry standard from the 1930s until 1970.[12]

In the post–World War II era, industry leaders began to realize that air pollution was gradually becoming a societal concern. They responded with the 1955 Clean Air Act, which recognized a growing awareness about air pollution but offered no remedy for the pervasive national problem. Twelve years later, after years of pleas from scientists and activists, the industry played a key role in penning another ineffectual clean air act in 1967.

In these years, mining interests feared federal intervention, arguing that air pollution was a local issue to be regulated locally. This strategy stemmed from an industrywide belief that the cost for upgrading smelters with scrubbers, acid plants, and other environmental technology would send financial shock waves rippling through the industry, resulting in plant closings, major layoffs, and even bankruptcy for some corporations. The nationalist imperative buoyed these arguments: mining had to be secured to ensure a healthy economy at home and abroad. The fear of financial dislocation, although greatly exaggerated, appeared repeatedly in the mining record.

The views of David Swan, vice president of technology for the Kennecott Copper Corporation, serve as an example of the industry's position on clean air. He testified before the Senate Subcommittee on Air and Water Pollution in 1970 and then elaborated on his concerns in an essay presented in 1972 before the Society of Economic Geologists. The copper company executive, first, revealed his fear that he and his colleagues would lose local control over emissions. "There is no reason to believe," he began, "that the federal government is in a better position than state and local air pollution control agencies to promulgate emission standards."[13] He rationalized, no doubt, that counties and states would not regulate the mining industry, which paid hundreds of millions of dollars in taxes throughout the interior U.S. West. Two years later, after the EPA began to enforce federal regulations for minimum standards, Swan established economic criteria as the yardstick for implementation of environmental technology: "If growth is low, then the primary goal tends to become fixing up existing plants and equipment [with so-called Intermittent Control Systems based on weather, periodic shutdowns, and self-regulation] to comply with new regulations . . . while in high growth industries, new processes can be economically considered."[14] This rationale allowed the industry to persuade legislators into grandfathering older, more toxic technology into the regulations.

Testifying in 1975 before the Senate Subcommittee on Environmental Pollution, Swan reiterated his economic concerns and then calculated that the $245 million proposed price tag to upgrade Kennecott's smelters at Hurley, New Mexico, and Bingham, Utah, to meet federal standards was too costly for the projected environmental benefits.[15] Expressed at the height of the economic recession in the 1970s, Swan's lamentations won sympathy among conservatives and western congressmen, who worked to postpone compliance until the mid-1980s. The result, after a hushed meeting between President Richard M. Nixon, the Copper Caucus—a politically based pro-copper lobbying group with support from Senator Pete Domenici (R-N.Mex.) and other powerful western senators—and industry leaders—was congressional passage of the 1977 amendment to the Clean Air Act. This act extended the compliance deadline to 1982.

In the meantime, Bartlit and other environmentalists–such as the Sierra Club and the Citizens Committee on Natural Resources–had figured out how to confront overconfident corporate attorneys at hearings and during testimony. They mobilized scientific experts, environmental lawyers, and concerned citizens, often turning intimidating corporate interrogation techniques against industry representatives with barrages of well-informed legal, scientific, and regulatory questions of their own. As purveyors of nature's imperative, they gladly testified before public hearings on the national, state, and local levels while also initiating letter-writing campaigns to government officials and submitting pro-environment editorials to newspapers across the Southwest. Grassroots environmentalism celebrated the nation's democratic tradition while simultaneously calling into question industrial practices formerly associated with capitalist free enterprise and the democratic right to exploit nature.

The battle lines were often blurred as well. Chano Merino, Local 890 representative of the United Steel Workers, for example, supported uninterrupted operation of Kennecott's Hurley smelter. "It isn't the smoke that bothers us," he testified in 1975 at an EPA hearing in Silver City, New Mexico; "it's when we don't see smoke that it bothers us."[16] In public, the local labor leader strongly championed the company's cause. The smelter's survival, which the company claimed hinged on the proposed expenses for environmental technology, translated into jobs and employment for fourth- and fifth-generation workers. But behind the scenes in miners' homes and at local taprooms, smelter workers debated the possible health risks of living and working near the smelter. Further blurring the situation was the inexactness of toxicological science, which at that time was still in its formative stage after more than a century of smokestack air pollution in the United States.

Despite industry opposition, nature's imperative made a dent in "business as usual." By 1975, Kennecott installed scrubbers, acid plants, and air pollution monitors and found a market to sell sulfuric acid, the principle by-product of the clean air technology. Likewise, Phelps Dodge opened its Hidalgo smelter in 1975 at Playas, New Mexico (with the latest environmental technology), on the border with Mexico. On other hand, the Arizona-based corporation kept delaying the shutdown of the most toxic smelter in the nation at Douglas. Using the 1977 amendment and litigation to delay the closing, Phelps Dodge did not stop pumping illegal levels of emissions into the southwestern skies until 1986.

Phelps Dodge finally shut down the Douglas smelter, claims John D. Wirth, author of *Smelter Smoke in North America* (2000), because of international pressures from U.S. and Mexican officials who were negotiating a trade agreement and potential antipollution strategies.[17] The Douglas smelter was on one corner of what air pollution experts called the "Gray Triangle," a corridor of smelter smoke from Cananea and Nacozari, Mexico, to Douglas, Arizona. American environmentalists, the EPA, and locals believed that if Phelps Dodge cleaned up the

Douglas smelter, Compania Minera de Cananea and Mexicana de Cobre would upgrade their smelters immediately south of the Mexico-U.S. border and therefore promulgate a transnational environmentalism. On a field trip to Cananea with a group from the Mining History Association in 1998, however, I noticed that the smelter there was still, twelve years after Douglas had closed, operating as an open hearth system, the most primitive smelter technology on the market and producing the most toxic air pollution on the border. More likely, Phelps Dodge continued to smelt copper at Douglas after federal deadlines because its low operating costs translated into high profits, and the EPA regularly extended the company's permits until the last possible date before eventually requiring a total shutdown.

Like jet pilots jockeying for position in an air war, environmentalists and industrialists likewise have made tactical maneuvers in the air pollution battle. Initially industry leaders gained the upper hand, instigating passage of weak clean air legislation in the 1950s and 1960s and intimidating upstart environmental critics untrained in the art of public confrontation. Once the environmentalists, such as the NMCCA&W and the Sierra Club, mobilized in the 1970s, however, and then grasped parliamentary strategy and how to use federal regulators to their advantage, the real dogfight was on. And even though Phelps Dodge smelted at Douglas until 1986 at the expense of air quality, vegetation, and wildlife, by 1975 the industry had installed environmental technology in nearly every copper smelter in the American West. By so doing, it helped to clear the western skies and improve air sheds over national parks, such as Grand Canyon, Zion, Saguaro, and Bandelier. This achievement on behalf of nature's imperative, although no easy task and certainly not a complete victory, marked a turning point in industrial emissions practices and in environmental history.

Story 2: "Libby's Dark Secret"

We should not get too overconfident, however, about the successes in the air pollution war. The battle to curb corporate mining abuses proves far too complex and far too prevalent in 2002 to close this chapter in environmental history.[18]

Perhaps the clearest representation of egregious mining industry abuse centers on Libby, Montana. A quaint industrial village nestled in the far northwest corner of the state, only a few miles from the borders of Idaho and Canada, Libby has a dark secret. The grim reaper has come to town to take away many former miners and some of their family members: the culprit, asbestosis! For more than half a century, the deadly disease has stalked miners who worked at W. R. Grace & Company's vermiculite mill and mine. Vermiculite is a potting soil and construction industry additive. But it is not the problem; asbestos is. In the mine shafts, deposits of asbestos lay next to those of vermiculite. Asbestos is the deadly mineral whose dust gets lodged in a worker's lungs; once in the pulmonary system, the steel-wool-like particles attach to alveoli in the lungs. White corpuscles then attack the minute foreign invaders, forming layers that block oxygen—carbon

dioxide exchange, causing asbestosis, an uncommon lung ailment that often pro-
gresses into cancer. Because many past and present miners and their families
smoke cigarettes, they have a 92 percent greater chance of contracting lung cancer than nonsmokers with asbestosis.[19]

Typical of the mining industry's mind-set, W. R. Grace's officials have deflected
fault for the town's tragedy since 1963, when the company acquired the operation. Journalist Mark Matthews, writing in the March 13, 2000, issue of *High
Country News,* revealed that "W. R. Grace knew its people were dying, but kept
the knowledge under wraps." But perhaps more distressing, he continued, "Federal
and state authorities also knew about the health dangers in Libby but did little
to help. Now, communities around the West are watching the outcome."[20]

Almost eighty years ago, the Zonolite Company began mining vermiculite
from a mountain near Libby. In the heart of the town, the company also operated a mill, which threatened the health of miners and townspeople who daily
breathed the deadly air. By 1969, the mill's smokestack daily spewed as much as
5,000 tons of asbestos into the atmosphere. And even though the first documented case of asbestosis was in 1956, Grace did not inform its workers until
1979 that asbestos was a health hazard, by then a well-known fact among the general population. In 1969, in fact, Grace's insurance company warned that "when
an X-ray picture shows change for the worse [in the lungs of an afflicted
employee], that person must be told and . . . must be gotten out of the environment which is aggravating his condition. Failure to do so is not humane and is
in direct violation of federal law."[21]

The news media, for reasons still unclear, ignored Libby's story for decades.
Even after publication of the book *A Civil Action* (1996), which was adapted into
a motion picture starring John Travolta, little attention was paid to the town and
its progressively grimmer story. Not until the summer of 1999 were reporters
lured to the scene, when Grace's officials asked the state of Montana to return
$67,000 of a $500,000 bond that was funding the cleanup of the mine and mill
after they were closed in 1990. Libbyites angrily protested what they perceived
as open greediness. They made public their disgust that contaminated company
buildings, former workers' homes, topsoil in gardens, and even the Little League
baseball field built by Grace all remained uninspected and uncleaned, thus per-
petuating the community fear that the next generation of children would also
be afflicted with the deadly disease.

The EPA also confronted the mining company. In 1999, the federal regulatory agency opened an office in Libby and began a criminal investigation of Grace
based on the company's hazardous waste disposal practices and the declining
health of its former workers and other residents of the town. Once on-site, EPA
officials realized they faced a grave situation: things had already progressed beyond
a risk. Wendy Thomi, one of the EPA investigators, commented in March 2000:
"Typically, when we first visit a [contaminated] site, we usually don't have people who are already sick and dying there. . . . [Libby already has a] high incidence
of lung disease."[22]

In the following media frenzy, reporters also uncovered the story of former mine manager Earl Lovick. Already afflicted with asbestosis, Lovick testified in a 1988 deposition that he hid the health risks from his men. Ironically, he succumbed to the disease in 1998.

Labor leaders were also disgusted with the course of events. Don Judge, executive secretary of Montana's AFL-CIO, claimed in 2000 that workers had complained of asbestos dust as early as 1964. Concerned unionists had requested that Grace install showers and change rooms to allow the men to wash off what they called "nuisance dust" and to remove dust-ridden work clothes, which their wives had been shaking off in their homes and thereby contaminating their household air. The company ignored their pleas for hygienic safety but did requisition several respiratory masks. Unfortunately, "they got easily clogged and the men didn't wear them." When the company finally informed workers in 1979 of the health threat, it decided to install two showers for more than 100 employees. Judge vented his frustrations: "Grace is going to have to own up [in 2000]. They need to pay for diagnosis and treatment, lost income, plus the pain and suffering of the victims of asbestos exposure. . . . They also need to pay the penalty for this intentional poisoning. Thousands of workers across the country were exposed to tremolite [asbestos] by Grace's callous actions."[23]

Grace responded to the criticism. First, the company pointed out to the media that it spent $14 million on dust-control technology in the 1960s and 1970s. Later, after the 1999 story hit the presses, Grace opened an office in Libby "to fund an independent medical monitoring program to provide medical coverage to anyone . . . diagnosed with an asbestos-related disease."[24] Since Grace's recent mill-site cleanup, the company denies any legal responsibility for the health problems, hinting that cigarette smoking was the principle source of the townspeople's lung diseases. "There are those who say there is a risk living in this town," Grace spokesman Alan Stringer stated in 2000, "but I don't think that's the case. . . . We'll work with the EPA and let them determine that. Our intentions are to do what is necessary."[25] As for the 140 lawsuits filed against Grace, company officials contend that regional law firms are just "trying to cash in on the human tragedy in Libby."[26]

Even more startling were the roles that the state of Montana and the federal government played in the historic cover-up. State officials, for instance, knew of asbestos poisoning as early as 1956, according to state documents uncovered by the Montana Environmental Information Center (MEIC). Even EPA officials discovered that their Washington, D.C., office was aware of the problem in the 1980s. "It [the document] didn't really get lost," investigator Thomi recently mused. "We're still trying to figure out what happened, why it got dropped. The agency has [also] found some documents showing that Grace wasn't as forthcoming as it should have been."[27] Even the U.S. Forest Service was aware of the dangers. Reporters uncovered a reference to a document in a draft of an environmental impact statement being prepared concerning one mining company's proposal to open another vermiculite mine on national forest lands near Darby, Montana. The document revealed that the people of Libby were found to have "excess mortality from respiratory cancer, nonmalignant respiratory disease, and accidents." An MEIC spokesman angrily reflected, "The government at all levels knew of the situation, but took no action."[28]

Libby's tragedy is no longer a secret. Rather, its dark story reveals a legacy of social and environmental irresponsibility. And for many of the town's residents, the future looks bleak. As Gayla Benefield, whose parents succumbed to lung disease, recently noted, "This isn't just the working men and their wives who are dying. . . . This could go on to the fourth generation within families. My grandchildren watched my mother die and they were terrified. They asked me if they would die of that, too."[29]

Obviously, mining requires damage to the environment. Miners penetrate deep into the earth. Truck drivers haul tailings to mountain-size dumps. Mills and smelters spew toxic emissions into the oft-thought pristine western skies. This industrial assault on the earth's ecosystems is part of the price of the nationalist imperative, a worldview that has trampled on voiceless nature for centuries. When W. R. Grace & Company arrogantly withheld essential information concerning the devastating health risks of working in the vermiculite mine and mill, the company proved that "business as usual" was more important than human lives. Libby's story, like so many other incidents of industrial injustice (faulty Firestone tires being the most recent case), illustrates the need for the corporate world to more diligently reformulate its philosophies and practices. Until this transformation takes place, more Libbys will come to light in the American West and elsewhere in the world. Their stories also must be told as part of the growing literature concerning mining and the environment.

Story 3: "Gripped by Gold Fever"[30]

Gold is the longest-standing measure of the nationalist imperative. From the earliest civilizations, the alluring metal has played a major role in the rise and fall of great societies. On the North American continent, the observer need only look to the Spanish conquest of Mexico, the U.S. dispossession of the Cherokees, and the rise of the American Far West for examples of national conquest in the search of gold. From the 1500s forward, "God, Gold, and Glory" went hand in hand with the worldwide spread of western civilization. Bullionist philosophy, with origins in mercantilism and strong adherents in the capitalist era, has driven miners and their supportive governments to fill the Fort Knoxes of the globe with the coveted metal.

Mining gold also became synonymous with the political development of democracy, especially in the American West. John Marshall's discovery at Sutter's Mill in 1848 launched the settlement of California and inspired the west-to-east migration of hopeful Americans and immigrants to the interior West in search of instant riches, not dissimilar to gamblers who today descend on Las Vegas. In the process, prospectors and miners disregarded the rights of Native peoples and sought military assistance from the nation's soldiery to ensure that their appetites would be sated with the "democratic" exploitation of the empowering metal. One of the United States' distinct regions was settled on this premise, leading to congressional passage of the Mining Law of 1872, the miner's version of the Homestead Act and one of the most controversial land laws in the twentieth century. Just as American exceptionalism expounded a belief in "free land," it also demanded "free" rights to mineral lands in the public domain. In short, the mining law offered individuals the opportunity to exploit the West's mineral and natural resources, an essential element of the nationalist imperative. Likewise, no longer was yeomanry the only measure of small *d* democracy. Now "free" enterprise in the capitalist system served as a similar marker for the proliferation of liberal economic and political ideals. Many Americans in the twentieth century came to believe that capitalism and democracy were synonymous.

Ironically, the mining law became a cornerstone of the late-twentieth-century corporate exploitation of the West's public mineral lands, especially in Nevada, the state with the largest amount of federal lands. During the 1980s and 1990s, in particular, multinational mining conglomerates with subsidiaries such as Barrick Gold, Newmont Gold, and Pegasus Gold have utilized the law to extract billions of dollars' worth of gold for nearly nothing: the law requires a five-dollar payment for each acre of land patented by the companies and no royalty fees (unlike oil, natural gas, and coal producers, who pay as much as 12.5 percent royalty on output). U.S. senator Dale Bumpers (D-Ark.), concerned with the national debt, in 1992 called the burgeoning gold rush "a license to steal."[31] In response, he sponsored a bill to reform the 120-year-old mining law. Until that year, Barrick, a Canadian-based corporation and one of several gold-producing giants in Nevada, California, and Montana, had paid no federal royalties on the $175 million worth of gold it had extracted from the public domain. The Bumpers bill called on the government to invest the estimated $200 million in new federal revenues that a 5 percent royalty would bring into environmental cleanup of old mines and the implementation of stricter reclamation standards for current operations. Bumpers's bill, which originally gained strong support from the Clinton administration, stalled in the Senate after passage in the House. The western congressional delegation, responding to the generations-old industry claims of financial ruin in the face of environmental regulations, galvanized in support of the "wise users" back home and fought hard to block passage of the proposed bill. At one juncture, westerners threatened to filibuster the Senate during the heated national debate. In the end, Secretary of Interior Bruce Babbitt's claim in 1993 that "a brand new era in land management" had dawned held little weight by the end of the decade, despite the secretary's insistence that the rush was "the biggest gold heist since the days of Butch Cassidy" and a "fleecing" of the American people.[32]

The discovery of "microgold" or "invisible gold" in 1962 in northern Nevada spurred the richest gold rush in American history as well as the subsequent debate over the mining law. That year geologists of the Newmont Corporation discovered billions of tons of gold-enriched mineral deposits, valued in the tens of billions of dollars, in the Carlin Trend. By 1965, Newmont poured its first gold brick, setting in motion a new era in western precious metals mining on the eve of the near collapse of the copper and iron industries. The federal government viewed the gold rush as an important national discovery. The U.S. Geological Survey (USGS), for example, spent more than $12.5 million for gold exploration in 1968 alone. Gold production was at the forefront of the nationalist imperative: according to USGS director William T. Pecora, "Uncle Sam badly needs [in 1968] new sources of gold. Not only is the dollar still officially supported by gold—our revenues at Fort Knox—but other demands far outstrip our production: for new industrial uses, for jewelry, even for spacecraft we're sending to the moon."[33] Furthermore, the ductile metal that neither corrodes nor dissolves served as a key element in atomic age computers and electronic devices. Gold still played a pivotal role in international affairs.

During the twentieth century, the gold industry slipped into a steady decline as early as the World War I era and did not recover until the 1980s, despite incentives in the 1872 law. This decline reflects the exhaustion of high-grade ores in the West, with exception of the Homestake Mine in South Dakota, which had been mined continuously since 1877, and the impact of the Gold Reserve and Silver Purchase acts of 1934. The Roosevelt administration believed that a new $35-an-ounce fixed price on gold would stabilize the monetary system during the Great Depression. But western senators convinced Congress to purchase virtually all the silver produced in the U.S. West.[34] The federal government prohibited gold mining altogether during World War II so that miners and engineers could be mobilized into the strategic metals industries, further contributing to the continued decline of the industry.[35]

For the next three decades, the price of gold remained fixed at $35 an ounce. Beginning in 1972, however, the federal government allowed market forces to determine the price of gold, which increased its value. Rising prices offered hope to gold-mining companies, especially subsidiaries of multinational conglomerates that had invested in the burgeoning Nevada gold fields. Beginning in the mid-1960s, Newmont and other outfits began mining microgold, or very low-grade gold ores (thirty tons of rock for one ounce of gold) by utilizing open-pit and heap-leaching technologies first used in the copper industry. Despite this early development, however, U.S. production lagged behind that of the South Africans, Soviets, and Canadians. Ultimately the 1970s recession, rampant inflation, and crises in Afghanistan, Iran, and elsewhere forced the price of gold to an unprecedented historic high of $850 in January 1980.[36] With this unbelievable price hike, multinational corporations took advantage of the Mining Law of 1872, first with major exploration efforts for invisible gold and then with the development of massive open pits and leach dumps.

During the 1980s, the price of gold remained high, varying from a high of $850 in 1980 to a low of about $350 in 1985. In general, the price hovered around $400 until 1997. Coupled with the development of the vast, low-grade deposits in Nevada, this relatively high price fueled the greatest gold rush in American history. U.S. production, for example, increased dramatically—from just under a million ounces in 1980, to about 5 million in 1987, to more than 10.5 million (or about double the peak year during the California gold rush) in 1997.[37] By the mid-1990s the United States ranked second only to South Africa in worldwide gold production.

The environmental consequences of the gold rush were dramatic. In the Tuscarora Mountains alone, in north-central Nevada, where the great Goldstrike and Gold Quarry mines are, Newmont, Barrick, and other multinational companies have been mining with modern open-pit techniques, using fleets of 100- and 140-ton, two-story-high haulage trucks, operating on a twenty-four-hour-a-day, seven-days-a-week schedule. These huge trucks remove hundreds of millions of tons of ore, with each truckload valued at about $2,200. The scale of the operations has increased dramatically since the inception of open-pit gold mining in the 1960s. The thirty-eight-mile-long Carlin Trend, the richest geological formation on public lands to date, turned into an environmental catastrophe. As one critic commented in 1988: "The five square miles of the Gold Quarry operation are sterile and arid, the vegetation long since gone.... Some two dozen metal buildings on the surface house crushers, furnaces, and other processing equipment. The pit itself looks like an amphitheater for giants: 3,000 by 4,000 feet, 500 feet deep, with wide 'benches' carved into its red stone to prevent the walls from collapsing."[38] And even though federal regulations require reclamation of tailings dumps and toxic waters, the pits will remain for millennia as monuments to western technocracy.

By the late 1980s, the visual degradation of the landscape had captured the attention of environmentalists, Senator Bumpers, and Secretary Babbitt. The traditional battle lines began to materialize as environmentalists, federal regulators, and environmentally conscious politicians confronted the mining corporations and westerners interested in protecting their economic stake in good-paying jobs. Of particular concern to environmentalists, aside from the awesome transformation of the landscape, was the issue of surface and groundwater contamination from heap leaching. As was common among copper-mining practices as early as the 1920s, the gold producers removed the ores from the giant pits and then dumped them into mountain-size heaps. Initially engineers lined the leach dumps with clay, which proved to be faulty in many cases. By the mid-1980s, therefore, the companies began lining their heap dumps with plastic liners to reduce the flow of fugitive cyanide-laden leach waters sprinkled on top of the dumps.[39] The toxic waters filtered through the dumps, capturing the gold. Workers then funneled the "impregnated" waters into leach ponds, where engineers had placed electrolytic plates for the gold to attach itself to. Some of the gold was smelted, refined, and then poured into bricks.

The water demands of these operations were monumental. Disconcerted environmentalists noted the excessive draining of the aquifer beneath the Nevada gold fields. Barrick alone pumped 68,000 gallons of water a minute, twenty-four hours a day, throughout the 1990s from the underground source. As a result, the water table in northern Nevada dropped more than 1,200 feet below the company's

Goldstrike Mine. This dewatering technique, company engineers claimed, created a "cone of depression," keeping floodwaters from inundating the pit and therefore allowing continuous blasting and removal of ores. Unfortunately, mining industry dewatering has dried up hundreds of square miles of the aquifer. By the end of the projected thirty-year life span of the operation, it will result in the loss of more than 1 million acre-feet of groundwater. Once dewatering ceases, the pits will fill up with toxic waters, endangering wildlife and deterring reclamation efforts.[40]

Environmentalists were also angry about what they considered the "giveaway" attitude of the U.S. Bureau of Land Management (BLM). They were upset, for example, about a 1986 General Accounting Office study that revealed the federal agency had flagrantly ignored environmental regulations. Of thirty mine sites requiring companies by law to clean up their industrial wastes and reclaim the land, only six had met the standards; the rest posed serious hazards to both people and the environment. Even more distressing to the environmental contingent was the BLM's regulations concerning small-mine operators. Agency policy exempted cleanup and reclamation of lands on claims of less than five acres. Unlike large operators, which were required to post bonds for future remediation, the smaller companies could mine one small claim, leave the devastated landscape, and move on to another small claim, loopholing their way across the public domain. "They're here today and gone tomorrow," Jim Jensen, director of Montana Environmental Information Center, complained in 1988. "They dredge the bottom of a stream, ruin it and move on." Coupled with the poor reclamation efforts of the larger operators, the costs for cleanup of public lands alone, as Philip Hocker of the Minerals Policy Center in Alexandria, Virginia, estimated in 1992, would reach $880 million: "Until we get the law [Mining Law of 1872] fixed, the taxpayer is going to bear those costs."[41]

Perhaps the best example of the abuse of the Mining Law of 1872 concerns 780 acres of Forest Service sand dunes on the Oregon coast. Claimed and patented by the Coosand Corporation for $1,950, the beach land was acquired in 1989, ostensibly to be mined. Realizing their error in charging too little, the Forest Service offered the sand company $700,000 in 1992 to repurchase the claim. Coosand declined the offer, even though state and local laws forbade mining the dunes. Noting that the transaction was legal, the General Accounting Office publicized the value of the beach lands at $12 million, thus ensuring that Coosand would wait for another, more lucrative offer. The Forest Service's second offer of more than $1 million was also rejected. "There is something wrong with the law," complained U.S. representative Peter A. DeFazio (D-Ore.) in 1992, "when the government is giving away $12 million in assets for $1,950."[42] The GAO estimated that year that from 1970 to 1989, the federal government patented lands worth about $48 million for a return of $4,500.

These environmental costs inspired the Bumpers bill. It called for reform of the Mining Law of 1872, especially in dealing with royalties and reclamation. After initially introducing the act in 1990, the Arkansas senator worked with other deficit-minded and environmentally conscious congressmen to pass the legislation. After passage in the House in 1990, the bill was voted down in the Senate 50–48. Thereafter, Senate committee delays kept the bill from coming to a vote. In response, Bumpers and his political allies successfully convinced Congress in 1992 and 1993 to impose two consecutive one-year moratoriums on mineral lands patenting. Something had to be done, the senator argued, because "the practice [of transferring title to public lands was] a flagrant giveaway."[43]

Regrettably, the mining industry won the battle over the 1872 mining law. Despite vociferous objections from Bumpers, Secretary of Interior Bruce Babbitt, the U.S. House of Representatives, led by George Miller (D-Calif.), and environmentalists, the Clinton administration caved in to pressures from western senators, headed by Democrat Harry Reid of Nevada, and the industry. The political winds were not changing in the West; jobs in mining paid well and came with what one Newmont executive called "gold-plated" benefit packages (which included college tuition for children of employees and cheap, company-built housing) and, although temporary, a reprieve from depressed strategic minerals industry woes. "The West is under siege right now," Senator Conrad Burns (R-Mont.) claimed in 1993. "We've got no other way to make a living than the areas Clinton wants to tax and raise fees on. We'll be left selling 20-acre ranchettes to fancy-pants Easterners."[44] Revealingly, opportunities to mine gold, even at the end of the twentieth century, were synonymous with the western perception of "free" and democratic exploitation of the public domain. The fight against royalties and environmental regulations, Senator Alan K. Simpson (R-Wyo.) added in 1994, "is not about money. We are defending our Western heritage."[45] Senator Ben Nighthorse Campbell (D-Colo.), illustrative of the western bipartisan stand against reforming the 1872 law, did not mince words as to why even Democrats in the West should oppose the Bumpers bill: "How would you go back to a public-land state facing an election in four years and say that you voted to basically end mining . . . and the using of public lands?"[46]

Undoubtedly, gold mining on the public domain will not cease until market conditions force a stoppage. Signs of the bust phase, endemic to all mining operations, began to surface in 1997, when the price of gold dipped below $300 an ounce for the first time since 1980. That year the Echo Bay gold company reported more than $400 million in losses, and Royal Oak Mines defaulted on a $44 million note. The following year, Pegasus Gold, one of the top three producers in the United States, cut its payroll from 1,020 to 600 workers and saw its stock plummet from $8.50 to $1.60 a share.[47] During the mid-1990s, gold also seemed to be losing its luster as a stabilizer of the international monetary system because of a glut on the world market. In response, the central banks of Great Britain, Switzerland, Canada, Australia, Belgium, the Netherlands, Argentina, and the Czech Republic began selling their gold reserves, in some cases relinquishing as much as 30 percent of their holdings. Ironically, the banks began purchasing U.S. Treasury bonds, a sure sign of a prosperous American economy but not very reassuring to a gold-mining industry facing the bust phase.[48]

For the environmental contingent, the battle to reform mining on public lands was lost in the 1990s. Millions of acres of public lands had been ravaged. Nothing could be done to turn back the clock, with little money now available to clean up the waste sites and reclaim the land.[49] As early as 1989, Philip Hocker of the Minerals Policy Center warned that "what we're seeing now is the boom. No one thinks the bust will come. But it will and when it does it will be at the public expense."[50] Environmentalist Susan Alexander of San Francisco in the October 6, 1994, *New York Times* editorial summed up the pro-environment viewpoint: "What do they [mining corporations] leave behind on our national heritage of public lands? Poisoned drinking-water wells, dead rivers and moonscapes of gaping holes that could bury the Empire State Building. Who pays to clean up the mess? We the taxpayers. . . . It [the failure to reform 1872 law] is also a frightening example of the power of the almighty buck to destroy the fragile environment that life itself—and future profits, for that matter, depend on."[51]

Conclusion

The environmental movement of the last quarter of the twentieth century clearly forced a rethinking of traditional mining practices. And as a result, nature's imperative collided with the nationalist imperative, leading historian Duane Smith to conclude: "For the first time in its history, mining generally admitted blame for creating environmental damage and for shirking its responsibilities for restoration once the operations were concluded."[52] Yet as this essay suggests, the corporate mining world still admits fault grudgingly, often delaying implementation of cleaner technology until federal regulators and environmentalists have incessantly pressured for reform. The emergence of environmental divisions in nearly all the major multinational corporations operating on American soil reveals the impact of the pressure.

Ironically, the actions of these companies' environmental engineers have often been motivated by their concern for good public relations rather than by a genuine concern for the environment. As Smith points out, "Realistically, government action was necessary to catch the industry's attention, to convince the industry that it had to be a steward of the land and its resources. For too long, mining had danced to its own tune. The governmental kick in the pants, though painful, had the desired result."[53]

By the end of the twentieth century, environmental successes were evident. The Kennecott Copper Corporation, for instance, published "Our Environment," the first comprehensive industry examination of the mining-environment costs in the 1970s. Then the company implemented reclamation plans in New Mexico and Utah to revegetate tailings dumps, recover toxic waters, and, in general, establish an industrial environmental program. Homestake in South Dakota initiated a similar program, the wild cherry tomatoes growing on sewage, sludge-covered dumps being one obvious result. But AMAX, one of Colorado's premier mining corporations, set the industry standard for environmental cleanup from the 1960s to the 1990s. During these decades, AMAX spent more than $200 million on its reclamation projects, bringing positive public relations to the company in the form of the 1981 National Environment Industry Award. One company executive optimistically predicted that "the mineral wealth of the earth can be utilized for human progress in complete harmony with conservation and recreation."[54]

Federal implementation of the Superfund system has also forced the cleanup of historic and current industrial waste sites. Because the social, economic, and environmental costs of abandoned mines are so prevalent (and have led to complicated legal nightmares and public lands controversies), Congress passed legislation requiring current operators to bond their industrial activities. That means that once the ores are exhausted or the company goes bust, funds are available to reclaim the postindustrial landscapes. The results of the Superfund program can also be controversial. Anaconda Copper's recent multi-million-dollar transformation of its historic waste dumps, which covered hundreds of acres near Butte, Montana, into a Jack Nicklaus–designed golf course is just one example. The beautiful verdant links, with distinctive black slag traps (as opposed to sand), have provided a recreational alternative to the former wasteland. However, environmentalists are concerned that the excessive water and pesticide needs of the course will lead to groundwater shortages and further contamination.[55] On the other hand, the American Smelting & Refining Company's reclamation of its long-standing smelter lands in Ruston, Washington, on Puget Sound proved very successful. There the company spent more than $100 million in the 1990s to transform hundreds of acres of toxic slag dumps into a beautiful seaside park.[56] Clearly the corporate response to environmentalism has been mixed, with the industry gradually easing into a new industrial philosophy concerning the environment. More stories about the clash between mining and the environment are needed to paint more fully this national and even international picture.

The global consequences of corporate mining, with the American West as part of that larger story, also need further examination. American and European companies in particular have exported the nationalist imperative (i.e., capitalist imperialism) around the globe. And because many of the nations in the developing world have not yet exploited their mineral and natural resources as thoroughly as the developed nations, the environmental consequences have been, and will continue to be, devastating, thus contributing to the perpetuation of authoritarian regimes, social displacement, and destruction of vast sections of the world's ecosystems.[57] One need only to observe past and current events in Brazil, Chile, Nigeria, and Indonesia to realize the potential consequences. This field of study is begging for attention, especially from a comparative point of view. Interestingly, the western exportation of capitalist imperialism in the second half of the twentieth century also went hand in hand with the exportation of the West's environmentalism since the 1960s. The results have often led to violent encounters between industrialists and supporting military regimes against environmentalists and grassroots leaders of the social justice movement.

Finally, uranium mining and the cold war should be mentioned. No mined mineral has been as directly linked to the nationalist imperative as uranium. The United States, in particular, invested billions of dollars in building the infrastructure of the interior American West to ensure prospecting and mining of carnotite and uraninite, specifically to produce U-235 and other atomic isotopes needed to construct the atomic bomb and nuclear energy facilities. The damaging implications of uranium form perhaps the greatest legacy that the mining industry has ever left: the atomic destruction of Hiroshima and Nagasaki, Japan, the meltdown at Chernobyl in Russia, and the near miss at Three Mile Island, plus the long-term threats to people and the environment at Hanford, Washington, Rocky Flats, Colorado, and elsewhere. The impact of nuclear contamination caused by underground atomic detonations in the U.S. West and in the waters of the South Pacific may never be known. The direct effect on uranium miners needs further study as well. Uranium mining clearly facilitated the rise of the United States and Soviet Union to superpower status, yet a definitive understanding of the ultimate environmental consequences remains conjecture.[58] Nuclear proliferation in India and North Korea also has possible future detrimental environmental and social consequences.

Obviously, mining and the environment is a very complex topic with national and international significance. Environmental historians and other scholars therefore need to pay more attention to this nascent subfield of environmental history. The emergence of the new ecological consciousness in the second half of the twentieth century has forced industry to rethink its practices. Now scholars must assess that ongoing relationship. In 1996, when Congress eliminated the U.S. Bureau of Mines, although motivated in part by concerns to reduce the deficit, the act sent a clear message that the federal government, in a nonpartisan way, no longer strongly supported the unbridled technological assault on the environment.[59] Times, they were changing. In a not so subtle way, the national legislature realized the will of the people: to do something tangible about the deteriorating environment. Ironically, however, it will be the development of even more environmentally friendly technology, not a reversion to a pretechnological age,[60] that will supersede the long-standing faith that the western world, and increasingly developing nations, has in smokestack technology. When Americans and other peoples of the global community come to this realization and accept that their daily lifestyles drive the machine in the garden, a change may take place. If this change does not occur, the human species may find itself facing its own extinction in the not too distant future.

Notes

1. This quote comes from Peggy Lee O'Neill, "Squeezing out the profits," *Albuquerque Journal*, 13 March 1995.
2. Duane A. Smith, *Mining America: The Industry and the Environment, 1800–1980* (Lawrence: University Press of Kansas, 1987), 159.
3. Ibid., 2.
4. I would like to thank Susan Johnson of the University of Wisconsin, Madison, for commenting on this essay for a presentation at the 2001 Western History Association Conference in San

Diego, California. In her comments and during the postpresentation discussion, it became evident that the nationalist imperative encompasses more than just capitalist imperialism. A case in point is the Soviet model, in which a communist state, for nationalist reasons, sponsored unprecedented industrial destruction in Russia outside the parameters of the capitalist model. As a result, the nationalist imperative reveals a potential investigative model for understanding the implications of national industrialization on the environment in capitalist as well as communist systems.

5. See Seymour M. Hersh, *The Price of Power: Kissinger in the Nixon White House* (New York: Summit Books, 1983), 258–96, for a discussion of American capitalist imperialism in Chile; Raymond Bonner, "U.S. May Try to Curb Diamond Trade That Fuels Africa Wars," *New York Times*, 8 August 1999; and Alan Cowell, "DeBeers Tries to Ensure Gems Don't Finance Insurrection," *New York Times*, 1 March 2000, for a discussion of the role of DeBeers Consolidated Mines, Ltd., in indirectly financing rebel military actions in West Africa through diamond purchases.

6. Smith, *Mining America*, 25.

7. Ibid., 55–58; Christopher J. Huggard, "The Impact of Mining on the Environment of Grant County, New Mexico to 1910," Mining History Association, *Annual 1* (1994): 1–8.

8. Kirkpatrick Sale, *The Green Revolution: The American Environmental Movement, 1962–1992* (New York: Hill & Wang, 1993).

9. Ibid.

10. Interview with John Bartlit by author on 14 December 1993; Christopher J. Huggard, "Mining and the Environment: The Clean Air Issue in New Mexico, 1960–1980," *New Mexico Historical Review* 69 (October 1994): 369–88; Katherine G. Aiken, "Not Long Ago a Smoking Chimney Was a Sign of Prosperity: Corporate and Community Response to Pollution at the Bunker Hill Smelter in Kellogg, Idaho," *Environmental History Review* 18 (summer 1994): 67–86.

11. Charles E. Hughes, "Progressive Reform in the Rocky Mountain West: Local Citizens vs. Big Business in the Smelter Cases of Salt Lake County, 1904–1906," *Journal of the West* 35 (October 1996): 25–27.

12. John D. Wirth, *Smelter Smoke in North America: The Politics of Transborder Pollution* (Lawrence: University Press of Kansas, 2000), 1–79.

13. U.S. Senate, Committee on Public Works, Hearings Before the Subcommittee on Air and Water Pollution, Air Pollution—1970 part 4, 91st Cong., 2d sess., March-May 1970, 1568.

14. Eugene N. Cameron, ed., *The Mineral Position of the United States, 1975–2000* (Madison: University of Wisconsin Press, 1973), 90.

15. U.S. Senate, Committee on Public Works, Hearings Before the Subcommittee on Environmental Pollution, Implementation of the Clean Air Act—1975, 94th Cong., 1st sess., April-May 1975, 1312.

16. *Silver City Daily Press*, 20 June 1975.

17. Wirth, *Smelter Smoke*, 192–97.

18. It should be noted that a federal court in Washington, D.C., ruled in November 2000 that the EPA's discretionary power to determine clean air health standards was unconstitutional; likewise, the U.S. Supreme Court ruled 5–4 (identical vote to that of the Bush decision) that the Clean Air Act did not have enforcement power over some wetlands in the United States; see National Public Radio report for 7 November 2000 and "Court Knocks Out Wetlands Rule," *Progressive Farmer* 116 (February 2001): 10.

19. Mark Matthews, "Libby's Dark Secret," *High Country News*, 13 March 2000, 12–13.

20. Ibid., 12.

21. Ibid.

22. Ibid., 13.

23. Ibid., 15.

24. Ibid., 13.

25. Ibid., 14.

26. Ibid.

27. Ibid., 15.

28. Ibid.

29. Ibid., 1.
30. Quoted from Jim Robbins, "Gripped by Gold Fever," *New York Times,* 4 December 1988, IV, 21:1. I would like to thank Jim Bailey for his assistance with data collection in this section of the chapter.
31. Dirk Johnson, "Digging for Ore Still Pays; Should Miners Pay, Too?" *New York Times,* 12 February 1992, D 25:1.
32. Interview with former U.S. senator Dale Bumpers (D-Ark.) by author on 22 September 2000; see also Jon Christensen, "Babbitt Attacks Mining Gold Heists," *High Country News,* 30 May 1994, 5; Gale Norton, the new secretary of interior, has a poor public lands record and will, no doubt, support continued mining abuses in the West; likewise, conservatives may successfully convince the U.S. Supreme Court to declare the enforcement powers of the EPA unconstitutional, forcing regulatory jurisdiction back to the states and even individual counties and municipalities.
33. Samuel W. Matthews, "Nevada's Mountain of Invisible Gold," *National Geographic* 133 (May 1968): 670–71.
34. Gerald D. Nash, *The Federal Landscape: An Economic History of the Twentieth-Century West* (Tucson: University of Arizona Press, 1999), 32–34.
35. Earle B. Amey, "Gold," in *U.S. Geological Survey, Metal Prices in the United States through 1998* (Washington, D.C.: GPO, 1998), 50.
36. Amey, "Gold," 51.
37. U.S. Bureau of Mines, *Minerals Yearbook,* 1975, 1980, 1990, 1998 (Washington, D.C.: GPO, 1975–99); Robbins, "Gripped," 21; Amey, "Gold," 49.
38. Robbins, "Gripped," 21.
39. See Robert L. Spude, "Cyanide and the Flood of Gold," in *Essays in Colorado History* 12 (1991): 1–35; U.S. Bureau of Mines, *Minerals Yearbook, 1990, Metals and Minerals,* vol. 1 (Washington, D.C.: GPO, 1993), 498–500, for a discussion and illustration of the heap-leaching processes.
40. Ernie Thompson, "Gold Mines Are Sucking Aquifers Dry," *High Country News,* 13 June 1994, 6.
41. Johnson, "Digging," D 25:1.
42. "Federal Land Sold for Very Little," *New York Times,* 12 February 1992, D 25:1; interview with Bumpers.
43. "Senate Rejects Moratorium on Cheap Mining Land Sales," *New York Times,* 23 October 1990, A 20:1.
44. Timothy Egan, "Sweeping Reversal of U.S. Land Policy Sought by Clinton," *New York Times,* 24 February 1993, A 1:6.
45. Timothy Egan, "Billions at Stake in Debate on a Gold Rush," *New York Times,* 14 August 1994, I 1:2.
46. Richard L. Burke, "Clinton Backs Off from Policy Shift on Federal Lands," *New York Times,* 31 March 1993, A 1:6. Campbell, by the way, has since changed his party affiliation, joining the Republican Party.
47. William R. Long, "Gold Industry Tries to Dig Itself Out," *New York Times,* 19 April 1998, III 4:1.
48. Long, "Gold"; Tim Pritchard, "As Gold Price Plunges, a Company Thrives," *New York Times,* 2 June 1999, C 4:3.
49. The larger gold companies have taken out bonds valued in the tens of millions of dollars for future cleanup.
50. Jim Robbins, "A New Kind of Mining Disaster," *New York Times,* 5 February 1989, IV, 7:1.
51. Susan Alexander, "Great Mining Ripoff Dodges the Bullet Again," *New York Times,* 6 October 1994, A 28:4.
52. Smith, *Mining America,* 152.
53. Ibid.
54. Ibid., 157.
55. See Jim Robbins, "Busted Town Pursues Industrial Recreation," *High Country News,* 5 September 1994, 4.
56. Karen Pickett, "Environmental Battlefield: ASARCO's Ruston, Washington, Smelter and Superfund," *Mining History Journal* 7 (2000): 45–63; Environmental Protection Agency, "Former

Asarco Smelter Facility, Ruston and North Tacoma, Washington," Superfund fact sheet (January 2000): 1–5; Thomas I. Aldrich, "Refining a Unique Remedy," *Mining Environmental Management* (December 1995): 15–18; see also Fred Quivik's publications.

57. See Donald Worster, *Rivers of Empire: Water, Aridity, and the Growth of the American West* (New York: Oxford University Press, 1992), for a discussion of empire building and the impact on the environment.

58. For discussions of uranium mining and the West, consult Eric W. Mogren, *Warm Sands: Uranium Mill Tailings Policy in the Atomic West* (Albuquerque: University of New Mexico Press, 2002); Arthur R. Gómez, *Quest for the Golden Circle: The Four Corners and the Metropolitan West, 1945–1970* (Lawrence: University Press of Kansas, 2000), 17–30; Raye C. Ringholz, *Uranium Frenzy, Boom and Bust on the Colorado Plateau* (Albuquerque: University of New Mexico Press, 1989).

59. Sandra Blakeslee, "Babbitt Likens Move to Kill Science Agencies to 'Book Burning,'" *New York Times*, 17 February 1995, A 16:1.

60. For example, Jerry Mander, *In the Absence of the Sacred: The Failure of Technology and the Survival of Indian Nations* (San Francisco: Sierra Club Books, 1991), argues that technology itself is detrimental to the global community and the environment.

Organized Religion and the Search for Community in the Modern American West

Ferenc M. Szasz

In late 1999, Harvard theologian Harvey Cox mused on the rise and fall of secularization during the twentieth century. In the course of his observations, he noted:

> Although religion neither causes nor is caused by the other factors in a complex cultural whole, it is often the most accurate barometer. . . . I am convinced that religion is the royal road to the heart of a civilization, the clearest indicator of its hopes and errors, the surest index of how it is changing.[1]

The religious history of the American West bears out Cox's observations. Indeed, religious tension lay at the center of the historic Native-Spanish, Latter-day Saint–Gentile, and Anglo-Hispanic encounters. By the dawn of the twentieth century, however, this overt antagonism had largely faded. Grudgingly tolerant of one another's positions, the organized faiths of the region seemed content to move on separate, parallel tracks.

With the outbreak of World War II, however, these tracks began to merge. During the 1941–45 conflict, the region's churches and synagogues actively sought out common ground in both goals and values, a position that held, more or less, until the mid-1960s. After that, the center lost its hold. From approximately 1965 forward, the world of western religion splintered steadily into a seemingly endless array of social/theological positions. What the twenty-first century will bring is anybody's guess.

Although overlooked by many historians of the modern West, the religious dimension is of utmost importance. In fact, the cultural tranquillity of the region depends largely on some form of general religious harmony. Although the West has long been a land of religious pluralism, that pluralism has been most effective when it shared a common goal toward which all faiths could strive. Thus the 1945–2000 religious search for community is fraught with social consequences. The Japanese attack on Pearl Harbor on December 7, 1941, instantly realigned the forces of western organized religion, uniting them, really for the first time, in a common cause. Virtually all denominations backed the Allied war effort, and the three-and-a-half years of conflict provided western clerics with a number of opportunities to voice their hopes for a better postwar world.[2]

These hopes proved decidedly ecumenical. In November 1943, a Salt Lake City Presbyterian described Jesus as "the world's first democrat," a champion of the poor of all races, Jews and Gentiles alike.[3] On Lincoln's birthday in 1944, the Congregational women of Oklahoma spoke out for improved race relations, decrying Hitler's attempt to set one American ethnic group against another.[4] Earlier, a Denver Catholic priest and a Denver rabbi had signed a common declaration of Judeo-Christian forces that called on world leaders to establish a just society after the conflict, one that would guarantee the rights of all minorities, economic justice, and the rule of international law.[5]

The numerous 1940s magazine photographs of New England churches on village greens represented "religious freedom"[6] to this generation, and this theme was strikingly brought home in the tragic story of the four chaplains of the torpedoed troop ship *Dorchester* (a Catholic priest, a rabbi, and two Protestant ministers), who gave their life jackets to the soldiers and, arms linked, perished with the ship.

From 1944 onward, the religious leaders of the American West began seriously to plan for the imminent postwar world. That year, seven Catholic bishops of the Southwest met and concluded that they had little faith in war, politics, or state action to bring about economic justice and goodwill among nations. They argued that any reconstruction of human society required active involvement by "believers in the Word of God," and, especially, by cooperation among all religious bodies. Moreover, said the bishops: "We can co-operate in this work of reconstruction *without* in any way compromising our religious principles or diminishing our loyalty to discipline."[7] In a similar fashion, the Episcopal bishop of Utah declared in 1945 that American Christians needed to understand other peoples and other faiths of the world. The bishop prophesized that the postwar world would not so much be an "atomic age" as one of "internationalism."[8] Likewise, the Presbyterian Synod of Nebraska asked its parishioners to accept the Japanese who had moved into the state after release from wartime internment camps. More than any other event, the war awakened western churches to the issues of ethnicity, race, and the need for increased cooperation.

During the conflict, the region's religious organizations expressed hopes that the churches might lead in the establishment of the postwar global world. Oklahoma Episcopalians presented this concept to their parishioners only three months after Pearl Harbor.[9] The state's Congregationalists joined in shortly afterward. Everyone agreed, however, that introducing justice into a postwar world would be problematic. People responded automatically to the military challenges of Pearl Harbor, Stalingrad, and Dunkirk, an Episcopal priest noted, but they reacted less spontaneously to the equally significant political challenges presented by the conferences at Bretton Woods, Dunbarton Oaks, or San Francisco.[10]

Rapid church growth during the late 1940s and 1950s, however, seemed to confirm these wartime hopes. In the two decades after 1945, every subregion of the West witnessed a genuine boom of church, synagogue, and parochial school building. During this "brick and mortar" phase, most western groups built fewer "symbolic" church buildings to focus on more functional designs, often adding ugly, boxlike "Christian education" buildings to their (usually) Gothic structures. Thus religious architecture of the day tended to expand "horizontally" with the addition of meeting halls, rather than "vertically" with lofty towers or steeples.[11]

The "queen city" of Denver embodied this building trend to perfection. A Denver survey in 1950 discovered that the cost of recent church construction—thirty-five new buildings in five years—had exceeded $1 million. From 1945 to 1957, Denver officials issued 177 building permits for churches, church schools, and other religious buildings, with a total valuation of more than $10 million.[12] During the last ten years, The Denver Post noted in 1969, more than 250 new churches and synagogues had been built at a cost of $25 million. Over half of these edifices were constructed in modern or contemporary design.[13] Drawing upon the motto "recreation is re-creation," a number of the mainstream denominations included gymnasiums, tennis courts, and other play areas as a part of their church complexes. The Latter-day Saints (LDS) excelled in constructing such recreation centers. Since sport is highly democratic, people from all denominations frequently used the various church facilities.

Other western cities echoed Denver's postwar building boom. Churches in Lincoln, Nebraska, expanded from 100 in 1930 to 123 in 1955. By 1950 Roswell, New Mexico, claimed sixty-six churches, whereas Amarillo, Texas, boasted 140. Lutheran pastor Erick Hawkins, who served in Salt Lake City from 1950 to 1957, put it succinctly: "Some pastors are called to teach or counsel; I have been called to build churches."[14] This postwar explosion in church and synagogue building, however, proved the last echo in the region's celebration of shared religio-cultural values.

In spite of all the war-inspired quests for common goals, the postwar era still harbored echoes of the earlier religio-cultural tension. Catholics and Protestants in New Mexico largely held each other at arm's length throughout the 1950s. As late as 1949, Screen Actors Guild president Ronald Reagan resigned from the prestigious California Lakeside Country Club because it refused to accept Jewish applicants. The ethnic restrictions of Los Angeles' elite Hillcrest Country Club led to Groucho Marx's famous quip: "I wouldn't want to be a member of any club that would have me."[15]

The deep-rooted Latter-day Saint–Gentile cultural standoff also took on new form during the postwar era, but it did so because of a splinter band of polygamist dissidents rather than the mainstream Salt Lake City church. In 1953 Howard Pyle, the governor of Arizona, authorized a surprise raid—with tacit mainstream LDS approval—on the outlawed polygamous Mormon community of Short Creek (now Colorado City) in the Arizona strip. The raid, which involved state police driving women and weeping children from their homes at night, turned into a public relations disaster that later cost Pyle his reelection. It also proved the last of its kind. For the remainder of the century, the state governments of Arizona, Utah, and Idaho have made few moves to round up Latter-day Saint polygamists. Although law enforcement officials keep a wary eye on the various polygamous groups—estimated in 1995 at about 30,000—except for cases of underage sexual abuse, the states usually leave them alone.

Still, the incidents of overt conflict proved relatively minor. The wartime spirit of holding to one's own faith perspective while seeking out religious cooperation merged easily with the Cold War struggle against the (officially) atheistic Soviet Union. From 1941 forward, "Judeo-Christian" became the adjective of choice to describe the national religious atmosphere. In the 1950s and early 1960s, the quest for religious community ran at full tide.[16]

But this "culture of consensus" could not last. The assassinations of John F. Kennedy, Robert Kennedy, and Martin Luther King, Jr., plus the quagmire of Vietnam, brought an end to the emphasis on shared values. What historians have termed "the Sixties" (c. 1963–c. 1974) inaugurated a sea change in western religion, one that remains much in evidence over three decades later.[17]

Many of these changes involved the infamous baby boomer generation (b. 1945–63), a group "so large [that] it seemed to have no parents and no memory."[18] Estimated at approximately 756 million worldwide, the religious quests of the baby boomers—"a generation of seekers"—helped realign the contours of organized western faiths.[19] Excluding the African American churches, which always retained a tight community focus, the boomers left the mainline groups by the thousands. Their spiritual searches led them in countless directions: to Jewish Orthodoxy, to traditional Catholicism, to a burgeoning conservative evangelical Protestantism, to various Asian faiths, especially Buddhism, to "New Age" gatherings, and to a wide variety of short-lived cults and sects.

Although the boomers' quest proved nationwide in scope, the American West attracted a number of high-profile religious organizations. It did so for good historic reasons. Sociologists have long noted that when a shared faith dominates a region (as, say, in the historically evangelical South), it functions as a means of social control. But many areas of the West had traditionally lacked this dimension of life. Although one can find western subregions with a hegemonic faith perspective—Mormon Utah, Protestant Texas/Oklahoma, Progressive Era Catholic/Jewish San Francisco, perhaps the Lutheran/Catholic northern Great Plains—the anonymity that accompanied the expansion of many postwar western cities and the vast isolated regions of the intermountain region meant that the urban and rural Wests provided a number of havens for religious experimentation.

From the 1960s forward, the San Francisco Bay area became a flashpoint of this "revolution in consciousness." The region abounded with nontraditional religious activity: "Jesus people," vaguely connected with some sort of evangelical Protestantism, the Hare Krishas, the Children of God, Scientology, Jim Jones's "People's Temple," and so on.[20] The historically underchurched Puget Sound region also housed a variety of nonconventional groups. The extremism of southern California faiths became notorious.[21]

The empty spaces of the rural West proved equally enticing to religious utopians. In 1982, Elizabeth Claire Prophet, founder of the Church Universal and Triumphant, established a ranch north of Yellowstone National Park.[22] The most-written-about western religious story of the decade of the 1980s dealt with the rise and fall of the middle-class utopian commune in Antelope, Oregon: Rajneeshpuram.[23] During the 1990s, eccentric groups of antigovernment, quasi-religious utopians sought refuge in Idaho, Montana, and Texas. Many harbored grim millennial expectations, as illustrated in the dramatic shoot-out between federal agents and the Branch Davidian compound in Waco, Texas (1993), or in the mass suicide in California of the Heaven's Gate communitarians four years later. The UFO phenomenon, which some sociologists consider a quasi-religious movement (modern angels?), found many supporters in the Dakotas, Arizona, and especially in Roswell, New Mexico, the famed site of an alleged UFO crash in 1947.[24] Extensive media coverage of these often bizarre sects kept western religion much in the public eye from 1965 to the end of the century.

The media's focus on extremist groups, however, presented a distorted view of the post-1960s western faith communities. The journalists simply overlooked the quiet responses that the more traditional groups made to social upheavals of the era. In spite of falling numbers, the largely middle-class churches proved genuinely creative. They established day care centers for working mothers and temporary shelters for runaway teens. They inaugurated a "motel chaplaincy" program to counsel suicidal businessmen and pregnant teenagers. They introduced free food distribution for the homeless. Hundreds of church basements served groups or housed twelve-step programs, ranging from Alcoholics Anonymous to Parents without Partners to suicide prevention.

The mainline groups created several new institutions as well. In Idaho and elsewhere, Protestants joined Catholics during the 1950s to begin the extensive Migrant Ministry program to assist the largely Mexican migrant agricultural workers. Throughout the region, but especially in Seattle, San Francisco, Los Angeles, and Denver, the Catholic Church maintained its far-flung system of parochial schools. In the ghetto areas of Los Angeles, the Jesuit-run high schools proved far superior to anything the public sector offered.

Some mainline groups seized on the cultural upheavals to try to heal centuries-old antagonisms. Western Reform rabbis in Oklahoma and New Mexico inaugurated formal Jewish-Christian dialogues in several cities. The Episcopal Church introduced a brief Christian/traditional Native American faith ecumenical movement on western Indian reservations. During his visit in 1993 to Mexico, the Pope formally apologized for his church's historic treatment of Native peoples. Five years earlier, an ecumenical group of Protestant and Catholic leaders issued a similar apology to the Indians of the Pacific Northwest, pledging to work together for common purposes.[25] Indeed, Christian-Native dialogue on environmental issues has emerged as one probable area of ecumenical cooperation for the future.

These low-profile efforts on the part of the mainstream churches, so vital to their local communities, never received the national publicity that the press accorded the extreme utopians. In fact, during the 1990s, several western newspapers, including the *Albuquerque Journal,* quietly dropped their religion page. When the churches and synagogues are doing their jobs, it simply isn't "news."

Probably the best term to describe the last thirty years of western religious history would be the old bromide "pluralism." But the increasing variety of "religious pluralism" has proven far less troubling than what sociologist Wade Clark Roof has termed a "moral pluralism."[26] Fellow sociologists Robert Wuthnow and James Davison Hunter have charted the major realignments in American religion. They agree that during the last quarter of the century, the traditional denominational cultures—Jewish-Catholic-Episcopal-Baptist-Methodist-Congregational, and so on—have lost much of their meaning. Increasingly they have been replaced by a bipolar set of "moral cultures." Advocates of "conventional morality"—from all the major religious groups—line up on one side against advocates of increased "personal freedom," usually centering around issues of sexuality and "lifestyle," on the other.[27] Indeed, the western regional churches have often emerged as the very focal points of these antagonisms. Some United Church of Christ (UCC) or Unitarian pastors have placed the "Open and Affirming Message" (i.e., the welcoming of gay and lesbian members) at the heart of their message. Similarly, on issues of abortion and sex education, the liberal Episcopalians and Congregationalists are not likely to have much in common with the more conservative Vineyard Fellowship or the Southern Baptists.

Studies have shown that baby boomers who stress personal autonomy and reject traditional gender roles and sexual norms are increasingly likely to have abandoned the mainstream churches of their youth. But among others, the conservative evangelical wing of western Protestantism has begun a major effort to win this group back. From the mid-1980s forward, evidence suggests that some baby boomers are returning, but often on their own terms.

The variegated evangelical Protestant community has reached out to the boomers through a variety of means. Two of the most successful have been the Denver-based Promise Keepers movement and the rise of various urban megachurches. The Promise Keepers idea began with an epiphany from William (Bill) McCartney, then head football coach at the University of Colorado in Boulder, the flagship university of the intermountain West. A prominent regional public figure, McCartney had earned fame and modest fortune. But, as he readily confessed, this success caused him to abuse alcohol and neglect his family. "I've caused a lot of undue pain and suffering," he admitted.[28]

His long acquaintance with athletics and the mass media led McCartney to the idea of holding men-only rallies in large arenas to reinforce a traditional moral outlook. Naturally, he thought of the often unused football stadiums. The first rally, held in 1991, drew a modest 4,200, and the movement remained exclusively a Colorado phenomenon until 1994, when it suddenly began to spread to both South and West. About 727,000 attended the mass rallies in 1995, and in 1997 more than twenty-one states housed Promise Keepers offices. Virtually everyone was astonished at their initial growth rate.

At the rallies, men gather to proclaim seven promises:

Honor Jesus Christ,
Have close male friends,
Practice spiritual, moral, and secular purity,
Be faithful to wife and children,
Support the church,
Defy racial and denominational barriers,
Encourage the world to do the same.

"Coach Mac," as he is now known, described the situation thus: "Mealy mouthed, weak-kneed, Daffy-Duck Christianity—there's a lot of that out there. [Promise Keepers] is a confrontation with the living God." Those who participate fully in the movement "encounter the living God . . . face to face."[29]

The opposition, however, was not long in forming. Gay rights organizations attacked McCartney's initial hard-line stance on homosexuality (he later modified his position), and feminist groups denounced the Promise Keepers' "not-very-cloaked misogynistic message." A woman pastor of the UCC church in Boulder accused the group of attempting to reverse the recent gains made by women. The American Jewish Congress and the Religious Coalition for Reproductive Choice have also been critical of what they perceive as reinforcement of the unequal status of men and women in family and society. Several professional counselors have attacked the Promise Keepers' central premise that men must first be broken of pride. Many reporters from the popular media have expressed similar doubts.[30]

A number of sociologists have tried to explain the appeal of the Promise Keepers movement. Their surveys have discovered that the median age of those attending is thirty-eight; that 88 percent are married and 21 percent have been divorced; that about half confess that their own fathers were largely absent when they were growing up. The movement seems to have its greatest appeal to members of the baby boomer generation, many of whom either grew up without a religious tradition or left the church of their youth. A significant number are single parents, and many have also been involved in some form of twelve-step program.[31]

In seven years, the Promise Keepers moved from obscurity to the front pages of the region's papers. In 1997, for example, the annual budget approached $22 million. Then, just as rapidly, the movement started to decline. In early 2000, attendance fell and the organization announced several cutbacks. Some observers believe that it may have passed its crest. Although their basic message retains its popular appeal, the Promise Keepers movement lacks a permanent institutional base from which to promulgate its positions.

The western megachurches, however, do have such a base. Thus they have been far more effective in responding to the needs of the boomer generation. These congregations, both Protestant and Catholic, are multifaceted. They usually have dynamic pastors and well-trained staff people able to provide for every imaginable need. They feature informal sermons, high technology, and energetic, music-filled services. Even more important, the new megachurches are tolerant of human frailties, especially divorce, depression, relationship difficulties, and various forms of addiction. As one large-church pastor observed, his congregation consists largely of the "walking wounded."[32]

These churches are nationwide, of course, but five of the largest ten are in the rapidly growing, increasingly impersonal western cities. First Assembly of God in Phoenix serves a congregation of 8,000, whereas the Calvary Chapels of Costa Mesa, California, and Albuquerque, New Mexico, have between 12,000 and 13,000 each.[33] Denver also boasts a number of large, nondenominational evangelical churches.[34] Calvary Chapel churches—several of which are bilingual—have considerable appeal to the Hispanic community. Sociologist Donald E. Miller has suggested that groups such as the Vineyard Fellowship and the Calvary Chapel may well be the "new paradigm" churches for the millennium.[35]

As any phone book will show, the large western cities contain the entire spectrum of organized religious faiths. Mormon Salt Lake City, Catholic/Jewish San Francisco, Protestant Lubbock, and "semisecular" Seattle might differ in religious "tone," but each harbors every major group. Three western cities, however, have taken on special significance in this regard: Las Vegas, Nevada, Los Angeles, California, and Santa Fe, New Mexico. Taken together, these cities reflect the variety of the modern western religious experience.

Las Vegas

After World War I, Nevadans in general and Las Vegans in particular found themselves on the economic ropes. Then in 1931, Governor Fred Salazar signed the bill to legalize gambling, the first state to make this move. As historians Russell Elliott and William Rowley have noted, Nevada's decision to open itself to "naughty fun" not available elsewhere proved much in line with the historic western past.[36] Aided by the 1971 decision to legalize prostitution in certain regions, Nevada emerged in "the Sixties" as a model of the consumption-orientated, tourist-directed society.[37]

The economy of pre–World War II Nevada had revolved largely around mining and ranching, neither occupation especially conducive to church influence. Given the size of the state, plus the scattered nature of the population, only the best-organized religious groups could make much headway. Official church attendance always remained low, and Nevada presented a unique religious profile. From the 1920s forward, Latter-day Saints and Catholics remained far larger than all the other organized religious groups put together.

Significantly, the region's two leading faiths have had minimal historic problems with the gaming industry. Although an LDS General Authority member visited the city in 1963 because of concern over "difficult conditions not conducive to religious growth," the Saints had in essence made their peace with the prevailing culture.[38] When the Mafia controlled the Vegas strip from the 1930s into the 1960s, it was widely rumored that they preferred to employ LDS managers because of their strong work ethic and their reputation for honesty.[39]

So, too, for Roman Catholicism. In 1963, strip casinos decided that their customers might wish to attend services on Sunday, so they donated more than $250,000 to help build the Guardian Angel Catholic Cathedral. Four years later, Nevada's newly installed third Catholic bishop, Most Reverend M. Joseph Green, told reporters that gambling was intrinsically not immoral. The church condemned only the *misuse* of gaming.[40] In 1981, Father Edward Anderson admitted that his church had become a "tourist parish," where visitors often dropped casino chips, rather than cash, in the collection plate (all cashed by Caesar's Palace). The churches and casinos did not compete for customers, he said, they simply shared them.[41]

Among the mainline denominations, only the Protestants seriously opposed gaming, but by the late 1950s they, too, had been forced to moderate their earlier stance. A newly arrived Methodist pastor declared in 1959 that he was "amazed" at Las Vegas, which he politely termed "a city of contrasts."[42] First Presbyterian Church of Las Vegas limited its response to gaming by providing counseling for those wrestling with gambling difficulties.[43]

Since the presence of prominent religious buildings in a city usually denoted "respectability," Las Vegas spokesmen were quick to parade their own postwar church construction. Local church leaders denied that Las Vegas deserved its "city of sin" reputation, one reporter claiming that "Las Vegas is perhaps more spiritually minded than most of the other cities in the country." In 1963, city officials boasted of their eighty different religious denominations serving 60,000 parishioners in the area.[44] The Las Vegas Mormon temple (constructed in 1989) continues to astound observers by its architectural splendor.

By the late 1980s, however, the public influence of most organized faiths in Las Vegas had become decidedly marginalized. The booming economy of the fastest-growing city in the nation proved far stronger than any historic theology. A survey in 1989 found church and synagogue attendance lower in Nevada than in any other state. Popular guidebooks indexed the brothel "Chicken Ranch" but rarely "Churches."[45] In 1995, when the new Hard Rock Cafe opened against a backdrop of religious symbols and the claim that the nation's true faith was "Rock and Roll," the only response the local Catholic bishop could make was to officially protest. (The casino later modified the design.) A reporter concluded in 1996 that the best term to describe Las Vegas culture was "pagan."[46]

In Las Vegas, therefore, the churches and synagogues have been forced to adapt to new social roles. Rather than controlling the public sphere, which seems to go its own helter-skelter way, the faiths have shifted their focus to providing for personal needs, both for parishioners and for visitors. They often have their hands full. Since the city traditionally attracts people with various past personal dilemmas, which often increase when they find themselves cut off from home and family support, the churches and synagogues continue to provide valuable local services, even in a "pagan" community.

Los Angeles

Shortly before the century began, entrepreneur Henry E. Huntington predicted that "Los Angeles is destined to become the most important city in this country, if not in the world."[47] By 1940, with 1.5 million people and Hollywood just next door, Los Angeles was on its way to fulfilling Huntington's prophecy. Visitors remained fascinated by the city's enormous energy. As critic Lewis Mumford observed in the 1930s, the key to Los Angeles was variety, "variety of biological and cultural stock, variety of wants, variety of opportunities, variety of institutions, variety of fulfillments. Where variety is absent, the city does not exist."[48]

Certainly the "variety of faiths" of this "centrifugal city" has proven Mumford an able prophet. A recent survey by cultural geographer Barbara Weightman discovered the following: "The capital of the third world" houses the nation's largest Hindu shrine, which serves an estimated population of 10,000. Similarly, it is home to a temple that functions as the center of the international Buddhist Progressive Society to train monks and nuns for the growing Anglo and Asian Buddhist community. Since about 1,500 American Zoroastrians live in the region, the community constructed a new Zoroastrian worship center designed to resemble the ancient Persian building that King Darius built. Five Islamic centers and eighty-two mosques serve the estimated 250,000 southern California Muslims, and a number of mosques have been built in predominantly black areas to better serve the converts from the African American community. The Catholic Diocese of Los Angeles officially lists ninety-three ethnic groups in its parishes, and priests offer Mass in forty-two different languages. The presence of more than 800,000 Jews (mostly Reform) marks the city as second only to New York in this regard.[49] Historian Deborah Dash Moore has argued that Jewish immigrants to Los Angeles have come close to creating a distinct version of their historic faith.[50]

The variety of religion in the Los Angeles area seems to defy description. In nearby Irvine, one may find the South Coast Community Church, which, with a staff of sixty-eight and membership of 10,000, ranks as one of the largest Protestant megachurches of the nation. In addition to powerful Catholic, Protestant, Jewish, and Mormon presences, the city houses numerous smaller bodies as well: Korean Presbyterians; "New Age" centers; Scientology centers; Zen centers; the Church of Religious Science; the Metropolitan Community Church, which ministers chiefly to homosexuals; various Wicca organizations; and even a society of Devil Worship. When former Jesuit Charles A. Fracchia surveyed California in the late 1970s, he described it as a veritable "spiritual explosion."[51] If anything, the "explosion" has increased in the two decades since Fracchia made his observation.

In such a panoramic world, religion in Los Angeles has emerged as almost another "consumer item." As sociologist J. Gordon Melton has observed, "Los Angeles is the only place in the world that you can find all forms of Buddhism. Not even Asian countries have all forms of Buddhism."[52] Another scholar, historian Eldon G. Ernst, notes that California never produced any religious "mainstream." From the onset, all organized bodies have been "minority" faiths. Thus

California has changed our whole understanding of what it means to be "religious."[53] It is relatively easy to suggest what it means to be religious in (say) Provo, Utah, Amarillo, Texas, or Mosquero, New Mexico. But what does it mean to be "religious" in Los Angeles?

Santa Fe

In its only entry on religion, the rather quirky *Atlas of the New West* lists twenty-three prominent western New Age centers, the best known of which is probably Santa Fe, New Mexico.[54] The hearty welcome that the "city different" gave to the New Age movement in the 1960s and 1970s had deep historic roots. Ever since the early twentieth century, Santa Fe has marched to its own drummer. In 1926, writer Erna Fergusson characterized the city as one that did not want a middle-class, Anglo-American Chautauqua (a popular, "uplift" lecture series). Although the mainline Protestant groups have made their presence felt in Santa Fe since the 1850s, the religious atmosphere remains dominated by the powerful Roman Catholic church, symbolized by the presence of Bishop Jean Baptiste Lamy's Romanesque cathedral, intermingled with the pervasive spiritual traditions of the nearby Indian pueblos.

Just as New Orleans represented a "non-mainstream" society for the 1890s, so too did Santa Fe play this role for modern America. As late as 1985, the Reverend Jay Spoonheim, pastor of the newly formed American Lutheran Church, remarked that the people of Santa Fe "do not connect easily with a mainline expression of the Christian faith." He continued:

In some ways, New Mexico is still an untapped mission territory for Protestant denominations. While a Roman Catholic church seems to be on every street corner here, Protestants like the American Lutheran Church target the state in much the same way we planned missions in Asia and Africa.[55]

Reverend Spoonheim had a point. Santa Fe has long served as a cultural magnet for a wide variety of nontraditional faith perspectives. In 1969, the first Krishna Consciousness Temple opened. Various versions of New Thought, as seen in Unity, Religious Science, and the Dispensable Church, continue to attract followers. In the early 1990s, several of these groups staged Christmas Eve services that blended their upbeat messages with celebration of the winter solstice. In 1999, a Victory Outreach evangelical pastor brought in a reformed murderer and drug dealer to help stage a "Stop the Violence" rally at the Santa Fe Indian School. A few miles to the north, a gathering of Penitentes staged a religious procession as a protest against the rise in black tar heroin addiction.[56] The advertisements on the community bulletin board at the downtown public library in Santa Fe show how this medium-sized city (population approximately 85,000) abounds with alternative spiritual offerings.[57]

The great historic faiths have long had to bend to this atmosphere. Respected

Santa Fe Reform rabbi Leonard Helman achieved local fame for his "Woody Allen" sermon, where he compared the insights of historic Judaism with several of Allen's movies. The *New Mexican* once described him as "the rabbi different for the city different."[58] In 1995, Rabbi Nahum Ward Lev organized a gathering of forty-five people at Temple Beth Shalom so that they could voice the hurts and alienation that they felt their historic Judaism had inflicted upon them. Many had tried other faiths—Buddhism, Christianity, Indian Mysticism, and Sufi tradition—in the interim. One woman confessed that when she cried out to Jesus in a moment of anguish, she saw him "manifest himself in her room." When she spoke with her rabbi about this profound experience, "he recoiled from me like I had a disease." "I am not a Christian," the woman said in tears, "but I am no longer what I was and there's no place for me." After a very emotional session, Rabbi Ward Lev had only one comment: "It sounded like prayer to me."[59]

In 1997, Rabbi Berel Leverton, a member of the Lubavitch branch of Hasidic Judaism, moved to Santa Fe. He expressed concern that only about 550 families of the approximately 3,000 to 5,000 Jewish residents had a formal affiliation with any branch of Judaism. Remarking that "many Jews in the New Age Mecca are searching for religion," he stated that he hoped to call Santa Fe Jewry back to its traditional roots.[60]

Ever since the sixteenth century, the powerful Roman Catholic Church has made its own compromises with the local Native faith perspective. Local priests seasonally bless the animals, and in 1996, a priest led a procession to San Ysidro Chapel, where he blessed the fields and all grain yet to be planted. As he noted, "Let us pray for rain, may God bless all the fields, to the north and south, to the east and west."[61]

"Pagan" Las Vegas, "multifaceted" Los Angeles, "New Age" Santa Fe. These cities offer three distinct approaches to religion in the contemporary West. In spite of their differences, however, the cities share one item in common: in each case, the religious traditions have reverted back to the separate, perhaps peripheral, and at times antagonistic tracks of the pre–World War II era. The shared sense of midcentury community values has seemingly disappeared.

Or has it? If one looks hard, one can still find examples of religious community. The Las Vegas churches and synagogues seem to have agreed that their primary function involves providing personal, rather than social, services. In the aftermath of the 1992 race riot in Los Angeles, numerous middle-class synagogues reached out to African American churches, and many Christian black churches continue to work hand in glove with nearby Black Muslim groups. Recently the University of Southern California has inaugurated an ecumenical social service program that draws on the resources of all the region's faiths.

The most successful community effort, however, has come from the city of Santa Fe. It emerged accidentally, through an attempt to restore the nearly 100 crumbling adobe churches that dot the region.

Built of sand, dirt, and water that had been molded into sun-dried adobe brick, many of these churches date back to the eighteenth or early nineteenth century.

Their architectural integrity, however, depends on a periodic replastering, usually done by village women. Today, however, most of the women have jobs elsewhere, and few have time to devote to the demanding task of refurbishing the crumbling outer adobe walls.[62] "Unless something is done now," complained Taos artist Harold Joe Waldheim in 1985, "most [churches] will not last the 15 years left to this century."[63]

Since these adobe churches are virtually all Roman Catholic, one might expect that this issue would remain a denominational problem. Not so. For years the adobe churches have played a genuinely symbolic role in northern New Mexican life. Countless artists—Georgia O'Keeffe is perhaps the most famous—have painted them to illustrate the spiritual intersection between the harsh landscape, the Native tradition, and Roman Catholic Christianity. Photographers such as Laura Gilpin, Ansel Adams, and Eliot Porter have done the same. Numerous writers have followed suit. *Santa Fe New Mexican* columnist A. Samuel Adelo once praised the region's adobe churches as symbols of cooperation and brotherhood. They reflected not just the Catholic faith, he said; they were "a part of the multicultural mosaic."[64]

Thus clerics and parishioners from several denominations joined with then archbishop Roberto Sánchez and various artists to mount a crusade to return these churches to their former glory. In 1992, a number of local artists, including some of the most famous, donated more than 100 artworks for a benefit exhibition: "New Mexican Artists Celebrate Historic Churches."[65] The effect bore fruit, and during the 1990s several of the churches have been restored.[66]

Modest though this effort may seem, the ecumenical Protestant-Catholic-Jewish-Mormon–Native American cooperation for restoring New Mexico's crumbling adobe churches is rife with symbolism. Such action makes observers hopeful that perhaps the West's faith communities might also try to come together on other pressing issues of the day: urban sprawl, increased population growth, pollution, environmental degradation, perhaps even sexual and lifestyle issues. If the organized faiths of the West hope to help mold the region's culture in the twenty-first century—as they did in the 1941 through 1960s era—each subregion of the West needs to find the equivalent of Santa Fe's ecumenical restoration of its ancient adobe churches.

Notes

1. Harvey Cox, as quoted in *Context* 31 (1 December 1999): 1.
2. For an overview, see volume 3 of Martin E. Marty's *Modern American Religion, Under God, Indivisible, 1941–1960* (Chicago: University of Chicago Press, 1996); the best denominational account is Thomas Noel, *Colorado Catholicism and the Archdiocese of Denver, 1857–1989* (Niwot: University Press of Colorado, 1989); the most insightful study of the war years is Gerald Sittser, *A Cautious Patriotism: The American Churches and the Second World War* (Chapel Hill and London: University of North Carolina Press, 1997); Ferenc Morton Szasz, *Religion in the Modern American West* (Tucson: University of Arizona Press, 2000), provides the latest survey.
3. *Salt Lake City Tribune,* 13 June 1943.
4. *Congregational District News* 8 (February 1944): 5.
5. *Rocky Mountain News,* 7 November 1943.

6. On the key role of church architecture, see Peter W. Williams, *Houses of God: Religion and Architecture in the United States* (Urbana: University of Illinois Press, 1997).

7. *Newsletter,* National Conference of Christians and Jews (1944).

8. *Salt Lake City Tribune,* 17 June 1946.

9. *Oklahoma Episcopal Messenger* 3 (April 1941).

10. *Oklahoma Episcopal Messenger* 7 (June 1945).

11. *Denver Post,* 9 April 1952.

12. *Denver Post,* 3 November 1937.

13. *Denver Post,* 16 January 1960.

14. "Religions of Salt Lake City," typescript, Utah Historical Society, Salt Lake City, Utah.

15. Groucho Marx, as quoted in Neal Gabler, *An Empire of Their Own: How the Jews Invented Hollywood* (New York: Crown Publishers, 1988), 276.

16. On the 1950s, see J. Ronald Oakley, *God's Country: America in the Fifties* (New York: Dembner Books, 1986), and David Halberstam, *The Fifties* (New York: Villard Books, 1993). See also the two studies by Gerald D. Nash, *The American West Transformed: The Impact of the Second World War* (Bloomington: Indiana University Press, 1985), and *World War II and the West: Reshaping the Economy* (Lincoln: University of Nebraska Press, 1990).

17. Tom Engelhardt, *The End of Victory Culture: Cold War America and the Disillusioning of a Generation* (Amherst: University of Massachusetts Press, 1995). A fine survey of this time period is David Farber, *The Age of Great Dreams: America in the 1960s* (New York: Hill & Wang, 1994). For the impact on religion, see Thomas and Dick Anthony, eds., *In God We Trust: New Patterns of Religious Pluralism in America* (New Brunswick, N.J.: Transaction Books, 1981); Robert S. Ellwood, *The Sixties Spiritual Awakening: American Religion Moving from Modern to Post Modern* (New Brunswick, N.J., Rutgers University Press, 1994); Sydney E. Ahlstrom, "The Moral and Theological Revolution of the 1960s and Its Implications for American Religious History," in *The State of American History,* ed. Herbert J. Bass (Chicago: University of Chicago Press, 1970), 99–117; James M. Gustafson, ed., "The Sixties: Radical Change in American Religion," a special issue of *The Annals of the American Academy of Political and Social Science* 387 (January 1970); and Daniel Bell, "Religion in the Sixties," *Social Research* 38 (autumn 1971): 447–97.

18. Frances FitzGerald, *Cities on a Hill: A Journey Through Contemporary American Cultures* (New York: Simon & Schuster, 1986), 43, as cited in Robert Wuthnow, *Growing Up Religious: Christians and Jews and Their Journeys of Faith* (Boston: Beacon Press, 1999), xxxv.

19. Wade Clark Roof, *A Generation of Seekers* (San Francisco: Harper San Francisco, 1994).

20. David Chidester, *Salvation and Suicide: An Interpretation of Jim Jones, The People's Temple, and Jonestown* (Bloomington: Indiana University Press, 1988).

21. See Eldon G. Ernest, "American Religious History from a Pacific Coast Perspective" in *Religion and Society in the American West: Historical Essays,* eds. Carl Guarneri and David Alvarez (Lanham, Md.: University Press of America, 1987), 3–39.

22. *U.S. News & World Report* (5 July 1982): 39–40.

23. On Rajneeshpuram, see Hugh Milne, *Bhagwan: The God That Failed* (New York: St. Martin's Press, 1986); Kate Strelley (with Robert D. San Souci), *The Ultimate Game: The Rise and Fall of Bhagwan Shree Rajneesh* (San Francisco: Harper & Row, 1987); Francis FitzGerald, *Cities on a Hill: A Journey through Contemporary American Cultures,* 247–381; and especially Carl Abbott, "Utopia and Bureaucracy: The Fall of Rajneeshpuram, Oregon," *Pacific Historical Review* 59 (February 1990): 77–103.

24. James A. Aho, *The Politics of Righteousness: Idaho Christian Patriotism* (Seattle: University of Washington Press, 1990); William E. Gibbs, "The Roswell Incident: An 'Unsolved' or 'Unsolvable' Mystery," in *Great Mysteries of the West,* ed. Ferenc Morton Szasz (Golden, Colo.: Fulcrum Publishing, 1993), 145–60.

25. *The Christian Century* (9 December 1987): 1114–17; *Seattle Times,* 22 November 1987.

26. Dorothy C. Bass, Benton Johnson, and Wade Clark Roof, *Mainstream Protestantism in the Twentieth Century: Its Problems and Prospects* (Louisville, Ky.: Committee on Theological Education, 1986), 13, 23, 33.

27. Robert Wuthnow, *The Restructuring of American Religion: Society and Faith Since World War II* (Princeton, N.J.: Princeton University Press, 1988); James Davison Hunter, *Culture Wars: The Struggle to Define America* (New York: Basic Books, 1991).

28. John D. Spalding, "Bonding in the Bleachers: A Visit to the Promise Keepers," *Christian Century* 113 (6 March 1996), quoted 263.

29. Paul Logan, "Christian Men's Group Touts N.M. Event," *Albuquerque Journal*, 6 August 2000. Jan Jonas, "Promises to Keep," *Albuquerque Tribune*, 17 August 2000.

30. *Guardian Weekly*, 4 June 1995; Spalding, "Bonding," 260.

31. *Time* (5 November 1995): 63; Spalding, "Bonding." See also *Christian Century* 113 (9 October 1996): 941–42. The analysis by James A. Mathisen, "The Strange Decade of the Promise Keepers," *Books and Culture* (September/October 2001): 36–39, is very perceptive.

32. The pastor prefers to remain anonymous.

33. *Christianity Today*, as reported in the *Rocky Mountain News*, 19 December 1994.

34. Linda Castrone, "Houses of the Holy," *Rocky Mountain News*, 21 December 1994; Charles S. Clark, "Tailoring Services for Boomers," *Rocky Mountain News*, 21 December 1994.

35. Donald E. Miller, *Reinventing American Protestantism: Christianity in the New Millennium* (Berkeley: University of California Press, 1997).

36. Russell R. Elliott, with the assistance of William Rowley, *History of Nevada*, rev. ed. (Lincoln: University of Nebraska Press, 1987), 374.

37. See the essays in Wilbur S. Shepperson, ed., *East of Eden, West of Zion: Essays on Nevada* (Reno: University of Nevada Press, 1989).

38. *Las Vegas Review-Journal*, 7 December 1962.

39. Interview with S. B., Las Vegas, Nevada, spring 1998. See also Susan Berman, *Lady Las Vegas: The Inside Story Behind America's Neon Oasis* (New York: T.V. Books, 1996).

40. *Las Vegas Review-Journal*, 25 May 1967.

41. *Los Angeles Times*, 10 May 1981.

42. *Las Vegas Review-Journal*, 10 July 1959.

43. *Las Vegas Sun*, 14 October 1963.

44. *Las Vegas Review-Journal*, 17 May 1963.

45. David Spanier, *Welcome to the Pleasure Dome: Inside Las Vegas* (Reno: University of Nevada Press, 1992); Shepperson, *East of Eden*, 8.

46. Maria Edmundson, "Las Vegas Rising," *Civilization* (August-September 1996): 37–43.

47. Huntington, quoted in T. H. Watkins, *California: An Illustrated History* (Palo Alto, Calif.: American West Publishing Company, 1973), 357.

48. Lewis Mumford, quoted in Watkins, *California*, 518; see also Rodney Steiner, *Los Angeles: The Centrifugal City* (Dubuque, Iowa: Kendall/Hunt, 1981), and David Rieff, *Los Angeles: Capital City of the Third World* (New York: Simon & Schuster, 1991).

49. Barbara A. Weightman, "Changing Religious Landscapes in Los Angeles," *Journal of Cultural Geography* 14 (fall/winter 1993): 1–15; Michael E. Engh, S.J., "A Multiplicity and Diversity of Faiths: Religion's Impact on Los Angeles and the Urban West, 1890–1940," *Western Historical Quarterly* 28 (winter 1997): 462–92.

50. Deborah Dash Moore, *To the Golden Cities: Pursuing the American Jewish Dream in Miami and L.A.* (New York: Free Press, 1994).

51. Charles A. Fracchia, "The Western Context: Its Impact on Our Religious Consciousness," *Lutheran Quarterly* (February 1997): 13–20.

52. Quoted in Gustav Niebuhr, "Land of Religious Freedom Has Universe of Spirituality," *New York Times*, 30 March 1997.

53. Eldon G. Ernst, "Religion in California," *Pacific Theological Review* (winter 1986): 43–51.

54. *Atlas of the New West: Portrait of a Changing Region* (New York: W. W. Norton and Company, 1997), 114–15.

55. *Santa Fe New Mexican*, 13 December 1985.

56. *Santa Fe New Mexican*, 25 March 1969; *Santa Fe New Mexican*, 5 December 1992; *Santa Fe New Mexican*, 11 July 1999.

57. The best study of this phenomenon is Stephen Fox, "Boomer Dharma: The Evolution of Alternative Spiritual Communities in Modern New Mexico," in *Religion in Modern New Mexico*, eds. Ferenc M. Szasz and Richard W. Etulain (Albuquerque: University of New Mexico Press, 1997).

58. *Santa Fe New Mexican*, 28 October 1997.

59. Kay Bird, "Local Jews Seek an Elusive God," *Santa Fe New Mexican*, 25 October 1995.

60. *Santa Fe New Mexican*, 16 February 1997.

61. *Santa Fe New Mexican*, 16 May 1996.

62. *Santa Fe New Mexican*, 1 July 1995, 7 December 1997.

63. "The Church as Art Form," *Albuquerque Journal North*, 7 June 1986.

64. Ibid. See also Marie Romero Cash, *Built of Earth and Song: Churches of Northern New Mexico* (Santa Fe: Red Crane Books, 1993), and Judith Torbin and Joan Brooks Baker, *Symbols of Faith: A Visual Journey to Historic Churches of Northern New Mexico* (Santa Fe: Judith Torbin and Joan Brooks Baker, 1993).

65. *Santa Fe New Mexican*, 26 June 1988.

66. *Santa Fe New Mexican*, 14 September 1992; James Brooke, "Rebuilding Community Churches," *New York Times*, 23 December 1996.

Angels and Apples: The Late-Twentieth-Century Western City, Urban Sprawl, and the Illusion of Urban Exceptionalism[1]

Roger W. Lotchin

An American Airlines traveler could spot the discrepancy on landing anywhere in California at any AA stop. It appeared at San Francisco, San Jose, Oakland, or Palmdale in the Antelope Valley north of Los Angeles. The California city was supposed to sprawl, but in fact it was now growing rather compactly. Large, two-story houses, shoehorned onto small, cookie-cutter lots prevailed and were supplemented by many apartment houses, which squeezed even more residents onto the small spaces. Trees were usually growing everywhere, especially in the suburban spaces. All this did not seem quite proper for cities that supposedly wasted space and denuded and destroyed the environment. California cities were not understood to be like this.

Above all, Los Angeles was not supposed to follow this pattern. It was presumed to be the king of American "urban sprawl," or rather the queen, being Our Lady of Los Angeles. For the last fifty years, Our Lady has been lambasted by critics of all kinds for its horizontal character and devastating environmental impact. Many modern observers, like Carl Abbott and Greg Hise, have entered reservations to the general critique of Los Angeles and, by implication, of western cities. In many ways they have found them well planned and functional rather than anarchic and dysfunctional.[2] Nearly everyone seems to agree, however, that California cities in general and Los Angeles in particular "sprawl."[3] That characteristic seems to be taken for granted. Still, there does seem to be some evidence to the contrary. This essay will investigate whether California and western cities actually do "sprawl" more than other American cities and inquire if the impact of western-style urbanization undermines western cities' "livability."

Although publicists and planners have long discussed the horizontal city, American historians have not devoted much time to the subject. The "sprawl city" appears in some historians' discussions but not much in-depth analysis of it. A search of the bibliography of *Writings on American History, 1979–1990; America, History and Life;* the *Urban History Association Newsletters;* and the *Journal of Urban*

History reveals virtually no titles on "sprawl." Despite the importance of the urban form of our cities, our neglect of the subject has been manifest. Perhaps this comparison of American cities will begin to eliminate that gap in the literature as well as to suggest questions for future study.

Since Los Angeles is so often pulverized by the rhetoric of her detractors, let us begin with Our Lady of the Angels. In 1994, Los Angeles spread much less than many American cities, east and west. The remainder of urban California was not even close to the top of the list in that category. For example, Atlanta, Georgia, is half as dense in population per square mile as Los Angeles.[4] New Orleans is even less dense than Atlanta, to give just one more southern example.[5] Los Angeles is not even the most spread out western city—it is just the reverse. Instead, the City of the Angels and California cities in general are the densest cities in the West. So much for the western myth of Los Angeles "sprawl"!

But what about the notion that western cities in general and Los Angeles in particular spread out more than any other American cities? This question has two different answers. California cities are more dense than all but the most compactly settled eastern urban entities. The remainder of western urban areas have low densities. Western cities certainly have fewer persons per square mile than do many Rust Belt cities. Among cities with over 200,000 population, New York leads in crowding, with 23,671 per square mile, followed by San Francisco and Jersey City, with roughly 15,000.[6] Of the nine major cities with populations over 10,000 per square mile, seven—New York, Chicago, Philadelphia, Boston, Miami, Newark, and Jersey City—are east of the Mississippi. San Francisco and Santa Ana, California, make up the rest.[7]

So the older areas of the country seem to be far more crowded than western cities, unless we consider the South. Southern cities often have very low densities. Table 1 directly compares the cities of the two regions, rank ordered by people per square mile.

Table 1: The Thirty-Four Largest Southern Cities and Largest Western Cities with More Than 100,000 Population

S. Cities	Pop.	PPSM	W. Cities	Pop.	PPSM
Jacksonville	661,177	74	Okla. City	453,995	746[8]
Chesapeake, Va.	166,000	487	Salt L. City	165,835	1,521[9]
Columbus, Ga.	186,000	860	Colo. Springs	295,815	1,615[10]
Huntsville, Ala.	163,000	993	Ft. Worth	454,430	1,617[11]
Nashville-Davidson	495,012	1,046	Aurora, Colo.	239,626	1,808[12]
Chattanooga	153,000	1,291	Corpus Chr.	266,412	1,973
Montgomery, Ala.	192,000	1,423	Tulsa	375,307	2,045
Little Rock	177,000	1,570	El Paso	543,813	2,216
Virginia Beach	417,061	1,680	Austin	492,329	2,260
Mobile	201,896	1,711	Phoenix	1,012,230	2,411[13]
Birmingham	264,984	1,784	Reno	139,884	2,433[14]

Table 1 *(continued)*

S. Cities	Pop.	PPSM	W. Cities	Pop.	PPSM
Jackson, Miss.	196,000	1,800	Tucson	415,079	2,658
Shreveport, La.	197,000	1,994	Mesa	296,645	2,732
Winston-Salem, N.C.	145,000	2,036	Arlington	275,907	2,967
Knoxville	167,000	2,167	San Antonio	966,437	2,902
Macon, Ga.	107,000	2,239	Dallas	1,022,497	2,986
Greensboro, N.C.	190,000	2,380	Albuquerque	389,492	3,014[15]
Memphis	610,275	2,384	Riverside	238,601	3,071[16]
Charlotte	416,294	2,388	Houston	1,690,180	3,131
Hampton, Va.	137,000	2,646	Denver	483,853	3,156
New Orleans	489,595	2,711	San Diego	1,148,851	3,546
Atlanta	394,848	2,996	Portland	445,485	3,572[17]
Baton Rouge	224,704	3,041	Las Vegas	295,516	3,548
Portsmouth, Va.	104,000	3,153	Fresno	376,130	3,795
Richmond	202,263	3,365	Sacramento	382,816	3,975
Raleigh	223,621	3,595	Stockton	219,621	4,175
St. Petersburg	235,306	3,975	San Jose	801,331	4,678
Hollywood, Fla.	122,000	4,459	Anaheim	274,162	6,189
Norfolk	253,768	4,717	Seattle	519,598	6,193[18]
Hialeah, Fla.	192,000	9,984	Oakland	373,219	6,653
Washington, D.C.	585,221	9,531	Los Angeles	3,489,779	7,436
Miami	367,016	10,309	Long Beach	438,771	8,775
			Santa Ana	288,024	10,628
			San Francisco	728,921	15,609

Source: *County and City Data Book,* 1994, 650–853.

This table indicates that southern urban populations per square mile are considerably lower than western ones. And if other urban areas are included, especially Los Angeles suburbs, the greater western urban densities would be even more vividly obvious and, given our long-standing custom of calling LA the capital of "sprawl," uproariously highlighted. For example, posh Beverly Hills, at 5,633 people per square mile, has a higher density than every city on the southern city list down to Hialeah, Florida. Counterculture Berkeley, at 9,631, has a higher density than every southern city save Miami.[19] Upscale Beverly Hills and radical Berkeley are not anomalies in Urban California. Los Angeles suburbs are particularly dense compared to the urban South. In fact, the densest LA suburbs, or even major California suburbs, are almost all more compact than the southern *center* cities listed in Table 1. This is a surprising conclusion but true nonetheless. The densest LA suburb, Maywood, is twice as crowded as Miami.

Table 2 shows densities of the Los Angeles, Bay Area, and other California suburbs with the highest densities of people per square mile, that is, populations per square mile of 6,000 and over, a density approximately twice that of Atlanta.

Table 2: Most Compact California Suburbs

W. Covina	98,777	6,097	Lakewood	76,144	8,100
Costa Mesa	96,240	6,169	Garden Grove	145,874	8,149
Placentia	41,393	6,172	Manhattan Beach	33,463	8,580
S. San Fran.	55,610	6,179	San Gabriel	137,538	9,156
Anaheim	274,162	6,189	Compton	95,608	9,373
San Bruno	39,780	6,216	Berkeley	101,122	9,631
Cerritos	53,527	6,224	Gardena	51,244	9,669
Burlingame	27,235	6,334	Redondo Beach	62,790	9,967
Imperial Beach	27,330	6,356	Norwalk	97,767	9,976
El Cajon	92,483	6,422	San Pablo	26,486	10,187
Whittier	80,533	6,443	Rosemead	52,451	10,285
Covina	44,890	6,506	Santa Monica	87,064	10,490
Torrance	135,642	6,653	Bellflower	64,503	10,574
Campbell	36,755	6,617	Santa Ana	288,024	10,628
Buena Park	70,936	6,692	Paramount	49,967	10,631
Cypress	44,590	6,756	Baldwin Park	71,047	10,765
Fountain Valley	54,043	6,972	La Puente	38,154	10,901
Hunt Beach	185,055	7,010	Alhambra	83,214	10,949
San Mateo	86,538	7,093	El Monte	106,935	11,256
La Habra	52,100	7,137	South Gate	88,622	11,976
Montebello	60,368	7,273	Inglewood	111,496	12,119
Alameda	78,940	7,387	Daly City	93,358	12,448
National City	57,408	7,554	Hawthorne	74,906	12,696
Pico Rivera	60,743	7,593	Lynwood	63,216	12,901
Culver City	38,999	7,647	Bell City	34,922	13,432
Foster City	29,060	7,647	Lawndale	28,542	14,271
Downey	95,250	7,681	Bell Gardens	42,651	17,060
Monterey Park	59,357	7,810	Huntington Park	55,450	17,887
Westminster City	78,185	7,819	W. Hollywood	35,209	18,531
Temple City	32,322	8,083	Maywood	27,836	23,197

Source: *CCDB*, 1994, 650-97.

As this table indicates, nineteen California suburbs have a higher population per square mile than Miami, the most compact city in the South. Put another way, only three southern center cities have densities of more than 6,000. Sixty-one California suburbs alone are more compact than 6,000! Even the wealthy suburbs of Rancho Palos Verdes and Los Altos have higher populations per square mile than does Atlanta, the uncrowned capital of the New South. If southern cities slosh about more than do California suburbs, perhaps we should change our minds about the question of Golden State "urban sprawl."

Most of these suburbs are either near the center cities or are in the zone between center cities and the suburban periphery. However, if we pushed the comparison outward, it would still make the same point. Even far-distant California suburbs are comparatively crowded. I will return to this point later in comparing western and eastern densities, but suffice it to say here that distant California suburbs, like pleasant Claremont, have densities of 3,015 persons per square mile, and equally charming Pasadena has 5,765 (compared with Atlanta's 2,996).

Since density figures are difficult to pin down, it is necessary to cross-check them as much as possible. One way of doing that is to compare urban counties as well as cities. Table 3 compares the populations per square mile of the counties in which the principal cities of the two regions are situated. These figures are necessarily much lower because few cities completely fill up their home counties.

Table 3: Urban Counties of Southern and Western Metropolitan Areas: County/City, Population, Density per Square Mile

Southern Cities			Western Cities		
Caddo/Shreveport	246,325	208	Washoe/Reno	268,540	42
Montgomery/			Pima/Tucson	690,202	75
Montgomery	214,996	272	Clark/Las Vegas	845,633	107
Hinds/Jackson	254,606	293	Riverside/Riverside	1,288,435	179
Mobile/Mobile	389,234	316	El Paso/Colo. Springs	421,187	198
Pulaski/Little Rock	353,394	458	Maricopa/Phoenix	2,209,567	240
Chesapeake/Chesapeake	166,005	487	Maricopa/Mesa		
Hamilton/Chattanooga	288,637	532	Nueces/Corpus Christi	300,815	360
Wake/Raleigh	457,138	548	Bernalillo/Albu.	499,262	428
Guilford/Greensboro	357,737	550	Arapahoe/Aurora	420,862	524
Jefferson/Birmingham	657,674	591	San Diego/San Diego	601,055	619
Bibb/Macon, Ga.	151,936	608	El Paso/El Paso, Tx.	628,472	620
Forsyth/			Travis/Austin	613,159	620
Winston-Salem	270,971	661	King/Seattle	1,557,537	733
Knox/Knoxville	347,583	684	Oklahoma/		
Hillsborough/Tampa	858,552	817	Oklahoma City	612,713	864
East Baton Rouge/			Tulsa/Tulsa	519,847	912
Baton Rouge	391,632	859	Bexar/San Antonio	1,233,096	989
Muskogee/			Salt Lake/Salt Lake City	763,526	1,035
Columbus, Ga.	186,369	862	Sacramento/		
Duval/Jacksonville	700,852	906	Sacramento	1,093,237	1,132
Mecklenburg/			Santa Clara/San Jose	1,528,527	1,184
Charlotte	537,735	1,020	Multnomah/Port	600,811	1,380
Davidson/Nashville	517,798	1,031	Tarrant/Fort Worth-		
Dade/Miami	2,007,972	1,033	Arlington	220,119	1,413
Dade/Hialeah			Harris/Houston	2,971,755	1,719

Table 3 *(continued)*

Southern Cities			Western Cities		
Broward/Ft. Lauder	1,301,274	1,076	Alameda/Oak	1,307,572	1,773
Broward/Hollywood			Dallas/Dallas	1,913,395	2,175
Shelby/Memphis	844,847	1,119	Los Angeles/		
Virginia Beach/			Los Angeles	9,053,645	2,230
Virginia Beach	417,061	1,680	Los Angeles/		
De Kalb/Atlanta	563,517	2,100	Long Beach		
Newport News	177,286	2,596	Orange/Santa Ana	2,484,789	3,146
Hampton/Hampton,Va.	137,048	2,646	Orange/Anaheim		
Orleans/New Orleans	489,595	2,711	Denver/Denver	483,852	3,156
Richmond/Richmond	202,263	3,365	San Francisco/		
Norfolk	253,768	4,717	San Francisco	728,921	15,609

Source: *CCDB,* 1994, 650–873, and metropolitan maps, appendix C, C-1 through C-79.

Some anomalies in this table require explanation. As in the case of cities, some of the home counties of large cities are absurdly extensive. Harris County (Houston), San Diego County, Maricopa County (Phoenix), Pima County (Tucson), Washoe (Reno), Clark (Las Vegas), and others are gigantic. San Diego, at 4,205 square miles, is just slightly smaller in area than the state of Connecticut, at 4,845. Maricopa County, at 9,204, is larger than the state of Massachusetts, at 7,838, and Pima County is almost the identical size of Maricopa, at 9,187. Washoe County, at 6,343, is slightly smaller than New Jersey, at 7,419. Clark County, Nevada, at 7,911 square miles, is larger than New Jersey and four times as large as Delaware, at 1,955. Harris County, at 1,729, is just smaller than Delaware, at 1,955, and El Paso County, Colorado (as distinguished from El Paso County, Texas) is greater, at 2,127 square miles. Obviously much of the land area of these counties is uninhabited. Thus the comparison is somewhat skewed in favor of lower western densities by the inclusion of these huge counties.[20]

Still, even with these counties included, Table 3 indicates that the West is not less crowded than the South. The least-compact western counties have densities below the least-crowded southern ones. However, from one-third of the way down the table, western densities are greater, until we reach the very end, with several denser southern cities, topped only by San Francisco. If the preposterously large, uninhabited western counties are excluded, the lower southern densities would be even more evident. Table 3, showing the populations per square mile of urban counties, confirms the lower densities of the southern cities themselves.

Of course, it can be argued that urban–density-per–square-mile figures are misleading because all cities and urban counties have different amounts of square mileage. That is true, and some western cities have very great square mileage. With the exception of Indianapolis and Jacksonville, most of the cities and especially the counties with huge square mileage are in the West, so comparing them to southern or eastern cities would not prejudice the comparison against western densities. The greater the square mileage, the lower the crowdedness. Even with that comparative advantage, however, western cities are more tightly settled than southern ones. Nonetheless, other measures will help to pin down the question more definitively.

Auto ownership is often given as a stand-in for low density and "sprawl." Historians have frequently compared the per capita auto ownership of Progressive Era Los Angeles to that of New York City. Obviously LA citizens owned many more cars per capita.[21] In comparing the West and the South now, we must ask whether western urban citizens own more automobiles per capita than southern urban citizens.

The West has slightly more vehicles available per household, but the disparity is not very great. The most striking differences for both regions are those within each regional category, ranging from 1.1 for San Francisco in the West and 1.1 for New Orleans and Miami in the South, up to 2.0 for San Jose in the West and 1.9 for Virginia Beach in the South. And on closer examination, the relationship between cars available per household and populations per square mile seems nebulous. Historians have usually assumed that greater per capita numbers of cars are tantamount to lower densities. In a case like New York City, with average crowding of 23,671 and auto availability of 0.6, a correlation seems to exist. However, such a consistent relationship does not.

Denver, with just under twice the people per square mile as Birmingham, has exactly the same ratio of autos available per household. And that is not the most striking contradiction of the idea that high per capita auto ownership equals low urban density. San Francisco and New Orleans both have auto availability rates of 1.1 per household. Yet San Francisco has a density of 15,609 and New Orleans has a density of 2,711. The City by the Bay has almost six times more population per square mile than the Crescent City! We might account for some of the difference by the relatively high levels of poverty in New Orleans, but not for that much. In 1989, 27.3 percent of New Orleans families lived below the poverty level, whereas only 9.7 percent of San Francisco families did. Thus the density difference was six to one, but the poverty difference was only three to one.

Other comparisons lead to the same conclusion. Anaheim, California, has roughly 60 percent of the density of neighboring Santa Ana but almost the same number of vehicles available per household, 1.9 to Santa Ana's 1.8. Los Angeles, the unofficially crowned "Queen of Sprawl," has a midrange number of vehicles available per household at 1.5. So does Sacramento, which is only about one-half as crowded as LA. The intersectional comparison of Hialeah, Florida, and San Diego, California, is equally illustrative. San Diego has 35 percent of the density of Hialeah but the exact same number of cars available per household. A final example will suffice to reinforce the argument that the relationship between density and auto availability is tenuous at best. Norfolk, hemmed in by rivers and competing cities, and Nashville, luxuriating in space by virtue of its consolidation with

Davidson County, have virtually the same auto availability, 1.4 to 1.6. Yet Norfolk has more than four and one-half times as much crowding. These are only some of the more striking contrasts; a systematic comparison of lists of western and southern cities would only heighten them.[22]

Thus the per capita availability of autos is not very much help in judging urban sprawl. Some kind of relationship must exist between the two, such as that of New York City. Yet this relationship is not consistent enough to be of much systematic analytical value. In any case, the difference between southern and western auto availability is not very great, so it cannot explain the differences in urban populations per square mile.

What about other measures of compactness, such as the number of single-family dwellings versus apartments or attached housing? Do they reveal a bias in favor of the South or West? Certainly the apartment-building percentage of a city's housing is an indication of crowding. A comparison of detached housing to large apartments of five units or more demonstrates once again the lower density of southern cities. Western cities have a larger percentage of housing with five or more units than do southern ones. The lowest apartment-prone southern city has fewer apartments and the highest western city has more. A comparison of the largest western and southern cities indicates that southern apartment percentages are 4 to 7 percentage points below those of the western cities. That is a big surprise, but the position of Los Angeles at the highest percentage of apartments is an even bigger one. Given its reputation for "sprawl," LA should be expected to contain a greater percentage of detached housing and a lesser percentage of apartments. Perhaps this figure will discourage the use of further sprawl metaphors about single-family dwellings stretching to the horizon and on to infinity. Los Angeles is not the paragon of single-family dwellings; it is the western urban epitome of large apartment buildings.

If we include all shared housing, duplexes, small apartments, and large ones (five units or over) in the analysis, the West again leads the South. It has more total shared-housing units. On total shared housing, Los Angeles does not quite lead the list because its great rival, San Francisco, does. But the number is again very high. So on this measure, too, southern cities appear more spread out. The distortion of "western sprawl" seems well documented.

Cities in New England, the Middle Atlantic states, the Border States, and the Midwest reinforce this interpretation. Western cities are often less dense than cities in these other areas, but interesting anomalies remain. Surprisingly, these figures do not break down on an East-West basis. There are two sets of figures for the West. Once we get beyond the cities of California, the reputation of the West for horizontal cities is more convincing. The western cities are usually more expansive than cities east of the Great Bend of the Missouri, starting at Kansas City, Missouri and Kansas, and north of the Ohio. Cities in Illinois, Wisconsin, Ohio, Michigan, Maryland, Pennsylvania, New York, and Massachusetts are less spread out than the extra-California Urban West.

California is the exception to this rule, and it is a very big exception. California contains about three-eighths of the entire western urban population, so any generalization about "sprawl" that cannot test successfully in California is burdened from the start.[23] California cities, especially in the Los Angeles region, are much more compact than many eastern urban places. For example, no Border State city, except Baltimore and Washington, D.C., has densities as high as those of Los Angeles, much less the LA supersuburbs[24] like Anaheim or Santa Ana or smaller Huntington Park and Maywood. Wilmington, Delaware, comes close, but no other Delaware city is even remotely near the California densities.[25] In Kentucky, no city population per square mile approaches that of Los Angeles. Louisville has the greatest number of persons per square mile at 4,365, which is just over one-half that of LA, and no other Kentucky city contains even half as many people per square mile.

Some of this discrepancy is due to the extraordinarily large square mileage of places like Lexington, which is consolidated with Fayette County. Lexington-Fayette contains a mere 817 persons per square mile. However, some western cities are extraordinarily uncrowded for the same reason. Not all eastern or Border State cities have such boundaries, and more suffer from the reverse.[26] Louisville contains roughly 20 percent of the territory of "sprawling" Lexington, yet it still has densities of only 4,365 per square mile. (Los Angeles has 7,436 persons per square mile.) The same is true of Missouri, another Border State. St. Louis, once a premier American city, is no longer in the category of larger cities because it lost huge numbers of its population to the suburbs. It still has 383,733 people, but its densities (6,199) do not equal those of Los Angeles. No other Missouri city comes close.[27] Maryland is more compact, but only Baltimore comes up to the LA standard. The Maryland metropolis has 8,986 people per square mile, slightly more than Los Angeles but not even up to those of suburban Santa Monica, at 10,490, or Redondo Beach, at 9,967.[28] West Virginia's urban entities confirm the point. Suffice it to say, Border States do not measure up to California's urban densities. With the exception of Maryland, the urban densities of Border States appear more akin to those of the non-California West.

It would perhaps tax the reader unduly to continue a systematic tabular comparison between western cities and those of other regions: the Midwest, Northeast, Middle Atlantic, and New England. But mention must be made of them if only to suggest the possibilities of studying comparative "urban sprawl." First of all, some of the cities in these states closely approximate the non–California West model of densities. Indiana, New Hampshire, Vermont, and Maine cities are very spread out. Those in Massachusetts are not, but they are not as crowded as California cities, either. The most compact city in Massachusetts is the Boston suburb of Somerville, at 17,635 persons per square mile, followed by the college town of Cambridge, at 14,618, then Chelsea, at 12,175—both suburbs—and only then by Boston, 11,398, Everett, 10,320, and Malden, 10,531. In other words, the greatest density of Massachusetts cities or suburbs is in Boston or its suburbs.[29] If the reader is not surprised that Boston has only a bit more density than Santa Monica, California, then he or she has lost the capacity for that sensation.[30]

Of course, the most compact cities in the United States straddle the Hudson River: Manhattan (52,432), Brooklyn (32,428), and the Bronx (28,443), New York, Union City (44,043); and West New York (37,483), New Jersey. Obviously no western city can match this crowding. However, even here interesting possibilities arise. Because of the lesser numbers of persons per square mile in the Queens and Richmond boroughs, New York's overall density is "only" 23,671.[31] This figure is only infinitesimally larger than that of the Los Angeles suburb of Maywood, at 23,197.

Figures for Michigan, Illinois, and Pennsylvania cities indicate more compactness than those of the non-California West, but they are not on a level with California. Chicago and Philadelphia have higher figures than Los Angeles city, but California cities in general are more compact than the cities of those two states.[32] And neither Chicago nor Philadelphia is as crowded as San Francisco or southland suburbs like Maywood, West Hollywood (18,351), and Huntington Park (17,887).[33]

Given the very high ratio of people per square mile of suburbs from East to West, we are entitled to wonder if the word *sprawl* really describes anything more than the initial light settlement patterns of the suburban frontier. Suburbs are apparently still growing in density, while cities decline. I doubt that we know what the optimum figure is or will be. Perhaps today's "sprawl" will be tomorrow's Maywood or Somerville. Yesterday's was.

These convergences of eastern and California cities raise interesting questions. One is how much of this picture has been enduring and how much of it has changed over time. Historians have long considered LA the capital of "sprawl"; yet we have seen that according to the 1992 census figures, it does not deserve that reputation. Still, it may have been a much more expansive city at an earlier time, for example, when Robert Fogelson wrote *Fragmented Metropolis: Los Angeles, 1850–1930* to describe the city.[34] The high densities of current California cities suggest that they might well have started low but are now converging. Again, great numbers of tables will be avoided, but the question of change over time must be addressed.

The analysis of historically changing densities is complicated by the important measures having been dynamic through time. With a few exceptions, in the South and West, for example, both the populations and the boundaries of cities have expanded. Because of this dynamism, we cannot easily compare the compactness of cities or metropolitan areas over time. If populations and city limits each expand, the later figures of persons per square mile are no longer directly comparable to the earlier ones. Fortunately the U.S. Census devised an estimate of density in 1950 that obviates these difficulties. Slightly modified in 1960, the category of "urbanized areas" seeks to measure the phenomenon of density directly by measuring people per square mile in urban areas that are actually built up with residences. Thus the urbanized areas category continually measures and remeasures density as both population and boundaries change and residences multiply.

Using this category of analysis, we see that western cities passed southern ones in density by 1990. In 1950 the West may have been marginally less crowded, but by 1990 it was markedly more so. In 1950 the median for the thirty-four largest western cities was slightly above the median for the thirty-four largest southern cities: 4,106 to 4,085 persons per square mile. However, the southern urban average was slightly higher, at 4,387 to 4,069.[35] So in 1950 the picture was muddied, with each section dominating one category of measurement. By 1990 the ambiguity had vanished as western cities became much denser. Both southern and western urbanized areas had declined in density, but southern urbanized areas had declined much more. In 1990, the mean for the South was 1,572 and for the West it was 2,366. The medians were 1,426 and 2,216 respectively. Even with the denser California cities left out, both the mean and median figures for the West were markedly more dense: 2,083 and 1,996.

The preceding discussion sought to determine if western cities are less dense than southern ones, to investigate particularly the situation of California cities, and to generate questions for fresh research. The investigation demonstrates that western cities are more dense than southern ones and that California cities are the densest in the West or South, and often, the densest of any in the country. I hope that other historians will take up these questions and build on these conclusions.

If the above indicates that western cities are not uniquely horizontal, what about the supposed consequences of their urban form? Horizontal cities have been charged with everything from denuding the environment to causing horrendous traffic jams to jacking up the price of housing beyond the reach of the average person. Urban historians should be especially careful about evaluating these charges because historians above all should have a greater perspective on the question. Progressive Era reformers were just as adamant about the city, but in a reverse way. They thought that cities were too crowded, and they argued that decentralization was the panacea for a host of urban ills, not the cause of them. And they had their own lengthy checklist of pathologies that stemmed from density. So we should be careful not to swing to the other extreme of imbuing decentralization with a host of ills for which compactness is the supposed panacea. If we do so, we run the risk of looking foolish at a time when the outside world already is skeptical of our efforts.

Undoubtedly, horizontal cities have their defects, but some of these have been exaggerated. One is environmental. Cities are not always dangerous to the environment; in fact, they can sometimes enhance it, as in the case of reforestation. True, cities transform the natural environment, but not always for the worse. In its natural state, the West is largely a desert. Still, trees abound in the Northwest, from California to the Canadian boundary, and usually in the region's mountains. Nonetheless, much of the interior is arid, a natural wasteland. Flying over the West, one sees mile upon weary mile of brown, gray, and tan land, mostly free of vegetation, broken only by the occasional irrigation circle or linear oasis along a river. Even on the Great Plains, where agriculture is possible, trees are scarce.

However, wherever cities appear, so do trees. People reclaim treeless land and begin to create "urban forests" on it. Dallas from the air provides a vivid example. Up to the urban outskirts the plains are open and treeless, but at the limits of the urbanized area, trees appear and grow ever more densely as one moves into town. The East Bay region of San Francisco Bay provides an even more striking illustration. Where streets and houses exist, so do trees. Outside these areas, except for man-made parks, trees are scarce. So instead of looking at the expansion of western city limits and the construction of urban outskirts, suburbs, and urban fringes as a total loss to the environment, we should see them as having the redeeming dynamic of creating urban forests.

Urbanization does not take up a very large part of the landmass of the United States, as we shall see; still, some of the figures are particularly arresting for the purpose of visualizing the extent of urban forests. The figures cited earlier in the discussion of "sprawl" indicate that very large amounts of land have come within city limits and therefore are eventually going to become urban forests. Of course, not every western city is subject to reforestation. San Francisco is too crowded over much of the city for extensive forestation, but urbanization promotes forests over much of the West. When nineteenth-century cities like Chicago created forest preserves beyond the city limits, it was thought to be an enlightened act. Yet cities themselves are much larger forest preserves and even more of an amenity in plains and desert areas where trees are scarce.

The supposedly "sprawling" western urban areas have also made home ownership available on a large scale. It is sometimes argued that "sprawl" undermines home ownership. One reads that "sprawling" Los Angeles has one of the lowest home ownership rates in the nation. However, the figures for home ownership demonstrate just the reverse. The City of the Angels has a lower home ownership rate not because it "sprawls," but because for the last fifty years it has become ever more dense. Home ownership there has consistently gone down as the densities have gone up.[36] Of course, New York is the epitome of this phenomenon. In Manhattan, where the densities are the highest in the United States, the percentage of home ownership is only 17.9 percent. It is the same in the Bronx, and the overall New York City average of 28.6 percent is very low. Los Angeles does not even compare. The same phenomenon is true all over the West. Of the seventy-four largest American cities, those in the West have a higher home ownership rate than those in the East, as Table 4 demonstrates. The difference is not striking, but it is enough to disprove the charge that "sprawl" undermines home owning. Western cities provide widespread opportunities for home ownership.

Table 4. Home Ownership in the Seventy-four Largest American Cities Compared among Western and Middlewestern, Border, Middle Atlantic, and New England States[37]

Western Cities		Other Cities	
San Francisco	34.5	Newark	23.1
Glendale, Calif.	38.7	New York City	28.6
Los Angeles	39.4	Jersey City	29.6
Austin	40.6	Boston	30.9
Long Beach	41.0	Cincinnati	38.3
Oakland	41.6	Washington, D.C.	38.9

Table 4 *(continued)*

Western Cities		Other Cities	
Dallas	44.1	Chicago	41.5
Houston	44.6	Buffalo	43.1
Fresno	48.2	Yonkers	43.5
Santa Ana	48.3	Rochester	44.0
San Diego	48.3	Milwaukee	44.8
Stockton	48.5	St. Louis	45.1
Seattle	48.9	Columbus	46.6
Denver	49.2	Madison, Wis.	47.0
Anaheim	49.2	Cleveland	47.9
Las Vegas	50.4	Baltimore	48.6
Sacramento	51.3	Minneapolis	49.7
Tucson	51.4	Dayton	51.0
Arlington, Tex.	51.8	Pittsburgh	52.3
Tacoma	52.7	Detroit	52.9
Portland	53.0	Lexington-Fayette	53.0
San Antonio	54.0	St. Paul	53.9
Fort Worth	54.5	Louisville	54.9
Colorado Springs	54.6	Indianapolis	56.7
Bakersfield	55.1	Kansas City	56.9
Lubbock	55.3	Akron	58.7
Tulsa	55.8	Fort Wayne, Ind.	59.6
Riverside	56.3	Grand Rapids	59.9
Corpus Christi	56.6	Toledo	60.7
Spokane	57.2	Philadelphia	61.9
Albuquerque	57.3	Des Moines	62.0
El Paso	57.6		
Lincoln, Neb.	58.1		
Huntington Beach	58.5		
Aurora, Colo.	58.7		
Wichita	58.9		
Phoenix	59.1		
Omaha	59.2		
Oklahoma City	59.5		
Mesa	60.9		
San Jose	61.3		
Garland, Tex.	64.2		
Fremont, Calif.	64.6		

Source: *CCDB,* 1994, 650-853.

Critics have also charged that "sprawl" wastes land. When cities are so spread out, it is claimed, they waste good agricultural land that would otherwise be available for crops. This argument is dubious at best. Even the Department of Agriculture admits that the United States is not running out of cropland. Actually, the country is gaining cropland and open space and creating parkland in large acreages. Thus the numbers are not supportive of this indictment, and the whole concept of waste is itself questionable. Most of the space in cities and suburbs is devoted to residences, and homes are not a waste of land. They satisfy someone's need for a home and shelter and solve for the homeowner one of the most fundamental problems facing urban populations. Moreover, suburbs satisfy this human need in a manner congenial to the residents, if not to many planners and politicians. People long for a little space, some separation from the hurly-burly of busy urban areas, and houses that they can afford. As shown above, low-density locales are home-owner locales. Americans do not want to live in high-rise residences, as these generate their own problems. We are now tearing down college dormitories and urban public housing because of the pathologies, inefficiencies, and nuisances of high-rise housing. To call suburbs wasteful because they avoid these ills and satisfy this basic human need for housing in a way faithful to the wishes of the residents is a total misperception of the situation.

The reality is population growth, and that is what is driving so-called urban and suburban "sprawl." Urban areas are growing, and these larger populations have to be put somewhere. With the amendments to the immigration laws in the 1960s, the United States has once again become home to many immigrants. Inevitably, many of these are poor people from the developing nations and are enhancing both their own fortunes and the U.S. workforce by migrating here. It is not entirely clear where the experts would place these larger populations. If cities expand onto good cropland, as do Fresno, Sacramento, and Stockton in the Central Valley of California, the critics complain about the loss of farming acreage. If cities and suburbs spread over bottomlands, like those in the Ohio, Missouri, and Mississippi valleys, the detractors complain about building on floodplains. If the cities spread into the desert, as Las Vegas does, the skeptics bemoan the loss of the fragile desert environment and its unique natural forms. If cities spread into forests, commentators deplore the loss of them, too. So where should we put these growing populations? On mountainsides? Into megastructures like Frank Lloyd Wright's proposed Mile High Illinois building or Paolo Soleri's equally immense arcologies? Cities are one of several legitimate competing priorities for land use, and they must be accommodated on some kind of geography.

Many western cities do not really stand on prime farmland anyway. For example, all of Colorado's urban areas receive less than twenty inches of precipitation per year. Reno catches seven and one-half inches and Las Vegas, just over four. Phoenix gets less than eight inches and Tucson, about twelve. Albuquerque captures just under nine inches.[38] Agriculture under these conditions requires a massive irrigation infrastructure. In many places in the Great Plains, the Ogallala Aquifer is being depleted, and so is the Granite Reef Aquifer under Phoenix. Given these difficulties, maybe cities, with their lesser demands for water, provide a more rational scheme of land use than farming. Moreover, heavy urbanization places minimal rather than maximal demand on either farm acreage or open space.

Finally, in their zeal to attack "sprawl," critics have tended to ignore the fact that urban areas take up a relatively modest portion of the landmass of America. One recent analyst puts the figure at only 4.8 percent. This figure includes all of the urban areas, plus the space used for highways and military bases. Another claims 5 percent.[39] A 1998 estimate, based on satellite photography, puts the figure for the urbanized places of the United States at 2.7 percent.[40] Another estimate puts the total land use of southern California urban areas at 4.5 percent of the total square mileage of the large state of California. Finally, the photo-imaging project establishes the total urbanized percent of California at 5.2 percent. This means that 93 percent of the population lives on this amount of land. It is perhaps impossible to set anything but arbitrary standards for optimum land use, but putting 93 percent of the thirty-odd million Californians on 5 percent of the land seems like a very efficient way of handling them. Such low percentages indicate that cities, horizontality and all, are very land-use intensive. It also overwhelmingly repudiates the concept of "sprawl," which suggests the massive and unnecessary (wasteful) utilization of ground for cities. In fact, the reverse is correct. Rather than being an enormous block of land, the urban part is more like a humble portion. Clearly urban areas do not use much of the earth's surface. Would it be better if 100 percent of California's population rested on 3 percent of the land? On 2 percent? Would such places be livable? How much more efficient do we want to get?

What is more, a historical perspective clarifies that the suburbs are growing in densities. This is true all over the United States, but it is especially evident in the Los Angeles area and in southern California. Critics of "sprawl" tend to assume that the current densities they are shocked by are the end of the line or the end of the story. This view lacks historical perspective. As we saw in earlier sections, today's supposed suburban sprawl is rapidly becoming tomorrow's highly compact area. Los Angeles suburbs are a classic illustration of the growing number of people per square mile in suburbia. If some LA suburbs have a higher density than center city Chicago and most other center cities, can we really claim that "sprawl" is the ultimate land use? Or is it just a point on the spectrum on the way to an ultimate use?

And although their water woes are often cited as another problem caused by cities, urban places are not the heaviest users of western water. By a wide margin, agriculture is the most prolific consumer of water. The breakdown usually given by water historians is 15 percent for cities, 85 percent for agriculture. Since the West is heavily urbanized, this low water usage is highly significant. California has been estimated to have 93 percent of its population in metropolitan areas. If this extraordinary percentage of the people can get along on 15 percent of the state's developed water, that seems anything but inefficient or wasteful.

It is also argued that western air has been declining in quality, just as its water has been declining in quantity. Smog is one of the things that western cities and especially Los Angeles are known for. Yet even smog, the much-vaunted defect of western, especially California urban places, is exaggerated. Of the metropolitan areas that the Environmental Protection Agency (EPA) monitors, the western cities scored higher than the eastern ones on the Pollutants Standards Index (PSI).[41] That is, the western cities experienced more days over the allowable score of 100 than did eastern ones. However, the difference was hardly striking: 13.0 to 11.5 days per year. Moreover, the West had many more cities, nine compared to one elsewhere, with absolutely no days that exceeded EPA standards. As the smog season of 2001 neared its end, the news that LA was about to reclaim its title from Houston as the smoggiest metropolitan area caused a mild media flare-up. However, air quality officials pointed out that the air was "cleaner than last year and that will continue the long-term trend."[42]

So the factor of "sprawl" cannot be all that great if it produces a difference of only a day and a half at most. Five of the six western cities with serious smog problems are in California, led by Los Angeles, with sixty-three days a year that exceeded EPA limits. The importance of horizontal form is further called into question because California cities are the most compact in the West, not the most spread out. Finally, every California and western city improved markedly over the period that the EPA measured, from 1988 to 1997. Many improved their record by 50 percent. Los Angeles did so by 74 percent, Bakersfield by more than 50 percent, Fresno by 45 percent, Houston by 35 percent, Sacramento by half, Ventura by 64 percent, and Seattle by a much larger margin. As of late 1996, Los Angeles area smog had declined steadily for twenty years. In 1976, the Southland had 212 stage-one smog alerts; in 1996 it recorded seven. That was the lowest number of stage-one alerts "in the more than 40 years [of] record keeping." The air quality control officials and the environmentalists of the region maintain that the region still has a long way to go, but they also agree that it has come a long way.[43] In 1997, the last year for which figures are available, nine western metropolitan areas—Albuquerque, Austin–San Marcos, Denver, Las Vegas, Oakland, Omaha, Portland-Vancouver, Tacoma, and San Francisco—had no days at all over the PSI 100 standard. Smog may be a problem in the West, but if it is more so than in the East, it is just barely.

Transportation provides another measure of the "livability" of western cities. Traffic is perhaps the most remarked-upon aspect of western urban life and the one most associated with the supposedly "sprawling" City of the Angels. However, comparing angels and apples does not bear out the pessimistic picture of western urban life. A comparison of Los Angeles, the putative epitome of "sprawl," with New York, the supposed paradigm of urban density, fails to demonstrate an advantage for dense cities. Of the seventy-four most populous American cities, excluding those of the historic South because of their own low densities, New York City comes out worst by a considerable margin. New York has the longest commute time of any of the major American cities, at 36.5 minutes per trip. That is a full ten minutes more than Los Angeles, at 26.5 minutes. Despite all of the LA bashing, freeway badgering, and California baiting by the modern critics, people get to work more quickly in auto-dependent Los Angeles than they do in New York, with its low availability of automobiles and highly elaborate system of mass transit. They arrive in 28.4 percent less time. Los Angeles commuters do not even have the longest metropolitan commute in the West, much less the country. Fremont, California, in the Bay Area, does. Even San Francisco workers commute slightly longer times than workers in Los Angeles.

If this were a mere aberration, one could not crow as loudly for the West, but it is not. In the seventy-four western cities, the western commuter averages 21.6 minutes a trip to work, whereas his eastern counterpart averages 22.2 minutes a trip. This difference is not very great, but it is fully enough to redeem the reputation of the section for unique commuting problems. In four eastern cities—Chicago, Boston, Yonkers, and New York City—commuters spend more time en route than do the slowest western urban riders. Looking at individual western cities is equally revealing. Houston, often pictured as a sprawling, automobile hell, lacking in grace or even (until recently) zoning laws, outperforms New York by an even wider margin of almost twelve minutes. San Jose, ridiculed as the "Los Angeles of the North," has commuting times 20 percent less than Chicago and Boston, two of the most famous cities of the other North. Denver, condemned for its noxious air generated by autos, nonetheless drives them fewer minutes than most of the leading Rust Belt cities. Phoenix, currently fretting lest it become "another LA," delivers its commuters to work in twenty-three minutes, less than the slowest ten Rust Belt cities, thirteen minutes quicker than New York City, and so forth.

Carl Abbott has pointed out that unheralded places like Lubbock, Texas, have something to teach us.[44] That principle might well apply to transportation. At 15.8 minutes, the Texas High Plains city has the second-lowest commuting time of the seventy-four largest cities (behind Lincoln at 15.6), yet it is not engorged with freeways like Los Angeles nor highly transit-dependent like New York. Less than 1 percent of the Lubbockers (Lubbockniks?) commute by transit.[45] In million-person San Antonio, 96.5 percent of commuters ride tires rather than rails, and they get there a full fifteen minutes quicker than do those in New York, where 53 percent of the commuters travel by transit.[46] This argument is not intended to settle the perennial controversy between auto and transit proponents, but it at least indicates that the western auto-dependent cities are not the least-efficient ones in which to commute. And although the West has often been caricatured as the capital of the traffic jam, if commuters are getting to work faster there than in the East, we might well reassess that assumption, too.

Although ethnicity is not basically connected to "sprawl," the kinds of communities usually considered congenial to immigrants are the kinds found in the Rust Belt. They are (or were) large and dense and church, tavern, and neighborhood focused. One wonders if modern ethnics have preferred these communities to the kind one finds out West, large, horizontal, open, and shopping center oriented. If horizontal cities are not congenial to immigrants, then that lessens their ability to attract a labor force and would undermine their reputations for prosperity and tolerance. Moreover, big cities have always had a social-justice dimension to them. It has usually been assumed by urban historians that although big cities have had pathologies, they have also provided an economic launching pad for ethnics. So it is important to ask whether horizontal western cities have been as attractive to immigrants and their descendents as eastern cities, long known for their cultural pluralism. Like commuting time, ethnicity is also a test of the "livability" of horizontal cities.

Both the census categories of foreign born and foreign language speaking indicate ethnocultural lineage, but foreign language speaking would seem to be a better measure of it. The percentage of the population speaking a language other than English in the home is indisputably a mark of attachment to an ethnic culture since language is the most important indicator of culture. In addition, since it is consistently greater in the census than the category of foreign born, language seems an indicator less likely to underestimate the presence of culture. By that measure, of the seventy-four largest cities in the United States, excluding those of the South, those in the West show considerably greater use of a non-English language. Western cities are nearly twice as foreign speaking as eastern ones, 24.7 to 12.9 percent. Moreover, New York City is no longer the great entrepôt of pluralism it once was. Los Angeles is more diverse, whether measured by the benchmark of foreign born or language spoken in the home. The latter favors Los Angeles city over New York City by 49.9 to 41.0.

And Los Angeles is not even the most foreign-language-speaking western urban place. One of its suburbs, Santa Ana, is. At 69.2, Santa Ana is 28 percent more foreign language speaking than New York City. In fact, residents in seven western cities are more foreign language prone than New York City: Corpus Christi, San Antonio, San Francisco, Los Angeles, Glendale, El Paso, and Santa Ana, in ascending percentage order. Several eastern cities retain some of the ethnicity that used to be associated with cities of that region. Boston, Chicago, Yonkers, Newark, New York City, and Jersey City are all more than 20 percent, with Jersey City leading at 41.3 percent. However, there are many more western places with greater than 20 percent foreign language speakers, twenty-three cities against six for the East. And western cities overall lead eastern ones, not just those close to the porous Mexican border. For example, Wichita, a city literally buried in the geographic middle of the country, has more ethnic speakers than formerly heavily immigrant cities like Baltimore, St. Louis, Cincinnati, Kansas City, and Louisville. Bakersfield is twice as immigrant derived as formerly polyglot Pittsburgh. Denver is more so than Detroit, Huntington Beach is more ethnic derived than Cleveland and Philadelphia, and the Bay Area suburb of Fremont is more ethnic derived than Boston.

Nor is it just large western cities that are more ethnic than the eastern ones. Relatively modest and relatively elegant western suburbs contain higher proportions of ethnicity than many of the formerly immigrant metropolises. For example, Rancho Palos Verdes, one of the most famous and upscale suburbs in the United States and the California suburb with one of the highest per capita incomes, is almost as ethnocultural as Chicago, at 27.9 percent to Chicago's 29.1 percent.[47] Again, this is not just the Mexican border phenomenon. Hardly any (3.6 percent) of the foreign language speakers of Rancho Palos Verdes converse in Spanish. In Saratoga, California, which has the highest median income and percentage of those earning over $75,000, 18.9 percent of the population speaks a foreign language in the home, hardly any of it Spanish. This is a higher percentage than all but the top six of the eastern cities. And there are many more opulent examples. Menlo Park (16.8), Manhattan Beach (9.3), Newport Beach (10.6), Mission Viejo (14.6), Foster City (25.4), San Ramon (12.1), Walnut City (not to be confused with Walnut Creek) (48.2), Yorba Linda (15.8), Beverly Hills (35.7), and San Marino (33.4) are some of the more outstanding examples of places both wealthy and having a significant immigrant culture. Moreover, in most of these places Spanish is not the principal foreign language spoken. Asian speakers sometimes dominate these foreign-speaking categories, but often do not. Western cities and suburbs are just diverse.[48]

So it would seem that these new western cities are not uncongenial to immigrants. American immigrants historically have made rather shrewd judgments about whether they wanted to migrate to America, whether they wanted to stay in the United States, and whether they wanted to move around within this country.[49] The appeal of western cities to current rich and poor immigrants indicates that these urban entities have passed these tests. Carl Abbott's assertion that "western cities have most often expressed the American democratic tradition of open communities designed to accommodate new immigrants" is well documented.[50]

And the generally optimistic view of western cities that Abbott, Greg Hise, Gerald Nash, and others have posited also seems to be true, at least for the "livability" measures employed in this study.[51] Western cities are not the most extended, or supposedly "sprawling," in the United States, and the consequences of their horizontal character are often either positive or not as bad as those of less horizontal places. This discussion does not assert that western cities have no problems, and smog may be one of the worst of them. Americans have a long tradition of looking only on the negative side of their urban history or their urban present, but there is another side that should be considered too. Gerald Nash first put the idea of the positive western city on the map of twentieth-century western historians.[52] A close reading of the evidence in the areas considered above validates his point. Western cities are as "livable" as any others in the United States.

Notes

1. The reference is obviously to the New York nickname and to the City of the Angels.
2. Carl Abbott, *The Metropolitan Frontier: Cities in the Modern American West* (Tucson: University of Arizona Press, 1993), xi–xxiii.
3. Robert Fogelson, *The Fragmented Metropolis: Los Angeles, 1850–1930* (Cambridge, Mass.: Harvard University Press, 1967), 142–43, 146–47.
4. U.S. Bureau of the Census, *County and City Data Book: 1994* (Washington, D.C.: GPO, 1994), 674, 710. Since the *County and City Data Book* is a compilation of all of the U.S. Census figures for cities, I have relied heavily on it instead of wasting time searching the entire census for the relevant urban materials. I have not used the commercially published *County and City Data Book: 1999* because it is less reliable than the federal census and because it computes population per square mile by kilometers rather than miles. Since earlier census reports computed population by square mile instead of kilometers, that measure is more convenient to use. (Hereafter referred to as *CCDB*.)

5. *CCDB: 1994*, 746.
6. *CCDB: 1994*, xxvii. Some LA suburbs are denser than those of San Francisco. The word *density* is used here as the opposite of "sprawl."
7. These comments are based on tables of density made up from the *CCDB: 1994*, 650–853, and do not include suburbs, some of which are denser than 10,000 per square mile. See below.
8. Oklahoma data, ibid., 806–17.
9. Utah data, ibid., 830–41.
10. *CCDB: 1994*, 686.
11. Texas city data, ibid., 18–41.
12. Colorado data, ibid., 686–709.
13. Arizona data, ibid., 650.
14. Nevada data, ibid., 770–81.
15. New Mexico data, ibid., 782–93.
16. California city data, ibid., 1994, 650–97.
17. Oregon data, ibid., 806–17.
18. Washington data, ibid., 842–53.
19. To somewhat offset that fact, it should be noted that college towns are usually denser than those in the "other America." See any college cities in the *CCDB*.
20. *CCDB: 1994*, 32, 60, 74, 354, 368, 452, 536.
21. Fogelson, *The Fragmented Metropolis*, 92; David Brodsly, *L.A. Freeway: An Appreciative Essay* (Berkeley and Los Angeles: University of California Press, 1983), 82.
22. Author's tables, drawn from *CCDB: 1994*, 650–853.
23. *CCDB: 1994*, 2.
24. The phrase is Carl Abbott's, *Metropolitan Frontier*, 143.
25. *CCDB: 1994*, 698.
26. Ibid., 734.
27. Ibid., 770.
28. Ibid., 746.
29. Ibid.
30. Ibid., 686.
31. Ibid., 782.
32. Ibid., 722, 806.
33. Ibid., 686.
34. Fogelson, *Fragmented Metropolis*.
35. U.S. Bureau of the Census, *Census of Population, 1950*, vol. 1, 1-26 to 1-29.
36. *CCBD: 1994*, 680; *CCDB: 1952*, 445.
37. Southern cities were excluded from this comparison because they, too, have very low densities. Using higher-density places gives a better comparison of the impact of low densities on home ownership.
38. *CCDB: 1994*, 697–709, 781, 661, 793.
39. Lloyd Billingsly, "Facts versus Fantasy on Urban Sprawl," *Action Alert* 17 (29 March 1999): 1–3.
40. Christopher Elvidge, William T. Lawrence, Marc L. Imhoff, and David Stutzer, *Land Use History of North America* (n.p.: A LUHNA Book, 1998), 1, 11. This is a very generous estimate because the definition of *urban* under this survey is only 1,033 persons per square kilometer.
41. The PSI indicates the number of days per year that metropolitan areas exceeded values greater than 100. The PSI measures five sources of pollution and calculates a score based on that. U.S. Environmental Protection Agency, Office of Air Quality Planning and Standards, "National Air Quality and Emissions Trends Report on Air Pollution Trends in Metropolitan Areas," http//www.bts.gov/ntda/nts99/data/Chapter4/4–45.html.
42. Gary Polakovic, "Southland on Course to Reclaim U.S. Smog Title," *Los Angeles Times*, 26 September 2001, pt. 2, p. 3.
43. Marla Cone, "Southland Smog Drops to Lowest Level in Decades," *Los Angeles Times*, 30 October 1996, A1; Robert Franciosi, "A Tale of Two Cities: Phoenix, Portland, Growth and Growth Control," *Arizona Issue Analysis* 152 (October 1998): 1–10, on-line; Timothy Egan, "Urban Sprawl Strains Western States," *New York Times*, 29 December 1996, 1:1.

44. Carl Abbott, *The Metropolitan Frontier: Cities in the Modern American West,* 128.

45. *CCDB: 1994,* 837.

46. Ibid., 789.

47. Ibid., 675.

48. *1990 Census of Population: Social and Economic Characteristics: California,* pt. 6, sec. 1, 841, 849, 856, 857, 858–59, 868–69, 874, 876.

49. John E. Bodnar, *The Transplanted: A History of Immigrants in Urban America* (Bloomington: Indiana University Press, 1985), 1–84; Dino Cinel, *From Italy to San Francisco: The Immigrant Experience* (Stanford, Calif.: Stanford University Press, 1982), 15–70; Ricardo Romo, *East Los Angeles: History of a Barrio* (Austin: University of Texas Press, 1983), 3–60.

50. Abbott, *Metropolitan Frontier,* xxiii.

51. Greg Hise, *Magnetic Los Angeles: Planning the Twentieth-Century Metropolis* (Baltimore, Md.: Johns Hopkins University Press, 1997), 1–13.

52. Gerald D. Nash, *The American West in the Twentieth Century: A Short History of an Urban Oasis* (Albuquerque: University of New Mexico Press, 1977), ix–x.

The American West, the World,
and the Twenty-First Century

Gene M. Gressley

In 1972, the ever-gracious, urbane Howard Lamar, Yale historian and then-incoming president of the Western History Association, sat at breakfast in the huge coffee shop of the Shoreham Hotel in Washington, D.C., where the Organization of American Historians was convening, discussing with his program chair the program for the upcoming WHA conference that autumn at New Haven. With a jolly laugh, Lamar commented, "Run that by me again—you propose a session on the West in the twenty-first century?" Assured that this was indeed the topic, Lamar's smile broadened as he asked the obvious question: "Do you think anyone will come?" His breakfast companion conceded that the answer was speculative. "Admittedly," the program chair confessed, "few of our colleagues are intrigued by even the twentieth-century West." Lamar, with his typical courtesy, said, "All right: go ahead."

The following autumn some 500 eager, scurrying western historians converged on the Yale campus for the thirteenth annual conference of the WHA. On Friday afternoon, October 13, the session "The West in the Twenty-First Century" convened. Earl Cook, a distinguished geophysicist at Texas A&M University, and eminent western historian Robert V. Hine of the University of California, Riverside, presented erudite and provocative papers to the audience—a select eight souls. President Lamar may not have been a futurist, but his judgment was absolutely on target: the WHA was not ready for theorization about the West's next century.

Nor are they, we venture, ready for such musings three decades later. However, thanks to the hormonal vibrancy of the New West adherents, our ears have received a dinning about the sins of the nineteenth- and twentieth-century Wests. At century's end, everyone seems eager to board the "Twentieth-Century Limited" to characterize the twentieth century.

In a magnificent tour de force on the twentieth-century West, Walter Nugent reminds us that historians are not futurists. Nugent writes, "Projections into such a distance [500 years] would be absurd, but some speculations might at least be entertaining."[1] Nugent, of course, is absolutely accurate. The terrain of historians is the past, not the sandbox of the future. That playground should be left to politicians and philosophers—both of whom frequently forecast coming events with cinematic ease devoid of knowledge.

Although one doubts that the august, white-starched American Academy of Arts and Science had an audience of mimes in mind when they created in 1969 the "Commission of the Year 2000," the resulting product, *The Year 2000,* by Herman Kahn and Anthony J. Weiner, with the hindsight of thirty years, provides much mirth.

A reader will trawl those pages with diligence to discover an accurate prognostication—biblical or not! Yet Kahn and Weiner had constructed their structure on a long heritage of avoiding the futuristic saints. Nostradamus usually initiates the secular (everyone yields to the Book of Revelation) futuristic lineage. Machiavelli, credited and blamed for so much that never entered his mind, contended that mankind's actions were an equal division of chance and self-government. Jumping past the utopian Edward Bellamy and Henry George into the twentieth century, we find futurists creating havoc everywhere. H. G. Wells led off the century with an obsession—on the revolution of technology and transportation to the futurism of totalitarian fright, which gathered an enormous readership for Aldous Huxley's *Brave New World* and George Orwell's *1984* (a year that came and passed sans a shudder).

After and between Wells and Orwell came a veritable host, some heavenly, some not, of cloudy dreamers such as Arnold Toynbee, more theologian than historian, sociologist Pitrim Sorokin, and the dour Oswald Spengler. Then in this dash, we conclude with the contemporary and the elusive Club of Rome, terrified by the absence of third world contraception, and the all-inclusive "Futuribles" projects of Bertrand de Jouvenel. Most of Jouvenel's more recent studies focused on dire warnings of social change, economic development, and even human nature. Futurists have served society usefully by reminding the locusts of humanity that nothing in the future is inevitable, perhaps even likely, and further that a new "supercivilization" of technology, which may soon arrive with turbo speed, breaking the stockade of war and poverty, may be more ethereal than real.

The question arises: Where does America, the West specifically, fit in this equation of futuristic tradition? One school of policy makers holds, along with Herman Kahn and the Gaullists, conveniently ignoring two-thirds of the world, that it is time for the United States to reverse the flow of influence between the United States and Europe; a veritable "re-Europanisation" is their chant. Another cult maintains that all dissent in twentieth-century America will be aimed at fleeing "technological domination and corporate gigantism"—what, in effect, they would label as "depersonalization." Francis Fukuyama, whose Hegelian *The End of History* created such an abnormal fever a few years ago, foresaw America's presentism as driven by technological (shades of H. G. Wells) and economic issues, specifically pointing a bony finger at the "baby boomer" generation, with its hallmarks of the pill, a female labor force, mobility of labor—all pushing enthusiastically into a postindustrial society.[2] One could with more ease than conviction enumerate dozens more generalizations from American soothsayers—whatever the discipline. Then one can conclude with the buoyant George Gilder, whose optimism is a rarity among futurists, that the world can only get better through technology, sending tremors through many an environmentalist.

A theme persistently debated is "American Exceptionalism." Journalists and the Eurocentric populace flag the nineteenth century as "the British Century." The founding father of publishing behemoth Time, Inc., modest Henry Luce, wrote a highly popular editorial in *Life* in February 1941 that labeled the twentieth century as the "American Century." Luce, carrying the banner of manifest destiny that infected nineteenth-century America, looked over his reading glasses with the admonition that it was nothing less than America's "duty" to lead the world. In essence, Luce perceived Lady Columbia, standing astride the office building of Time, Inc., guiding the world.

Luce's jingoism, totally or in part, dominated American policy until the 1960s, when student leftist agitation, propelled by Watergate and Vietnam, threw cold water on the hot radiator of American exceptionalism. How could a nation disgraced by the killing fields (and presumed morally corrupt) lead the world? Mulling such thoughts in the mid-1970s proved humiliating. The exceptionalist debate rages on in the teacup of the academic cosmos. Some historians see the entire idea of exceptionalism as an illusionary figment of the left, or perhaps Michael Kammen speaks for the mainstream when he answers the question, "How exceptional was America?" with, "Very."[3]

Wherever one stands in the philosophical spectrum of exceptionalism, America persists in exporting its presumed superior economic and political systems to the third world. Now, this is manifest destiny in its finest formal penguin attire—especially since exporters-importers have conflicting fashions.

One can dispute the moral philosophy of exceptionalism. Less contestable is the fact that the United States enters the twenty-first century unrivaled in its power and dominance. David Landes has recently contended that, the swagger of America aside, the nation's spirit remains embedded in its global policy. Henry Kissinger, taking the *longue durée* view of Talleyrand (and the more recent Annalists), insists on a Nixonian balance of power—or at the very least a "compatibility" of political and economic accommodation between nations. So where do we stand in this Ringstrasse? As the American economic/political juggernaut rolls into the twenty-first century, few are the nations that can offer competition. By 2150, perhaps China and India might transform American confidence into humility, but only a handful of prophets would argue from that premise today. The query persists: Where does the American West fit into the economic jigsaw puzzle? One picks his/her seat at the economists' faro table and places bets on "rational choice," with the expectation that the next roll of the dice will position our player to react to the markets—be they stock or stacked. The comforting notion of our gambler is that by selecting "rational choice," he/she will escape the dictation of Keynesian philosophy manipulating economic policy. Or our raffler may select the table of century-old individualistic neoclassicism. Or our plunger, if a devotee of the New Economy, might place his wager on the New Growth Theory of brilliant young Stanford economist Paul Romer. Romer makes a lot of sense to contemporary economic commentators with his laconic statement that the current economic milieu is the result of "a long string of chance outcomes." Then another high chair participant might place his chips on Darwinian natural selection. After all, if you are a farmer standing in the middle of your wheat field in North Dakota experiencing a 50 percent decline in the price of wheat, survival of the fittest may seem as realistic as a Lutheran sermon was on Sunday morning.

Mergers typified first by the $79.5 billion takeover of Mobil by Exxon and BP Amoco's $28.5 billion purchase of Atlantic Richfield lay even beyond the Progressive nightmares of Theodore Roosevelt. Darwinism strides down Wall Street again. For although the Street no longer hungers for oil reserves, the market continues to covet profits. As Daniel Yergin notes, big oil's competitive atmosphere is increasing exponentially month by month.

The recent rush to judgment and to merger was not restricted to petroleum companies. The AOL–Time Warner combination stunned the media world, even more than the previous WorldCom–MCI marriage. Indeed, the world of dot.com produces virtually a merger per day.

Merger mania flourishes according to these entrepreneurial behemoths because of the efficiencies necessitated by competing in a global economy. Few can argue the impact of globalization on the world, though paradoxically the preachments of politicians, corporate chieftains, and labor leaders result in long pauses at any attempt at reasoned argument. Merely leaf through the pages of the congressional debate on our China trade policy to reassure yourselves of the inanity of ignorance.

The consequences, whether positive or negative, of globalization abound. Dissenters are few when it comes to the presumption, not of innocence, but of the opportunities presented for economic betterment. Nor can nationalists reasonably dissent with the proposition that globalization has undermined the capacity of individual nations to manage their economies. Although the Milosevics of the world try, societies are no longer in isolation. Economic growth induced by globalization remains the only perceived way to reduce the poverty of the third world. In a global economy, firms select their options from a region, and industries in turn base their attractiveness on the health of the urban sector. The teller-like technology of globalization has already begun to integrate financial institutions and dismantle territorial frontiers. The information age craze of the twentieth-first century, symbolized by the miracle of the Internet, erases the memory of the nineteenth-century global syndrome, an era when information flowed easily between nations in capital and financial markets with minimal impediments. Amazingly enough, only two countries (Turkey and Russia) in the age of Napoleon III demanded passports.[4]

Globalization has attracted a "crazy rhythm" of opponents playing discordant tunes. One of the most vociferous and self-contradictory has been that of American labor. Between 1947 and 1957, 337 major strikes occurred annually, but the number declined to thirty-four strikes in 1998. What happened? Workers realized that they had a Nike-like interlaced future with their companies. Furthermore, although Mercedes, Toyota, and Honda might dot the American landscape with their plants, their workers were commonly nonunion. Dramatically, the new slogan of the twentieth century became Capitalists and Workers of the World, unite. Democrats and Republicans alike have uncovered an electorate that increasingly finds common cause—economically speaking.

Instead of ostensibly being anxious about their Friday night paychecks, American labor has taken up the war cry of global labor exploitation. Although the sincerity of labor leaders' commiseration (versus competition) might be questioned, few would doubt the intensity of their anger as evidenced against the World Trade Organization's (WTO's) most recent round of talks in Seattle, where protestors hammered the International Monetary Fund (IMF) and World Bank for their programs of economic shock therapy of devaluating currencies, raising interest rates, and elimination of subsidies. The IMF and the World Bank insist that their policies, in the long term, will raise the standard of living in the third world.

As remarkable as the diversity of their agenda, the WTO attracted an eclectic mixture of 25,000 agitators united only by their opposition to economic globalism. The protestors included socialists, union members, a scattering of intellectuals, human rights activists, Luddites, eco-warriors, farmers, and above all, a frenetic contingent of anarchists from Eugene, Oregon, who seemed remarkably potent in deed and impotent in ideology. The Seattle scene was reminiscent of a Mabel Dodge salon, perhaps not as vociferous but every bit as chaotic, on lower Fifth Avenue a century earlier. One would be silly to suggest that globalization presents no vexations for American workers. "Barfshevism" was the epithet most flung about by the Seattle dissenters. Someday in the twenty-first century when Congress is legislating, not investigating (grandstanding is so much more fun), it will have to confront the working-class issues of portable health policies, wage insurance for those laid off, job retraining (including adult education), as the Claremont clarion, Peter Drucker, has so recently discovered, and an expansion of the earned income tax credit. In brief, the argument in Seattle focused on the economists' contention that the liberalization of trade permits a "win-win" scenario for the global economy. Environmentalists vociferously said *au contraire:* free trade would result in lower prices, stimulate economic demand, and induce disaster for the ecosystem. In spite of all the raucous behavior and oratory, the question left unaddressed, let alone answered, was, How can trade policy be used to improve the lives of labor in poor countries?

Lost in the stars of Seattle was the fact that the environmental movement, as inflexible as some segments often are, has been an enormously effective force in realizing their agenda, especially in the last half of the twentieth century.[5] The environmental surge comes in all shades and hues. Some are devoted latter-day Henry George espousers, biodiversity advocates, and feel that land policy is the central question, whether in the American West, or around the planet, particularly the preservation of endangered fauna and flora. Some daydream of "Olmstedian" parks to provide social space so that the citizenry can dance with a sense of freedom. The livestock community frets about loss of grazing to a public commons. The "tree huggers" or "tree sitters" splinter with industry over clear-cutting of American forests. Atomspheric purifiers, especially agriculturists, perceive the exhaustion and misuse of water. Then the Club of Rome leftovers exclaim about the horrors of the population bomb—the list of individualistic babbling is endless. All humanity is at risk.

In common with many societal institutions, contemporary environmental philosophy is ever evolving from the days of John Muir, whose Sierra Club desired nothing less (or more) than the wilderness all around us. The late David Brower, longtime (1952–69) voice of the Sierra Club, once blurted out at a factious gathering of conservationists, "We should stand for something we believe in and hang with it," a laudable if somewhat humorous edict, if we can be forgiven our iconoclasm. In the 1970s, Herbert Marcuse, Michel Foucault, and Martin Heidegger, whether as permanent or temporary European expatriates, injected a strong element of "cultural pessimism" into global environmentalism—strains of which play out today in the American West's environmental crusades. A split in the environmental ideological tournament is symbolized by the clash of "hard greens versus "soft greens." Basically the Peter Huber "conservative manifesto" for the hard greens reduces to the naked (an arresting metaphor) Teddy Roosevelt premise: We stand in awe of our scenic western grandeur and let the marketplace rationalize all other problems. In essence, the soft greens ferret out a spiritual kinship with all of "God's creatures"—the snail darter, the spotted owl, and the Wyoming toad. Hating growth and having more than a small dash of sentimentality, they in essence worship at nature's altar. The hard green/soft green dichotomy undermines much of the West's environmentalism. Richard White, with his usual perception, united both hard and soft greens in the same sanctuary. White suggests that contemporary environmentalists have failed to appreciate "that human beings have historically known nature through work."[6] The founding father of the history of environmentalism, Sam Hays, has devoted a lifetime to the proposition that Americans value nature not as a commodity but as an amenity.

Whether you worship with White or Hays, the hard and soft greens frequently sing from the same hymnal. For instance, they united (though their victory was a Pyrrhic one) behind the Interior Department's fight with Charles Hurwitz over California's Headwaters Forest of redwoods. One of the major premises for the Interior Department's surrender to Hurwitz was his chilling intimation of filing a legal challenge in the courts, a threat that could take years to resolve. The intensity of the antagonism between environmentalists and their opponents shows little sign of abatement. Eco-terrorists spotlight Edward Abbey's "monkey wrench" strategy by simply blowing up what offends. As a result, in the last five years thirty-three explosive events have sent tremors through westerners, causing private and government damages of $28.8 million. Two incidents alone amounted to more than $20 million—the $12 million fire at the Vail, Colorado, ski resort and the $9 million fire at the nearby forest district ranger headquarters. Abbey disciples are unlikely to win many converts to their cause with such destructive capers.

Two ecological issues, water and population, dramatize the West's present predicament and cloud the West's future well into the twenty-first century. Three decades ago, Paul Ehrlich published *The Population Bomb* (1968), predicting mass starvation by 1975 unless a magic potion slowed the growth of the world's population. That sleight of hand came from an Iowa agricultural geneticist, Norman Borlaug, whose "green revolution" enabled third world countries to break the chain of starving multitudes.

The buzz phrase "sustainable agriculture" encompasses an elemental concept (seldom defined with any precision) that humanity could balance resource utilization with consumption—so as to not exhaust the American West (or the world's) resource base. Immediately sustainability became the popularization of politicians; here was a Rooseveltian "freedom from want." Western politicians merged sustainability with the looming threat of overpopulation, exhaustion of their state's tax base, and in general turning the environment into a junkyard. In 1971, Governor Tom McCall of Oregon (whose grandfather had been one of Wall Street's less successful buccaneers) was one of the first to capture the West's (and the nation's) imagination. McCall showed little hesitancy in driving Oregon real estate developers to the suicidal brink with his histrionic slogan, "Come visit us again and again, but for God's sake don't stay." Twenty-eight years later, as Californians continued to invade the Northwest, an Oregon state senator, John Lim (ironically, a Korean immigrant), introduced a bill to erect signs at the Oregon State border: "You are welcome to visit Oregon, but please don't stay." As Oregonians enter the twenty-first century, it is doubtful that the Lims of 1997 will be any more successful than the McCalls of 1971 in damming the population deluge currently flooding the Oregon border.

The American West is among the most rapidly growing regions of the world. Some western cities have boomed by twentyfold in the last three decades—Boulder, Colorado, Santa Fe, New Mexico, and Las Vegas, Nevada, are among the most chanted examples. Portland, Oregon, Seattle, Washington, and Salt Lake City, Utah, trail not far behind.

The relationship between urban sprawl and water is self-evident, as it is crucial to the survival of the West of the twenty-first century. Donald Pisani in his ongoing, monumental analysis of western water policy and federalism observes, "At the state level diversity of western water laws was potent evidence of the power of federalism." Further, Pisani notes that aridity defined the West as much as any other one dimension.[7] Neighbors contested with neighbors to grasp a resource that their grandsons, with rampant greed, would treasure far more than the gold their grandfathers so rapaciously extracted from the hills of folklore.

Western water policy, often a bureaucratic circus, has the capacity to induce monomania in western states. Case history after case history, dam after dam illustrates the absence of political direction or simply abdication by western leaders.

The Oahe Dam in South Dakota is but one dramatic example. The United Family Farmers violently objected to the bureaucratic bullying of the Army Corps of Engineers and the Bureau of Reclamation. Nothing less than their environment and economy was at risk, so claimed the bib-overall agrarians. Amazingly enough, Nixon's Environmental Policy Act of 1970 presented the farmers with the legal discovery weapon that enabled them to carry on their fight. Then Jimmy Carter weighed in by putting Oahe on his infamous dam "hit list," thereby doing what everyone thought was politically impossible—deconstruct a legislative project already blessed by Congress. Ronald Reagan, playing the "Gipper," insisted that the urban sector bear some of the cost of replacing Oahe. To the rescue rode George McGovern, hero of liberals, Vietnam antagonist, and friend of the South Dakota construction industry and chambers of commerce, to frustrate via legislation the coalition of environmentalists and small farmers. The Oahe project survived, with McGovern serving as its Lone Ranger.[8]

Sixteen hundred miles south of Oahe, Tucson, Arizona, presents yet another drama in western water policy. Arizona's political godfathers, from Carl Hayden to Barry Goldwater, trumpeted the merits of the $4.7 billon, 330-mile-long Central Arizona Project—designed presumably to cure Arizona's liquid addiction to groundwater exploitation. After a year and a half of receiving polluted Colorado river water from the Central Arizona Project, Tucsonites, discovering their water heaters destroyed and thousands of water pipes corroded, sent up howls heard not around the world, but all the way to city hall. The city fathers threw down their water pistols and reverted to exhausting the groundwater table. Yet citizens were warned by developers—no more CAP water, no more growth. Few Tucsonites beseeched the gods on that urban prayer.

Whether the West's concept of space will be defined by water, as Walter Prescott Webb claimed a half century ago, is debatable. But the West of the twenty-first century will certainly be circumscribed by a ring of water and by the contest between the urban and rural West—well into the twenty-first century. Twentieth-century irrigation has consumed 80 percent of western water resources. That ratio, legally frozen for so long, is about to be altered as the judicial system increasingly sides with urban development. Further, agrarians shifting from micro- to macroeconomic agriculture have discovered that water rights are their most valuable asset.

Meanwhile, change in the rural West is moving more rapidly than *The Last Picture Show.* Initially, holistic resource management, advocated by wildlife biologists in Zimbabwe three decades ago and by Aldo Leopold in his classic *Sand County Almanac,* mesmerized the conservation community, though their fixation has attracted more missionaries than disciples. Now less than 3 percent of America's population is left tilling the soil. Donald Pisani, Gilbert Fite, and others have quantified the agricultural calculus: "Should America have more farmers in poverty or fewer farmers in prosperity?"

In the year 2000, American agriculture flirts with the halfway house of economic measures: one, a revisitation of the populistic rhetoric of the late nineteenth and twentieth centuries (which never attracted a long-term survival mode), and two, globalism. A worldwide wheat glut has depressed, for the third year, wheat prices in the American Northwest. In 1996, farmers trucking to their grain elevators received $5.63 per bushel of wheat. In 1999, a bushel of wheat fetched only $2.89. The commodity press page recorded a similar decline for other products—soybeans and cotton futures plummeted to their lowest record in twenty-five years. Domestically, farmers basically lacked economic clout.

The fundamental threat facing western (and eastern, for that matter) farmers was weak export demand. Globalization represents both the challenge and the solution. In the nineteenth century, farm communities survived to the extent that they were "railroaded." In the twentieth century, interstates might bypass towns, but as long as their produce found a world market, deliverance was at hand. In the twenty-first century oceanic shipping represents the highway of agrarian redemption. Not that the global deity's prayer book is any more omnipotent than the German Lutheran's liturgy in Minnesota. A U.S. trade representative succinctly summed up the conundrum, "You have to consider that agriculture has never been integrated into the global system." If the French and German farmers, who have enormously powerful lobbies (and of course numbers), have their say, several generations will fade into the sunset before Colorado wheat reaches German tables. Other global provocations confront western agriculture. The North American Free Trade Agreement promised far more than it delivered.[9] A strong dollar has undermined agricultural exports. Back among the Nebraska fencerows, farmers are increasingly hard-pressed to amortize their capital-intensive operations. Book after book and funeral-like documentaries ("The Farmer's Wife") on PBS record the dirgelike atmosphere of rural life. Even twenty-first-century science and technology seem impotent. Biotechnology, reputedly the next green revolution, has faltered as global competitors and consumers raise "cane" over the health hazards of biotechnology. Doomsayers chant the unthinkable: that a starving world may force a revolutionary wave of mass migration, carrying with it disease and environmental degradation that heretofore has only appeared in science fiction.

Nationally, the "days may be dark and dreary," but a political sunshine, temporarily at least, shines down on the farm. After renouncing the enslavement of farm subsidies "to balance" the budget, Congress passed and President Clinton reluctantly (so he said) signed a "safety net" to undergird agricultural prices. But back among the red barns, a long-term twenty-first-century harvest will arrive for American agriculture only when the Germans, French, and Chinese start swallowing American wheat.

If William Inge's *Picnic* portrays rural America at midcentury, then Leonard Bernstein's *West Side Story,* with its urban tensions, Jets versus Sharks, and asphalt jungles graphically depicts inner-city America. In 1938, Lewis Mumford thundered urban despondency in his now canonical *The Culture of the Cities.* In Mumford's eye, cities, west or east, would not last much longer. A couple of decades later, Jane Jacobs in her *Cities and Wealth of Nations* found *Candide* more to her liking. Jacobs discerned a feudalistic future between cities and their hinterlands as metropolitan centers reached the twenty-first century. By 1999, the eighty-four-year-old Jacobs had not substantially altered her beliefs. In her *The Nature of Economics*, Jacobs insisted that cities are natural phenomena and should be left to grow "naturally." English urbanist Peter Hall, while more repressed than the spontaneous Jacobs, maintains that the city will be the engine of civilization. Simultaneously with Hall's pronouncements came yet another installment, in a long gray line of bureaucratic reports from the Department of Housing and Urban Development (HUD). In contrast to Jacobs and Hall, HUD found the images of metropolitanism in the West "mixed." Indeed, the twenty-first century held optimism, with a flourishing economy, joblessness, and a population decline, although many cities of the West also faced a loss of the middle class, poverty, and income inequality. Even older suburbs in Los Angeles, Phoenix, and Kansas City, for example, suffered from the blight that Bernstein focused klieg lights on in the mid–twentieth century.

No issue in the contemporary urban scene, and for the foreseeable future, causes more anguish on the part of urbanites than "urban sprawl." On this subject, HUD repeats the same refrain that it has for the last quarter of a century, pleading with urban planners to come up with strategies to solve the structural decline of cities and older suburbs. Almost fifteen years ago, John Herbers wrote eloquently of the urban blight about the "lost chord" of the western city center[10] and of a moral decay that commentators ascribed to the Vietnam generation, "You can't trust anyone over thirty."

Brooks Brothers emotionality aside, urban leadership created show window growth in many western cities: Phoenix, Houston, Portland, and Seattle were the most notable. In the twenty-first century, urban leaders must decide how to equate economic livelihood with quality-of-life issues. Instead of restoring flagging downtowns of cities, all too frequently this generation of Quigg Newtons (referring to the mayor of Denver in the 1950s) are sinking cash into strip malls.

Are suburbs the answer to the burgeoning urbanism in the twenty-first-century West? As suburbs blossom, that elusive attraction that seduced the suburban migration appears more illusory than ever: Lexus drivers pulling away from bucolic subdivisions named "Pheasant Meadows," "Cherry Hills," and "Paradise Valley" launched themselves into a stream of traffic congestion that forced up their blood pressure and put in play their credit cards. More than one commuter lamented that he was spending more on his commute than on his son's college tuition. All this pent-up frustration, unless siphoned off by CDs and recorded books, will only increase road rage. In spite of Martha Stewart's unctuous advice on suburban living, suburb developers have clearly not solved the habit of metropolitanism.

Notwithstanding advertisements on the latest "New, New Thing," telecommunication and computer fixation, most jobs remain in the cities and adjacent industrial parks. Although constantly scorned in the politicians' world, mass transportation, as San Francisco and Washington, D.C., have proved, can be efficient and effective in moving the masses. Furthermore, politicians (bless them) need to listen to western constituents and breach the barrios of bureaucracy that impede regional cooperation. The vexations of urban sprawl endure—like Fermat's the-orem—defying answer or reason. How will westerners cope with developers' desire "to play leapfrog with a bulldozer"? As the twenty-first century dawns, sub-urban westerners are devising a myriad of answers. Many responses are designed to limit sprawl (instead of encouraging homesteaders to flee it and create more). In 1998, voters found 240 antisprawl initiatives on their ballots. Some western cities such as Boulder and Portland are simply putting in place draconian measures to limit growth. "The Great Wall of Portland" has become immensely popular with the citizenry, but newcomers' frustrations boil when they attempt to locate a rea-sonably priced home within its confines! Developers across the country, urban and suburban, offer a variety of enticements to potential residents. One suburban architect compressed his objective into a melodic sentence, "We are trying to romance the buyer." And just what does this "Stardust" melody play? Well, the first waltz consists of playgrounds, walking trails, lakes, public transportation, exercise rooms, tennis courts, clubhouses, on and on—a veritable mini-Aspen resort. If the clients' ardor is still elusive, all they have to do is express their desires (and pay for them), and their dreams are reality. Urban planners are also bent on enticing city dwellers to return, by offering riverfront parks, creative apartments in abandoned railroad yards, and artistic lofts in high-rise warehouse buildings.

Finally, environmentalists are attacking urban sprawl in their own inimitable way. Waving the Endangered Species Act (1973), environmentalists have crafted 250 habitat plans. Former Interior secretary Bruce Babbitt led the charge with the silver-toned call that cities of the West have no other option, if we are to con-serve both wildlife habitat and open space. Whatever urbanites of the twenty-first century select as their future, the West, as Gerald Nash and Earl Pomeroy wrote years ago, is increasingly becoming an "urban oasis," an urbanism tempered by accommodation with environmentalism—especially water conservation.

Historically, western cities have been the focal point for making decisions, with their colonial eastern or foreign partners, on the future of western hinterlands. Twentieth-century western economists have scorned the "objectivism" of Ayn Rand. The western economic policy has increasingly been in lockstep with the eastern economic leadership, especially the venerable economic spiritualism of one of Rand's most ardent disciples, Alan Greenspan. Whether the twentieth-century economy has smoothed the West's boom-and-bust cycles is open to a free-swinging-door debate. One thing appears certain: the wild fluctuations that so infected the nineteenth-century West are no longer guided by the laissez-faire philosophy of Adam Smith, if for no other reason than that those mineral, live-stock, and timber resources of the nineteenth- and twentieth-century Wests are either exhausted or verging on extinction.

During the last half of the twentieth century, seers worried over, commented on, and prognosticated the West's future. What is so evident about the Wagnerian crescendos of so many of these journalists and an occasional novelist thrown in—Carey McWilliams, Bernard DeVoto, Joel Garreau, Marc Reisner, Ian Frazier, John Gunther, Rick Bass, John Steinbeck, Ivan Doig, Robert Gottlieb, et al.—

is the extreme pessimism and cemetery-like gloom of both their outlook and predictions of the West's future economy and livability. In contrast, historians such as Gerald Nash, Earl Pomeroy, and Walter Nugent commonly achieve the "big picture" with wet glass plate clarity.

We have no intention, from space constraints or inclination alone, to joust with these journalistic knights at the green felt Las Vegas round tables. I do hope, though, by taking a few snapshots of some state economies in the West, to add a dash of faith to the recipes of despair. I begin with a statement of Frank Lloyd Wright (also ascribed to Aldous Huxley, both borrowing from a Hendrik Van Loon metaphor) that if United States were tipped sideways, Los Angeles would be where everything would land. In many ways California is to the West what Jackson Hole is to Wyoming—a separate nation. With its 34 million population, as former governor Gray Davis was so fond of reminding us, California has the seventh-largest economy on the planet. Indeed, California alone defines "mega" for the rest of the western economy. In California, regionalism is clung to with life preserver intensity. Southern Californians insist that the San Francisco Bay population ignores them—and vice versa. The Central Valley castigates both their houses, declaring that they are treated with contempt by northern and southern California. Urban developers continue to spread their sprawl, convinced that another California water plan will float their dreams, watery trances that evaporate with the heat of the noonday sun, just as newer malls cannibalize older malls, providing the business elite with affluent visions for the future.

Sometime in the twenty-first century, Los Angeles will become the largest city in United States. Already the City of Angels is one of the leading urban areas of the Pacific Rim, and by the end of the twenty-first century, Los Angeles will surely be christened as one of the ten megacities of the world. Credibility of these prognostications is not all that difficult when one realizes that Los Angeles already represents the largest multicultural region in the world. These utopian nightmares were not lost on Mike Davis, whose *City of Quartz* and *Ecology of Fear* updated the shattering chaos of Nathanael West's *Day of the Locusts.* Like West, Davis discovered a city of bubbling blacktop, overpopulation, rampant crime, and social disruption—a land of disaster and paranoia. Davis, presumably scared stiff by threats, fled for the relative calm and peace of the State University of New York at Stony Brook, where all that he had to plague him was academic politics as usual. Whether western cities in the twenty-first century will mirror eastern cities in the twentieth with their urban cores being transformed into entertainment centers/residential apartments, with the poverty neighborhoods getting poorer and less powerful, is debatable. The urban twenty-first-century West of the foreseeable future still represents the elite leadership of the regional West, especially in the financial institutions.

Nothing symbolizes the New Economy as much as California, home of such dot.com companies as Oracle, Hewlett-Packard, and Intel, all clustered in, or close to, Silicon Valley. Just the name Silicon Valley conjures up the "New, New Thing,"[11] which translates, for many, into the second industrial revolution/the information age. Forget for a moment the tea leaves of the future for the foretelling of the past. Freeze 1920, when Thorstein Veblen arrived at Stanford University, where Veblen was about as comfortable as "a playboy in a European monastery."[12] Veblen quickly constructed a cabin hideaway, not unlike Fernando's of the popular song, where he could meditate on the power and social structure of a technocratic future, serve tea, and seduce Stanford coeds. What would this "playboy of the western world," this explorer of conspicuous consumption, have thought of mass upon mass of glass office boxes, where secrecy is so highly valued, where the workers still stare at their monitors, hoping against hope that inspiration will strike and lead to the next IPO à la "Doonesbury"? Not that money is an end all, be all, for many. Far too much capital drifts about the valley to impress. As one venture capitalist was heard to mutter, "The hardest part of financing is agonizing about whom to let in!" (A sociologist has discovered an arresting fact: more than half of the venture companies in California are incorporated by expatriate capitalists from India.)

If money fails to have an impact on the Silicon Valley entrepreneur, what does? One word—*passion*. As many have noted, a gold rush is on, though in contrast to a century and a half ago, the unemployed of this gold rush are confident to the point of being cocky. The next business plan comes with the next click on the screen; all it takes is luck. Risk doesn't exist, or so the syllogism went until the Nasdaq uproar of 2000.

This cybercapital of the future originated in the fertile imagination of brilliant technologists such as Robert Noyce, William Shockley, David Packard, William Hewlett, and James Clark. Two men, whose names not one American in a hundred thousand could recall, T. G. Reid, who invented the integrated circuit, and British physicist Tim Berners-Lee, who took the Internet (which had been in existence for two decades) and invented a golden path by networking distant computers, were pivotal to such dot.com success. In essence, Berners-Lee beheld the World Wide Web. The stampede to the information age was on! Most interpreters of the high-tech revolution agree that investors, the general public, and technologists are blinded by the power of the Internet and that the impact on economic distribution, let alone on our culture and politics, is profound. Few concur on what the future foretells. The question is simply, What's next?[13]

While the broadband of the Internet is still shrouded in ether, another golden bounty has shone down on the California landscape for generations. As California moves into the twenty-first century, Californians reap the benefit of a $27-billion farming economy. One-third of all agricultural labor in the nation calls California home—an electrifying fact, since less than 3 percent of America's workforce is agriculturally grounded. The wrath of John Steinbeck in the thirties, plus the strikes of César Chávez in the sixties, are not forgotten. But they seem less relevant in the year 2000, not solely because of the low unemployment in the "factories in the fields," but also because of the commodity shift from wheat and cotton to the higher-value fruits and vegetables. Additional sources of income have cropped up that Steinbeck, McWilliams, and Chávez could never have envisioned. California growers learned to their amazement and that of their workers that well-treated farm laborers are more productive. So much of the righteous indignation of the past saints of the soil has been plowed under. The substandard living conditions and low wages have not all vanished, but they are no longer the norm. Low unemployment and better labor conditions, all combined with the California water project, have resulted in one of the most flourishing agricultural regions in the world.

Other than a mining heritage, the California and Montana economies have little in common. Economically, contemporary Montana represents more plight than prospect. In 1976, the average wage in Montana was $26,000. Adjusted for inflation, today it is barely $20,000. A recent analysis of Montana's economy and future borders on fatalism.[14] Montana's landscapes and communities, no matter how attractive they may be to residents of Tarrytown on the Hudson, do not hold the promise of a flourishing future. In fact, the irony is that more jobs, which ratchet up immigration, only serve to "hammer down the wages." Montana's scenery, society, and sense of place have been popularized and publicized through the immigration of a bevy of creative literary talent. Literary Montana is, or has been, their dwelling place if not their residence, as Richard Etulain noted years ago. Ivan Doig, William Bevis, Richard Hugo, Norman Maclean, Thomas McGuane, Dorothy Johnson, Wallace Stegner, Leslie Fiedler, John K. Hutchens, William Kittredge, Michael Malone, Dan Cushman, Mildred Walker, and A. B. Guthrie, Jr., are only a few of the glittering literati that any place would be proud to claim as its own. The style and the message of these writers have contributed, in no small measure, to the "epiphany" of Montana, the tourist influx, and the arrival of the residential affluent, symbolized by the trim mustachioed Ted Turner.[15] "The Last Best Place[s]," to steal William Kittredge's apt phrase, are found throughout the West. Stunning landscapes, small populations, nearby neighbors, if not neighborhoods, which lend that undefinable "sense of community," can be found around the next bend or down the straight lane of many a western state.[16]

The old economy triage of timber, mining, and livestock, in common with much of the West, is rapidly vanishing from the land of the "Big Sky." Ironically, the Old Economy is not missing out entirely on the New Economy. Montana Power, once a major voice in the fabled Montana twins, the Anaconda Copper Company and Montana Power, whose political power held captive the Montana legislature as part of their corporate fiefdom, has taken up the new economy dance. Montana Power, "the poster child when you look at utilities with hidden gems" and the onetime mouthpiece for eastern colonialism, has transformed its industrial structure, almost as swiftly as Moore's law. Currently Montana Power is auctioning off its old economy assets of oil, coal, natural gas transmission, and electricity to create a sleek new telecommunications company, "Touch America."

One state east of Montana, North Dakota flounders as it searches for its twenty-first-century future in a nineteenth- and twentieth-century past. Taking a leaf from the playbook of other western states, which have seen their destiny reflected in the eyes of their visitors, North Dakota looks desperately toward tourism. With wheat prices as flat as its prairie and gas/oil reserves all but exhausted, the old economy has "fossilized." So one finds North Dakotans with the dreams of Garry Greff, an ex-schoolteacher in the southwestern North Dakota town of Regent. Confronted with the knowledge that the tourist from Clyde, Ohio (Sherwood Anderson's fabled *Winesburg*), would be driven to drowsiness by the arrow-straight highways bleeding into the horizons of North Dakota, Greff decided to wake up these tourists, not with Starbucks coffee, but with the knowledge "that no one is going to stop for the norm." Greff sat about to festoon US 94 into an "enchanted highway," Walt Disney style. Using oil barrels as his medium, Greff created Paul Bunyan–size iron sculptures—grasshoppers, ants, oil field drillers—all calculated to jolt the tourist driver out of his numbing reveries and, above all, persuade him to stop at the nearest town and stay awhile.[17] The muse of Greff follows Hal Rothman's stimulating concept of the tourist as primarily "a colonial creature." Western states perpetually strive to balance their budgets. Western businesses are easy prey for the easterner searching for that elusive western "experience."[18] One wonders, though, if the western polemic, traditionally about cows and mines, has simply changed its focus to tourism.

Fling open the doors to Nevada, with the flamboyance of a neon-lit strip, populated with a colorful cast of gangster characters reminiscent of *Guys and Dolls* (though far more violent than the benign musical), typifying a crime-propelled, high-stakes casino. This dazzling existence largely ceased in the 1960s, when casinos encountered the pressure of law enforcement agencies to take a bath and sweep organized crime out of their corporate worlds. Enter Howard Hughes, who took plenty of baths, and his Mormon entourage, who veritably reeked moral and physical cleanliness. Soon Hughes's snake eyes success lured other investors, many interested in creating a faux heritage replete with Roman baths, gargantuan hotel suites, and enormous replications of Caesar's world or Times Square. It made little difference as long as "the prospect's" imaginations were boggled and the eyes of the slot machine beholder popped out. The master builder of the new Las Vegas, Steve Wynn, afflicted with health problems and overexpansion, sold out to eighty-year-old Kirk Kerkorian, whose high-stakes interests included the boardrooms of the casino MGM and the Daimler-Chrysler Corporation. Rumors to the contrary, a third major player, hotel czar Barron Hilton, divorced his casino and hotel business but refused to exit the faro tables.

Another far less exciting Nevada that decades ago produced the pawing, snorts, and bellows of the livestock industry has fallen victim to low cattle prices and bureaucratic infighting in Washington. More than fifteen years ago, a vigorous rancher/state senator, Dean Rhoades, launched one of the most successful grassroots protests to ride out of the range. Christened "the Sagebrush Rebellion" for a brief time, the Sagebrushers of the 1970s and 1980s, through a combination of media attention and legal action, contrived to attract the attention of Congress, whose debates on same were recorded with deadly prose in *The Congressional Record*. The Sagebrushers' goal, a minor one, was to convince the federal government to turn over title to all federal lands in the West to the states. The modesty of the proposal shook the staunch pro-western delegations. In the autumn of 1999, Sagebrushers, with the announced objective of demonstrating their pulse, if not their blood pressure, held a protest gathering in the Jarbridge Wilderness. Out of an anticipated 1,000 attenders, less than fifty faces showed up. This western rebellion had registered its last gasp.

Nevada and Wyoming have a complementary historical and philosophical ethos, be it "rugged individualism" or mineral resources. In Nevada, gold predominated, at the turn of the century in the south and by midcentury in central Nevada, with the fabulous Carlin low-grade gold discovery by Newmont. The black gold of oil and coal have prevailed in Wyoming since the turn of the century. But above all, the economies of both states have been, and are still, dominated by colonialism. Trainload after trainload of coal rolls out of the 2.5-million-acre Powder River Basin, the richest coal province in the world, to stoke the utilities in the Midwest and South. The latest blast of the Wyoming mineral boom-and-bust cycle is methane gas. Enticed by profit margins of 40 percent or more, gas producers are climbing over each other in a frantic lease hunt, reminiscent of the east Texas oil boom of the 1930s.

Not all landowners, especially ranchers, are pleased with the latest mineral gyration. To reach the gas reserves, producers have to pump to the surface millions of gallons of water. Where wrestling a living from a recalcitrant land is an everyday defiance, these stoic, weather-beaten cowmen are appalled by the squandering of huge, gushing streams of water that erode their arroyos. They remind some old-timers of the days when Salt Creek oil roared down creek beds, untamed and unused. The Wyoming legislature or political officialdom is not likely to cap the latest mineral roar, just as they avoided tightly regulating the early mineral development of uranium, oil, gas, and coal. The governing elite of Wyoming is as eager for the tax revenues as the Wyoming landowners are to cash their royalty checks. Although eastern colonialism doesn't lord itself over the capital in Cheyenne as omnipresently as the Wyoming wind whipped down Warren Avenue in the nineteenth century, today's colonialism—read globalization—dominates Wyoming's coal industry. Overseas corporate branch offices appear in Gillette, Rawlins, Cheyenne, and Lander, planetary testimony to Arch Minerals merging with Ashland Coal, which, in turn, flirts with British investors. Arco Minerals, operating two of the largest coal mines in the Powder River Basin, is now a component of British Petroleum/Amoco. Kennecott Energy, long one of the major giants of the copper world, hid in the corporate skirts of British-based Rio Tinto, a company whose interests rival the stretch of the nineteenth-century British empire. Peabody Coal, which claimed some of the earliest open-pit coal mining in the West, found its future in the arms of German mining conglomerate RAG International Mining.

Although global colonialism does not totally dominate Wyoming's range or urban scene, Jackson Hole, with its lordly Tetons as a stunning backdrop, is doing its best to attract the Jay Gatsbys from the Hamptons of Long Island. Three years ago, fifty home permits were issued by the planning commission in Jackson with evaluations of over $1 million *each*. And this past year saw the creation of the $40-million Amnagami Hotel, a structure reflecting an unlikely combination of minimalist architecture with a tinge of western bravado, replete with sawdust saloons and $500-jeans-wearing faux cowboy/consumers at the bar. Ersatz all— for a day, a week, or perhaps a month, but who cares seems to be the motto. Owen Wister, who spent some twenty summers in the Tetons, might experience the same wonderment that Thorstein Veblen did when looking across the Silicon Valley, only there would have been no seduction in the Wister cabin! Ah, yes, $10,000-a-week "city slickers," perched on a mountainside, sipping their scotch, absorbing the incredible view of the Teton range and thinking of telling their cohorts at 300 Park Avenue about their incredible western atmosphere. Not a hundred miles to the south of Amnagani, another western happening, the stunning Star Valley could be theirs, but it is doubtful that they will ever know that West.

One Cheyenne businessman equivocally and memorably noted that Wyoming was "the hole in the doughnut" in the prosperity of the Rocky Mountain West. Yet in more than one way, Wyoming typifies the West. David Broder, in his nationally syndicated column, succinctly diagnosed the malaise under the banner "Without Leadership, Wyoming Is Floundering!"[19] Even though Broder fingered Wyoming's "political angst," mirrored by its absence of leadership, as the prime culprit of the state's economic illness, he would not have had to limit his palliative to Wyoming. As the West enters the twenty-first century, increasingly the leadership question, regardless of the political level, will be posed and perhaps answered.

All of which brings us after this random snapshot-after-snapshot view of the West in 2000 to the eternal query: *Quo vadis* the twenty-first-century West? Although prognostication, as Daniel Bell, Herman Kahn, and many others have ascertained, is not only a dangerous, but frequently a ludicrous occupation, some overall trends are distinguished with chardonnany-like clarity. Someone said that history is "just one pass through the possibilities." If historians are poor predictors, which indeed they are, it is an almost impossible task to portend "discontinuities." So with that warning shot, not over the bow, but at the starting gate, we are off (some might uncharitably suggest in more ways than one).

What rivets the imagination of many historians is that the future is now—as George Bernard Shaw's socialists were wont to scream at the coal-streaked faces of British miners. More than a decade ago, Paul Kennedy, in his oft-quoted *The Rise and Fall of the Great Powers,* told Americans, and they believed him, that because of "an imperial overstretch," America in the twenty-first century would fall to a second-rate power. But by the year 2000, Americans were far too happy consuming the dividends of the "wealth effect" to pay the syndicated Kennedys much mind. Nevertheless, since the United States is king of the hill, America can anticipate that the twenty-first century will be fraught with attempts by countries around the globe to dethrone it.

In this picture, the American West's population is increasingly darkening in pigmentation. Multiracial, multilingual, multicultural, multiethnic are not just predictions for the West's future; that future is already here. Less and less will the West accommodate Pete Hamill's remark, "Today too often I find Americans, whose essential slogan is, 'I am offended, therefore I am.'" This is not to campaign for a

West of homogenization, which is obviously illusory in a vat of increasing diversity. But it does suggest that westerners might leave the barn dance past for the telecommunications of tomorrow. If we follow this fishing rod line out, we catch Katherine Morrissey's very useful idea that a region is not confined to a physical territory, but is a "mental landscape . . . a series of settlements tied together by mental concepts."[20] Tolerance may not be the tsunami of the twenty-first-century West, but a multicultural West will find far less room for the bigotry that once walked and talked on the muddy "sidewalks" of the nineteenth-century West.

I would suggest, then, that the West of the twenty-first century will not be one of uniformity, but more and more a vista for consensus. Not because westerners will slide down the slippery slope of fantasy to a fictional land of Oz, but because in the twenty-first-century West, inhabited by multipolar constituencies of environmentalists, tribalists, Old West mythologizers, communtarians, and old and new economy proselytizers, all will hunt for unification rather than division. Whether they locate that common ground will be one of the major puzzles of the coming century. In sum, westerners will seek to balance the West's sovereignty of the old-time religion of colonialism and the new Aztec hymn to the sun of globalism.

Little is the risk in proposing that the West of the twenty-first century will increasingly be one of metropolitanism and that the rural West will continue to be chewed up by the bulldozers of urban sprawl, communitarianism aside, for here optimism surrenders to pessimism—westerners will insist on escalating their demands for the services and culture of urbanization. A dichotomy, though, is present on the marquee of western living. Westerners may delight in urban lights, but they also are reluctant to forswear the pastoral ideal of the nineteenth century, a century in which American writers mythologized the West, nature, and rural existence. This theme is being carried forward into the twenty-first century by Cormac McCarthy, Kent Haruf, and Annie Proulx, among others, as the literary "New Mythic West." Whether the myth of Proulx or the antipastoralism of Hamlin Garland, Willa Cather, or Ole Rölvaag will triumph in twenty-first century will be arguable. Less open to dissent is the wrangling, removed from the rodeo/political arena, over land and public domain policy, between bureaucrats and westerners, which will continue well into the twenty-first century.

Several years ago Gerald Nash astutely wrote that the West was no longer a colonial West, but rather a region that set the agenda for much of the nation. Nash's words resonate with emphasis, for western ecology is built from the bottom up, and the health and vitality of the land, as well as the communities that dwell on that land, will be contested for with a nonstop fervor. In spite of the free-enterprise spirit of some western gubernatorial ventures, the West refuses to be held hostage to national priorities, such as toxic waste dumping and nuclear tailings. One scenario of the public lands tourney between national interests and western individualism perceives a diminishing battle. We have our doubts. True, the curtain has descended on the extractive West, embodied by the steep decline of the timber, cattle, and mining Wests. Yet whether the West, with its block of western senators, ever attuned to defending its regional suzerainty, will triumph is a matter of intense debate. It is our conjecture that as the West moves into and through the twenty-first century, globalization and national self-interest will make it increasingly difficult for the West to exercise its regional power. To lift a scene from that wonderful, campy 1943 scenario *Casablanca,* the Captain Renaults of contemporary western protesters are busily "rounding up all the usual suspects"— the polluters, the exploiters of the downtrodden, the contractors of foreign labor, and the violators of human rights. The causes are unlimited, the campaign results problematic. We owe the New West proponents a debt for prompting our memories that the James Hills, the Verner Z. Reeds, the Daniel Jacklings, with their entrepreneurial zeal, greed, power, and capital, ruthlessly built the western dream of today. But that dream would not have been theirs or ours sans the slave labor of thousands of backs, with herniated disks, be they Chinese, blacks, Mexicans, or poor Caucasians. Power and place are twins on the same western stage; only the actors vary.

So demographically, as Walter Nugent so devastatingly documents, western neighborhoods of the twenty-first century are likely to be ones featuring more and more diversity. This diversity, if seasoned and perpetuated, will demand a comparative methodology.

As stated above, another self-apparent demographic challenge, requiring boldness and imagination for the westerner of the twenty-first century, will be the Club of Rome's preoccupation with overpopulation. Admittedly, the problem is more acute for Zambia than Nevada, but in the intertwined world of the twenty-first century, the futures of Zambia and Nevada may be tied together by trade, disease, and poverty. No one knows the "carrying capacity" of the American West. What will be the effect of pollution on the West's burgeoning population? Diminished natural resources force change, but what will be the nature of that change? On the cusp of the twenty-first century, it is obvious that much of the third world cannot feed itself. These emerging nations, which seemingly shift their waves of refugee boundaries monthly, if not daily, are already importing 100 million tons of foodstuffs, primarily cereals.

Change? Inevitably, but since that transformation will be triggered by human nature, how original will the solutions be? The banishment of nutritional problems for 6 billion people makes all but the ignorant bewildered. Three alternatives present themselves: slaughter (which tribes, whether in Africa or southern Europe, are doing with genocidal glee), disease, or biotechnology/chemicals. Are any of these choices viable? As I write, European governments and populations are vigorously damning biotechnology.

The gulag mentality, although demonstrably effective on a short-term basis, carries within that psychology the seeds of its own execution. Even though a body of peace proponents prophesy the end of warfare (at least on a global World War III scale), one may be forgiven for expressing skepticism about the banishment of tribalism, terrorism, and biological bloodshed. Without the benefit of clergy, these aberrations of human nature will not vanish from our destiny in the twenty-first century. Banal as it may be for one to say, globalization alone cannot ensure the promise of the future. We the people tend to chloroform history. Partly this is due, as noted above, to the enthusiastic search for exceptionalism in our nation's history, all of which cauterizes the comparative approach. To revisit the exceptionalism polemic is akin to entering a nineteenth-century landscape maze of an English manor house garden. The most recent expression of exceptionalism popped up in Seymour Martin Lipset and Gary Marks's study of American socialism.[21] Why did socialism skip (that hoary query) the body politic in America? Lipset and Marks argue the unoriginal position that it is because of the divergence between society and "Leftist" politics in the American political cosmos. One doubts that numerous readers will be converted, for many reject American uniqueness as intellectual isolationism.

The funeral of socialism aside, until recently the westerner on the Rio Grande or in the San Joaquin Valley, convinced of his or her regional character, remained segregated from the inequality of other areas of the United States. Comparative methodology, which might expose this regional jingoism, brings a tepid response at best for most historians of the West[22] (in sharp contrast to the history of slavery, where David Brion Davis, George Frederickson, Stanley Elkins, and Frank Tannebaum have employed the comparative perspective with sophistication and success). Although converts to comparative methodology are few among western historians, other pundits are scattered about to consider the future of the twenty-first-century West. One westerner, Dan Kemmis, gazes from his office window in Missoula, Montana, in search of his optical West. Not a West of boundaries, but one where the world stage and the actors are in constant flux.[23] Kemmis is not a solitary sermonizer in perceiving the American West as a global player, as the recent and volatile congressional debate on awarding China a permanent favored-nation trade status illustrates. A witness of the congressional debate could, with ease, see the all-too-visible "wires" being pulled by an Internet entrepreneur in San Francisco or a manufacturer in Denver. How many times was the satiated "couch potato" informed that China represented a consumer market of more than a billion people! Nothing so graphically imprinted the westerner's mentality of the reach of globalism into Salt Lake City as the China trade argument.

Gerald Nash, with his usual perception, wrote in one of his most recent books of the impact of not only global policies on the West, but also of the federal government's role "in transforming an erstwhile economic colony, a colony dependent on the exploitation of its natural resources, into a trend setter on the cutting edge of new technology."[24] Whether prophet or fool (or a combination of both), one doesn't have to be an admirer of Hoagy Carmichael to be excited by the American West's global presence in a performance of an economic ballet in Tokyo or by an arthritic pipeliner on the frozen steppes of Siberia. In writing finis, a word not for our sponsor, but a nod to Clio, we can ask, What will the historian of the twenty-first-century West be up to? Will he or she be tweaking the noses of presentist historians—always great fun? Historians, regardless of the generation, tend to be such serious souls. Or will the historians of 2150, full of the religion of the Enlightenment or perhaps the romanticism of Chopin, look back to the twentieth-century West with as much nostalgia as some twentieth-century western historians now chronicle their views on the nineteenth century? Perhaps, for those who labor in the vineyard, this is the riskiest speculation of all.

Every decade or so, when historians feel especially unread, unloved, and impotent, another study appears on how historians can reach out to the great unwashed—the general reader.[25] The conclusions reached are past repetition; only the personages and the phraseology rotate. The lamentations can easily be listed: (a) historians should emulate the style of Macauley, Treveylan, or Becker; (b) if historians are to write for the masses, they must entrance them with topics that have wide appeal—the history of Niobrara County will no longer do; (c) in essence, historians, as we all know but ignore, insist on writing for each other (even if they don't read what their colleagues write), not for God and country, but for deans and promotion. The wailing wall could carry an interminable list of inscriptions, for the list is never ending.

Whether the global publics will embrace the wisdom of the twenty-first-century western historian is beyond even our daring to contemplate, but it would quicken our pulse to know. Good luck and erase those frowns, for even we aren't clowns!

Notes

1. Walter Nugent, *Into the West* (New York: Knopf, 1999).
2. Francis Fukuyama, "Commentary," *Times Literary Supplement* no. 4960 (18 June 1999): 5–6.
3. Michael Kammen, *In the Past Lane* (New York: Oxford University Press, 1997), 1, 98.
4. William Leach, *Country of Exiles: The Destruction of Place in American Life* (New York: Pantheon, 1999), 11.
5. In this essay, *conservation* and *environmentalism* will be used interchangeably, though self-evidently the two terms have variant implications as well as meanings.
6. Richard White, *The Organic Machine: The Remaking of the Columbia River* (New York: Hill & Wang, 1998), x.
7. Donald Pisani, *To Reclaim a Divided West: Water, Law and Public Policy, 1848-1902* (Albuquerque: University of New Mexico Press, 1992).
8. The arresting tale of the Oahe project can be found in Peter Carrel's excellent study, *Uphill Against Water* (Lincoln: University of Nebraska Press, 1999).
9. James P. Dickenson, *Home on the Range: A Century on the High Plains* (New York: Scribner, 1999).
10. John Herbers, *The New Heartland: Americans' Flight Beyond the Suburbs and How It's Changing Our Future* (New York: Times Books, 1986). Herbers recently wrote on urban sprawl, "The answer is yes yes. I don't see any end in sight. . . . But still it keeps on spreading and all you hear is build more and wider highways." John Herbers to Gene M. Gressley, 25 May 1999.
11. Michael Lewis, *The New, New Thing: A Silicon Valley Story* (New York: Norton, 2000).
12. John Patrick Diggins, *Thorstein Veblen: Theorist of the Leisure Class* (Princeton: Princeton University Press, 1999), 167.
13. Commentators on the "Second Industrial Revolution" have not confined themselves to the electronic slate to comprehend what is more often than not incomprehensible. I found more enlightening as well as entertaining from a "pop" standpoint to be Michael Lewis, noted above; Charles Ferguson, *High Stakes, No Prisoners* (New York: Times Books, 1998); and P. O. Bronson, *The Nudist on the Late Shift* (New York: Random House, 1999).
14. Liz Claiborne and Art Oretenberg Foundation, *Montana: People and the Economy* (New York: privately printed, 1999).

15. William Kittredge and Annick Smith, eds., *The Last Best Place: A Montana Anthology* (Helena: Montana State Historical Society, 1988).

16. Ed C. Marston, "Sense of Community," *High Country News* 31 (21 June 1999): 1.

17. A couple of decades ago, Nebraska successfully strove to slash the monotony of Interstate 80 with a series of beadlike "poetic lakes" strung along that interminable belt of cement.

18. Hal Rothman, *Devil's Bargains: Tourists in the Twentieth Century American West* (Lawrence: University Press of Kansas, 1998).

19. David S. Broder, "Without Leadership, Wyoming Is Floundering," *Albuquerque Journal*, 10 October 1999, 8.

20. Katherine G. Morrisey, *Mental Territories: Mapping the Inland Empire* (Ithaca: Cornell University Press, 1997), 7–8.

21. Seymour Martin Lipset and Gary Marks, *It Didn't Happen Here* (New York: Norton, 2000).

22. Howard Lamar, Walter Nugent, Gerald Nash, Roger Adelson, Jerome Steffens, and W. W. Savage have been notable exceptions to the comparative silence of western historians. Nor can those who know him have anything but admiration for Earl Pomeroy, who tends to think about everything in a comparative mode.

23. Daniel Kemmis, "Learning to Think Like a Region," *High Country News* 32 (10 April 2000): 18.

24. Gerald D. Nash, *The Federal Landscape: An Economic History of the Twentieth-Century West* (Tucson: University of Arizona Press, 1999).

25. The literature on the public role of history is as diffuse as it is frequently amusing. Some of the more representative titles are Patricia Nelson Limerick, "A How-to Guide for the Academic Future Going Public," *Perspectives* 31 (December 1997): 1, 17–20; Richard Freeman, *The Over-Educated American* (New York: Academic, 1976); Gary B. Nash, Charlotte Crabtree, and Ross E. Dunn, *History on Trial: Culture Wars and the Teaching of the Past* (New York: Knopf, 1997); Roy Rosenzweig and David Thelen, *The Presence of the Past* (New York: Columbia University Press, 1998); John Bodnar, ed., *Bonds of Affection: Americans Define Patriotism* (Princeton: Princeton University Press, 1996); Tom Engelhardt, *History Wars: The Enola Gay and Other Battles for the American Past* (New York: Henry Holt, 1996); Mike Wallace, *Mickey Mouse: History and Other Essays on American Memory* (Philadelphia: Temple University Press, 1990); Bessie L. Pierce, *Public Opinion and the Teaching of History in the United States* (New York: Knopf, 1926); Michael Kammen, *Mystic Chords of Memory: The Transformation of Tradition in American Culture* (New York: Knopf, 1991); and American Historical Association, "History and Publics," *Perspectives* 38 (May 2000).

Gerald D. Nash and the
Twentieth-Century American West

Richard W. Etulain

When Gerald D. Nash's pioneering book *The American West in the Twentieth Century* appeared in 1973, it received decidedly positive reviews. Readers saluted the overview volume as the much needed study of a hitherto neglected subject. As one commentator noted, Nash's insightful synthesis would now "be the starting point for future serious scholarship" on the modern American West. Nash's pathbreaking study, wrote another reviewer, "as lively as it is informative," provided "a splendid synthesis . . . of the history of the American West in the twentieth century."[1]

Until his death in 2000, Gerald Nash remained the most prolific and notable scholar on the post-1900 American West. From his earliest essays in the late 1950s, through his books in the 1960s, 1970s, and 1980s, and on to his most recent studies, Professor Nash continued to explore new themes even as he provided trenchant overviews of more familiar topics. Taken as a whole, his numerous publications provide the most thorough and valuable body of historical work on the modern American West. Without a doubt, Gerald D. Nash was our leading interpreter of the twentieth-century American West.

Nash's backgrounds make his emergence as a specialist in western history all the more remarkable. Born into a German-Jewish family in Berlin in 1928, Nash and his parents fled Nazi Germany in 1937. After a few months' stay in Palestine, the Nash family arrived as new immigrants to the United States in 1938. The Nashes relocated to New York City, where Gerald, their only child, entered the third grade at age ten. He quickly learned English, did well in elementary school, and then entered the highly regarded Stuyvesant High School. After gaining a bachelor's degree in history at New York University and a master's from Columbia University, he realized his need to know more of the rest of the United States. That opportunity came when he landed a fellowship for doctoral work in history at the University of California at Berkeley.[2]

In California, Nash became acquainted with the American West. There he began doctoral work at one of the country's most prestigious universities, especially known for its emphasis on the American West and the Southwest Borderlands. Eventually Nash wrote his dissertation for eminent historian John D. Hicks, who had already written trailblazing books on the Populists and was then working on modern American and California topics. Hicks encouraged Nash to study modern California. Marrying his new interests in the modern West to his previous work in economic history and policy studies, Nash completed his dissertation in 1957, titled "State Government and Economic Development in California, 1849–1911."[3]

The next few years became a transitional period for Nash. He taught one year at Stanford, another at Northern Illinois, and returned to Stanford on the promise of a tenure-track position. Then he traveled east for a postdoctoral year at Harvard with noted historian Oscar Handlin, during which time he turned his dissertation into a book. After working in four different positions in four years, Nash secured a tenure-track position at the University of New Mexico in fall 1961. At New Mexico, he rose quickly through the ranks, became departmental chair, and was named Presidential Professor (1985–90) and Distinguished Professor (1990–95) before his retirement in 1995.

Early on, Gerald Nash published like a man determined to make his mark in his field. Even before his first book appeared, his revised dissertation in 1964, Nash had authored nearly twenty essays on a variety of subjects. Three of those articles came from his master's thesis on John H. Reagan, a Confederate cabinet member, and several others reflected his growing interest in California and in modern western economic and administrative history. Already Nash was pursuing historical topics on land, labor, and transportation issues as well as on fiscal and other bureaucratic subjects.[4]

After several delays, Nash's much revised dissertation appeared as the book *State Government and Economic Development: A History of Administrative Policies in California, 1849–1933* (1964). As he made clear in his preface, Nash wanted his study "to examine persistent institutional relationships in [the California] state government's administration of economic policies." He was convinced that the early 1960s were an especially auspicious time "for probing into the history of the relations between government and economic life, an important strand in American institutional development" (viii, vii).[5]

Nash divides his thorough volume into three sections. After noting the failures of the Mexican government to deal effectively with economic development in California, Nash shows how the new state addressed its dynamic, explosive economic affairs between 1850 and 1870. Part two reveals the ways in which Californians, from 1870 to 1900, dealt with agriculture and industry through newly implemented administrative procedures. Continued agricultural and industrial growth from 1900 to 1930 demanded even more innovative administrative methods, as part three demonstrates. In these three sections, the author discusses such topics as agriculture, transportation, land policies, corporations, mining, and state-owned and operated enterprises.

State Government and Economic Development reveals a good deal about Nash's career-long interests. First of all, the book illustrates the author's pronounced interest in economic and political history, his fascination with administrative and public policies, and his grounding in the history of California. The volume also foreshadows several hallmarks of Nash's later publications. His book is thoroughly researched, clearly organized, and smoothly written.

Attentive readers of Nash's first monograph will also notice other facets of his scholarship. His footnotes reveal an extensive use of government documents and reports. Indeed, one would be hard-pressed to locate *any* materials pertinent to the subject not cited in his notes and bibliography. The volume contains extensive sections on oil policy, banking, land and labor policies, and transportation—topics frequently covered in Nash's later books and essays.

Organizational and stylistic patterns evident in Nash's subsequent writings also abound. Especially notable is his masterful talent of framing discussions. Within each chapter, introductory and concluding paragraphs always bracket major topics, and short, clear topic sentences elaborate on the subjects introduced in these opening sentences. Nash's close attention to organization is also evident in the surveys of historical trends with which he opens each of the book's three major divisions. This contextual technique appeared in many of his subsequent works.

Finally, the notes and bibliography attest to Nash's diligent research. Combined, they serve as something of a "Research Opportunities" essay for further research on the volume's subject. Nash does not shy away from strong statements about these sources, going so far as to remark that some books on the subjects he has researched should never have been published.

Those acquainted with Nash's first monograph will realize how much his second study, *United States Oil Policy 1890–1964: Business and Government in Twentieth Century America* (1968), builds on the first. The author's preface in the second volume makes clear this linkage: "My main objective has been to place in historical perspective the many changes that affected the developing consensus concerning needed cooperation between the [federal] government and the [oil] industry" (viii). Moreover, Nash also adumbrates one of the central themes of all his works: although conflict assuredly marks all human affairs, conversation and cooperation are even more evident. In this vein, he writes: "The prime purpose of this study is to analyze and describe the growth of cooperation as a prime characteristic of public policy in the petroleum industry" (vii).[6]

A close reading of Nash's initial volume hints at what his second study might contain. Discussions of national oil policy are scattered throughout *State Government and Economic Development,* but two explicit references in the bibliography foreshadow the volume on oil. "One of the surprising gaps in California historiography," Nash writes, "is the absence of studies on the development of the petroleum industry which grew to major proportions during the twentieth century." Two pages later, he reinforces his earlier statement: "Somewhat surprisingly, the fascinating history of oil lands in California during the twentieth century has attracted attention only from legal students" (369,

371). In 1968, Nash himself provided the thorough volume that helped fill this historiographical gap.

In his second book, Nash argues that the New Nationalism of President Theodore Roosevelt, more than any other administrative policy, proved the necessity of the federal government's serving as the arbiter in formulating national oil policies. Hoping to balance public and private interests, to conserve oil supplies, and to eliminate waste, the first Roosevelt encouraged a spirit of cooperation that later administrations often followed. As Nash adeptly shows, Franklin Roosevelt and Harry Truman, like Theodore Roosevelt, were intimately involved in fostering a continuing spirit of cooperation between the federal government and the burgeoning oil industry.

Nash's analysis of American oil policy takes a slightly different tack from his first book. In the earlier volume, he moved from territorial and state arenas toward federal influences; in the second, he began with federal policies and demonstrated their influences on state, local, and private policies. As he did throughout his career, Nash interweaves national-regional and regional-national stories, pointing out the explicit ways in which Congress and the presidency have influenced Sacramento and, conversely, the manner in which states have helped to shape federal oil decisions.

Not surprisingly, Nash devotes a good deal of attention to oil policies of the American West. The powerful, oil-rich states like Texas, Oklahoma, and California receive extensive treatment, as do important western figures such as Albert Fall, Lyndon B. Johnson, Robert S. Kerr, Joseph C. O'Mahoney, and Sam Rayburn. Western presidents Herbert Hoover and Dwight D. Eisenhower also played major roles in shaping the nation's oil and natural gas policies.

Gerald Nash's career spiraled upward in the decade following the publication of his first books. Moving quickly through the ranks at the University of New Mexico, he became a full professor in 1968 and in 1974 began a six-year term as chairman of the History Department. Meanwhile he remained busy as a writer. In addition to his book on oil policies, Nash wrote a brief study titled *Perspectives on Administration: The Vistas of History* (1969), a lengthy college text on the United States in the twentieth century (*The Great Transition,* 1971), and edited a brief study of President Franklin Delano Roosevelt (1967). The book that gained the widest circulation was his edited classroom reader, *Issues in American Economic History* (1964), which went through several subsequent editions.[7] He also wrote nearly ten essays during these years.[8]

The volume Nash published in 1973, however, established a new field in western history and gained him notable stature in the new area. *The American West in the Twentieth Century: A Short History of an Urban Oasis* provided the pioneering scholarly overview of the post-1900 American West.[9] Although a few journalists and historians had previously dealt with the modern West as part of larger western studies,[10] Nash's volume was the first full-length book to focus entirely on the twentieth-century American West. Additionally, it advanced several provocative themes, important interpretations followed or challenged in the next quarter century of western historiography. For nearly two decades this synthesis remained the only scholarly study of the modern West. It clearly shaped the first generation of books and essays written about this time period.

Nash's pacesetting volume furnished both an overview and a fresh interpretation of the modern West. Drawing on a variety of sources, including dozens of pertinent monographs, government documents, and accounts by journalists and lay historians, Nash provided a new chronological overview of the twentieth-century American West that included extensive discussions of economic, political, and sociocultural subjects. These chronological and topical divisions covered the major subregions of the West: California, the Pacific Northwest, the Plains and the Rockies, and the Southwest. The treatment of California was particularly full.[11]

For Nash, the history of the post-1900 West broke into two major periods. From 1900 to World War II, the West largely served as a colony of the East, controlled by Wall Street, big government, and eastern economic interests. But World War II, like a catalyst, broke many of the eastern economic chains binding the West. Uncle Sam, during the New Deal thirties but especially during World War II and on into the Cold War era, poured hundreds of millions of dollars into the West, thereby jump-starting the region's economy. New industries in booming western cities, plus jobs with federal installations in the West or their satellite connections, drew west floods of new immigrants.

In the early 1960s, California surpassed New York as the country's most populous state. But the importance of this demographic trend, according to Nash, was more than just that of a westward-moving people. The Far West, particularly California, became a pacesetter for American society and culture. The growing metropolitan West—for the region had become the most urban section of the United States—showcased a "sybaritic," "barbecue culture" that emphasized informal, outdoor living in a western suburb or urban cluster.[12]

By the early 1970s, Gerald Nash was telling readers a new story: the modern American West had rushed past the urban East as the most significant region of the United States. Henceforth, Nash added, increasing numbers of Americans would look west rather than east for their social and cultural cues.

No historian, before or since, has written a book that so shaped our thinking about the post-1900 American West. Indeed, from this volume, and from other, later studies, the "Nash thesis" emerged. In this view, the history of the twentieth-century West pivoted around World War II; after that dramatic series of events the West was no longer a "plundered province." With the boom of the 1940s, the region increased in economic and political power, as well as in social and cultural influence. It is now clear that the historiography of the modern American West began with the publication of Nash's pathbreaking book in 1973.[13]

During the next dozen years, Nash's reputation continued to grow. In addition to placing nearly twenty essays in scholarly journals, he also published a valuable brief overview of American history during the 1930s and 1940s, *The Great Depression and World War II* (1979). Increasingly Nash was heralded as a leading historian of twentieth-century America.[14] Meanwhile he continued to serve as chairman of his department, took on the editorship of *The Historian,* and taught a heavy load of courses. His colleagues at New Mexico recognized his major contributions to American history and to his home department and named him Presidential Professor of History, a post he held until 1990.

Nash's next major book on the American West, *The American West Transformed: The Impact of the Second World War* (1985), became a second high point in his career as the leading authority on the twentieth-century American West. Five years later, he produced a companion volume, *World War II and the West: Reshaping the Economy.*[15] Taken together, these two books furnish a comprehensive account of the early 1940s as a watershed period in modern western history. They also illustrate the balanced, indefatigable research and writing that characterize Nash's scholarship.

The American West Transformed enlarges Nash's bold thesis that World War II revolutionized the West. The author restates his argument in the opening words of the work:

This book has a simple theme: that the Second World War transformed the American West. No other single influence on the region—not the Mexican War, not the Civil War, not World War I, nor even the Great Depression—brought such great and cataclysmic changes to the West (vii).

After providing introductory sections on economic backgrounds, Nash focuses on sociocultural topics, devoting full chapters to immigration to the West, California cities, urban experiences in other parts of the Far West, blacks, Hispanic westerners, Indians and Japanese, science in the West, and Hollywood. No one previously—or since—has given such full coverage to these western topics during the World War II period.

This volume attracted more attention than Nash's previous books. It became a featured History Book Club selection and was named a *Choice* Outstanding Academic Book. The publishers quickly put it into paperback, where it gained wide adoption in western and modern U.S. courses. Still in print after nearly twenty years, *The American West Transformed* expanded Nash's reputation as the leading scholar on the twentieth-century American West.

The strengths and attractions of Nash's volume are as clear as the author's thinking and writing. Not only does Nash support his thesis on the transforming power of World War II on the West, he fills his chapters with illuminating stories of men and women who shaped this world. One encounters tragic as well as inspiring anecdotes of Native Americans, Hispanic Americans, and Japanese Americans rising above wartime biases and difficulties to prove their loyalties to a country that, under the pressures of war, was not always fair-minded in its treatment of them and other peoples. African Americans, Hispanics, and Indians, as Nash points out, all experienced prejudices, disruptions to their lives, and other war-related traumas. Even worse was the tragic relocation of Japanese Americans from their coastal homes, farms, and stores to inland detainment areas that some likened to concentration camps.

Yet as Nash likewise makes clear, positive results also emanated from these war times. "New economic opportunities, wider social contacts, and a heightened sense of ethnic and cultural identity"—they too emerged from World War II. The war also "hasten[ed] integration" and thus acted "as a catalyst to break down various barriers in the way of racial equality" (152). These chapters on minority experiences in World War II illustrate Gerald Nash's balanced approach to the past. They remain the best concise introduction to these important subjects two decades after they were written.

Nash's second volume on the impact of World War II on the West focused on economic topics. Here the author devoted separate chapters to mining, shipbuilding, the air industry, aluminum, and the environment and another chapter to magnesium, steel, and oil. Other full sections are titled "Westerners in Washington," "The View from Western States and Cities," and "The Private Sector." The opening and closing sections, illustrating Nash's proclivity for restatement, provide a useful introduction and conclusion.

With an exception or two, the topics covered will sound familiar to those acquainted with the author's analyses of western economic history. Fact filled and solidly researched, these chapters are valuable commentaries on economic developments in the American West during the early 1940s. Much more than that, however, these discussions remain the most thorough introductions to those topics yet available.

Other sections of this volume move beyond Nash's traditional areas of concern. The chapter "World War II and the Western Environment," for example, details the red-hot controversies over water power, grazing, national parks, and federal jurisdictions during World War II. On center stage in these embroglios, where Nash appropriately places him, is Franklin Roosevelt's redoubtable secretary of the interior, Harold Ickes. Doing battle with a hostile and western-minded foe like Senator Pat McCarran of Nevada, Ickes tried to steer a difficult line between the conservation of, as well as the careful use of, natural resources for war needs. For leaders like Ickes, Nash writes, "the war . . . did much to crystallize as well as institutionalize a growing awareness of the need for improved management of the West's environmental heritage" (162).

The closing chapters in this volume also deal with regional-national economic configurations and postwar planning that emerged during the world conflict. In discussing these eastern-western, federal-state, large-small business, and federal government–private enterprise entanglements and conflicts, Nash draws a large-canvas picture that remained in flux during World War II and soon thereafter. These descriptions of emotional competitions rely heavily on the attitudes and involvements of such figures as Ickes; McCarran; Senators James E. Murray (Montana), Joseph C. O'Mahoney (Wyoming), and Harry Truman (Missouri); and Congressman Maury Maverick (Texas) as well as a host of writers and bureaucrats like Thurman Arnold, Wendell Berge, and Adolph A. Berle. This cast of lively characters, as well as dozens of federal and regional organizations, allows Nash to tell complex and interlocking stories about the impact of the war on western economic developments and planning.

Indeed, *World War II and the West* merges two of Nash's longtime interests. His first book had delved primarily into policy and planning, especially the interrelationship between government and business. Later his coverage broadened into the larger field of economic history. Here these two subjects are brought together in a probing study of the molding power of wartime events and trends on policy making, planning, and economic developments. These diverse topics achieve the sharpest focus when Nash brings them together in the American West.

A prominent figure in Nash's pioneering studies of the modern West was A. P. Giannini, the dynamic founder of the Bank of America. Deciding that Giannini merited further attention for his crucial impact on western history, Nash produced a sound biography of the banker in his next book, *A. P. Giannini and the Bank of America* (1992).[16] In Nash's scenario, Giannini played a vital part in the expansion of the West as a pacesetting region. Put succinctly, Nash's biography demonstrates how Amadeo Peter Giannini (1870–1949) grew up with the West. A. P.'s career paralleled California's transformation from a promising periphery at the end of the nineteenth century into a powerful economic core by the mid–twentieth century. Concurrent with the Pacific Coast's gradual emergence as *the* subregion of the West, Giannini established and directed a bank that mushroomed into a powerful global institution.

Nash's brief biography, in steady, clear strokes, limns Giannini's rise to power. The son of an Italian immigrant farmer/rancher, A. P. early demonstrated his ambition, diligence, and frugality. As Nash shows, Giannini recognized the restrictive and sometimes selfish policies of earlier bankers and decided to center his attentions on ordinary citizen investors. A. P. democratized an entire economic field through pioneering branch banking—first with his Bank of Italy and later in his mammoth Bank of America.

Nash's Giannini continued to innovate throughout his long and active career. He always made the resources of his sprawling institution available to large businesses, the federal government, and even to movie moguls while simultaneously catering to wage earners, small investors, and home builders. Nash notes that A. P. was both idealist and opportunist, two impulses that impelled the Bank of America forward to become one of the world's largest banks by the late 1940s.

As Nash narrates this intriguing success story, he never overlooks his subject's blemishes and limitations. Often impatient with competitors and bank workers with whom he disagreed, Giannini frequently coerced employees to march to his drumbeat or drop out of his band. At times his monumental self-assurance, his driving ambition, and his dogmatism alienated his friends—and even family members.

Nash's readable life story of this titanic figure of the recent American West reveals his skills as a biographer. In the only biography he wrote, Nash provides a revealing and fair-minded study. More than any other biographer of the banker, Nash clarifies Giannini's central role in the economy of the modern American West. This volume adds to Nash's stature as the leading interpreter of the twentieth-century West even as it details the career of one of the region's most influential citizens.

In addition to his emphases on economic history, governmental policies, and the modern West, Gerald Nash maintained a lifelong interest in historiography. Even before the appearance of his first book, he published several essays that dealt with historiographical trends or research opportunities in a variety of fields.[17] Such essays continued to appear throughout the 1970s and 1980s.[18]

Then in 1990, Nash turned his hand to a full-scale evaluative overview of historical writing about the American West. First delivered as part of the distinguished Calvin Horn Lectures in Western History and Culture, the book appeared one year later as *Creating the West: Historical Interpretations 1890–1990*.[19] It remains the only book-length, single-author examination of the shifting interpretations of western history.[20]

In his provocative overview of western historiography, Nash adopts a dual approach—chronological and thematic. Following a theme that his mentor John D. Hicks referred to as the "ecology of historians," Nash emphasizes "the relationship between changes in the contemporary environment and the shifting views of historians" (vii). That is, Nash stresses generational transformations between 1890 and 1990 and explains how these shifts influenced changing interpretations of "the West as frontier," "the West as region," "the West as urban civilization," and "the West as utopia and myth." This method allows Nash to discuss, for example, how such major events as the two world wars, the Great Depression, and the 1960s clearly shaped the historiography of the American West.

Seen in the larger cultural-intellectual contexts in which Nash places them, the views of numerous major western historians take on larger meaning. We see within clearer circumferences the frontier interpretations of Frederick Jackson Turner and Frederic Logan Paxson, the regional historiography of Walter Prescott Webb and Herbert Eugene Bolton, the reinterpretations of Henry Nash Smith and Earl Pomeroy in the 1950s and 1960s, and finally the revisionist views of post-1960s historians. Nash's technique demonstrates, too, how the national optimism of the pre–World War I period encouraged adherence to Turner's well-known theses, whereas the pessimism of the depression decade undercut Turner's popularity. After World War II, in the buoyant 1950s and early 1960s, Ray Allen Billington helped to refurbish Turner's reputation, but the significance of these frontier interpretations suffered once again during the more pessimistic decades following the 1960s.

Creating the West, like his earlier biography of Giannini, illustrated Gerald Nash's versatility as a historian. His previous books had catapulted him to the forefront of specialists in twentieth-century western history; now he proved he was equally adept at biography and historiography. In the next decade he continued to enlarge his reputation.

For a time in the early 1990s, however, it looked as if Gerald Nash's career might be abruptly foreshortened. Seriously ill, he was unable to carry out new research and writing projects. But he soon fully recovered and quickly produced two additional books on the modern American West.

The Federal Landscape (1999), a volume in the Modern American West series that Nash coedited, illustrates his sure grasp of several western topics.[21] Subtitled "An Economic History of the Twentieth-Century West," Nash's broadly based volume organizes the twentieth century into seven periods, within which the author discusses important economic issues. In developing the major theme of his volume—how the power and influence of the federal government repeatedly reshaped the West—Nash again echoes the region's journey from colony of the East to a more independent pacesetter. The author illuminates this transition through discussions of water policies, reclamation projects, developments in transportation, and the administration of western lands. In addition, Nash treats the government's influential part in military and defense planning and its involvements in natural resource management, the exploitation of resources, and conservation. Finally he includes important sections on national parks and tourism.

Notably, Nash discusses topics that economic historians previously overlooked or underemphasized. We see, for instance, the impact of government policies on minority groups, including Native Americans and Hispanics, and on women's changing roles in the West. Nash also includes a section on the intriguing role that air-conditioning played in the rise of the region. Readers also will be drawn to the author's stimulating use of theory to structure his narrative. Nash was the first to suggest the usefulness of Nicolae Kondratieff's "wave" theory in discussing the huge federal impact on the development of the modern West.

In several ways, The Federal Landscape illustrates many of the major concerns that animated Nash's career. From the first to the most recent of his books, Nash always emphasized the central function of the federal government in helping to determine regional policies. This national-regional configuration is apparent throughout this volume. But powerful narrative strategies are at work here too. Apt anecdotes, a variety of judiciously selected quotes, pen portraits of important participants, and dramatic events invitingly described—all serve as effective storytelling devices.

Nash's economic history of the modern West provides an appealing, balanced mix of generalizations and specifics. Most important, he convinces us that the federal government has been the central player in the economic development of the post-1900 American West. The discussions of water uses, transportation, reclamation, and land policies, as well as his treatments of national parks and tourism, illuminate and support his central thesis of western economic development.

Nash's final book, A Brief History of the American West Since 1945 (2000), is the only overview that focuses solely on the West during the past half century.[22] As he had in several previous volumes, Nash utilizes chronological and thematic divisions to structure this work. The opening section discusses economic, urban, cold war, and environmental developments between 1945 and 1960. Then, in part two, Nash treats several racial and ethnic groups and presents a provocative chapter on literary, cinematic, and television representations of the West. The concluding section includes a lively chapter on computers, another on tourism, still another on Asians in the West, and a final chapter titled "Political Issues and a Shrinking

Natural Environment." A concluding section provides valuable comparisons between the West of 1945 and that of 2000.

Nash's last work juxtaposes his traditional concerns with other, newer subjects. The chapters on economic and political affairs and minority groups provide solid, substantial discussions of these topics in recent western history that Nash knew as well as anyone. But the chapters on tourism, environmental concerns, and especially his delightful discussion of computers in the West will strike readers as yet another example of Nash's versatility as a historian.

In the book's introduction, Nash describes his study as the beginning of a "dialogue" about the period, not as an "end" to the conversation. In this regard, most readers will be pleased with the balance of the author's assessments. Although Nash clearly points to the waste, greed, and environmental disasters that characterize too much of recent western history, he also elaborates on the important achievements of science and technology, urbanization, and efforts to build a fair multicultural society. Nash's aim of providing a balanced, two-sided account of the recent West is apparent throughout this brief volume.

The closing chapter skillfully summarizes Nash's findings, even as it reveals the author's point of view. The demographic, economic, and sociocultural changes of the last half century, Nash makes clear, pose numerous challenges for westerners as they peer anxiously into the new century. Because of these looming dilemmas, the author adds, "many commentators . . . express less optimism about the region's future than they had a half century before." But Nash seems to speak for himself, and other like-minded historians, when he expresses his hope "that an understanding of the issues before us as westerners will allow a new generation to overcome the difficulties and to express the optimism that has been the hallmark of the American West throughout its history" (161). For Gerald Nash, the American West in 2000, despite the apparent problems it faces, remains nonetheless a place of hope. It is still a region that can serve as an inspiration for an entire nation and all its peoples.[23]

Gerald Nash's overall impact on western history becomes clear when one takes a full view of his career. In more than forty years of energetic activity as a researcher and publishing scholar, he succeeded in doing what few even attempt. He pioneered work in a new field—the history of the twentieth-century American West. At his death in October 2000, he was the preeminent authority in that scholarly area.

These contributions won Nash several notable awards. His home institution, the University of New Mexico, honored him as Annual Research Lecturer, as Presidential Professor, and as Distinguished Professor. He also served as departmental chair and as editor of *The Historian*. In wider circles, Nash was similarly honored. In 1990–91, he was named to the prestigious Fulbright position of George Bancroft Professor of American History at the University of Goettingen in Germany. In the same year, his contributions to western history were saluted when he assumed the presidency of the Western History Association.

But other facets of Gerald Nash's exemplary career were not so well known. He gave his life to the history profession through his many publications, his dedicated teaching, his participation in historical organizations, and his leadership in local and regional groups. He represented the dedicated university professor. One is also struck with the balance of his achievement. As his students and colleagues contributing essays to this volume will attest, Gerald D. Nash epitomized the ideal historian—a person committed to sharing his understanding of the tangled web of the modern American West.

Notes

1. Reviews of Gerald D. Nash, *The American West in the Twentieth Century: A Short History of an Urban Oasis* (Englewood Cliffs, N.J.: Prentice Hall, 1973), in *Western Historical Quarterly* 5 (April 1974): 196, and *Journal of American History* 61 (June 1974): 234, 233.
2. For more extensive coverage of Nash's life, see his autobiographical essay in this volume.
3. Nash is third in line of a trio of distinguished historians who have specialized in frontier or western history, as well as modern America, and who have become authorities in modern western history. Frederic Logan Paxson, who replaced Frederick Jackson Turner at the University of Wisconsin in 1910 and then moved west to the University of California, Berkeley, began the tradition. John D. Hicks, Paxson's student and his replacement at Wisconsin, followed his mentor to Berkeley, where he also did work on the post-1900 West. At California, Nash became Hicks's student. Another of Paxson's students, Earl Pomeroy, also moved into the twentieth-century West and helped steer several of his students into the same area of research.
4. Of special note among these early essays by Nash are "Herbert Hoover and the Origins of the Reconstruction Finance Corporation," *Mississippi Valley Historical Review* 45 (December 1959): 455–68; "Problems and Projects in the History of Nineteenth Century California Land Policy," *Arizona and the West* 2 (winter 1960): 327–40; and "Western Economic History as a Field for Research," *Western Economic Journal* 3 (fall 1964): 86–98.
5. Gerald D. Nash, *State Government and Economic Development: A History of Administrative Policies in California, 1849–1933* (Berkeley, Calif.: Institute of Governmental Studies, 1964). All page references to this and subsequent books will be in the text.
6. Nash, *United States Oil Policy, 1890–1964: Business and Government in Twentieth Century America* (Pittsburgh, Pa.: University of Pittsburgh Press, 1968).
7. Nash, *Perspectives on Administration: The Vistas of History* (Berkeley, Calif.: Institute of Governmental Studies, 1969); Nash, *The Great Tradition: A Short History of Twentieth Century America* (Boston: Allyn and Bacon, 1971); Nash, ed., *Franklin Delano Roosevelt* (Englewood Cliffs, N.J.: Prentice Hall, 1967) and *Issues in American Economic History* (Boston: D. C. Heath, 1964), 2d ed., 1972; 3d ed., 1980.
8. Key essays during the period were Nash, "Bureaucracy and Reform in the West," *Western Historical Quarterly* 2 (July 1971): 295–305; Nash, "Oil in the West: Reflections on the Historiography of an Unexplored Field," *Pacific Historical Review* 61 (August 1970): 321–40; and Nash, "California's Economic Growth, 1870–1970: An Interpretation," *California Historical Society Quarterly* 43 (February 1973): 270–84.
9. Nash, *The American West in the Twentieth Century: A Short History of an Urban Oasis* (Englewood Cliffs, N.J.: Prentice-Hall, 1973; Albuquerque: University of New Mexico Press, 1977).
10. For example, journalist Neil Morgan's *Westward Tilt: The American West Today* (New York: Random House, 1961, 1963) and historian Earl Pomeroy's *The Pacific Slope: A History of California, Oregon, Washington, Idaho, Utah, and Nevada* (New York: Alfred A. Knopf, 1965). For a general overview of historical writing about the modern American West, see Richard W. Etulain, "A New Historiographical Frontier: The Twentieth-Century West," in *The Twentieth Century West: Historical Interpretations,* eds. Gerald D. Nash and Richard W. Etulain (Albuquerque: University of New Mexico Press, 1989), 1–31.

11. Several reviewers argued that Nash overemphasized California in his *The American West in the Twentieth Century*. Revealingly, they were not reviewers from California. Other scholars who have emphasized California's huge role in the modern West (understandably enough) have often been targets of similar criticism.

12. Nash's sections on modern western society and culture owe much to the superb work of journalist—lawyer—historian Carey McWilliams, especially his *Southern California Country* (New York: Duell, Sloan and Pearce 1946) and *California: The Great Exception* (New York: Current Books, 1949).

13. On the so-called Nash thesis, consult Paul Rhode, "The Nash Thesis Revisited: An Economic Historian's View," *Pacific Historical Review* 63 (August 1994): 363–92, and other essays in the same issue of this journal. See also William G. Robbins, "The 'Plundered Province' Thesis and Recent Historiography of the American West," *Pacific Historical Review* 55 (November 1986): 577–97.

14. Etulain, "A New Historiographical Frontier"; Jack L. August, "The Future of Western History: The Third Wave," *Journal of Arizona History* 27 (summer 1986): 229–44; Gene M. Gressley, "The West: Past, Present, and Future," *Western Historical Quarterly* 17 (January 1986): 5–23.

15. Nash, *The American West Transformed: The Impact of World War II* (Bloomington: Indiana University Press, 1985), and Nash, *World War II and the West: Reshaping the Economy* (Lincoln: University of Nebraska Press, 1990).

16. Nash, *A. P. Giannini and the Bank of America* (Norman: University of Oklahoma Press, 1992). The textual comments on this volume draw on Richard W. Etulain, "Series Editor's Preface," ix–x.

17. For titles of some of these "research opportunities" essays, see notes 4 and 8. Nash later coedited a book-length collection of such essays: Nash and Richard W. Etulain, eds., *Researching Western History: Topics in the Twentieth Century* (Albuquerque: University of New Mexico Press, 1997).

18. For example, see Nash, "The American West in the Twentieth Century: Prospects and Problems," in *The Modern West*, ed. Thomas G. Alexander (Provo, Utah: Brigham Young University, 1979); Nash, "California and Its Historians: An Appraisal of the Histories of the State," *Pacific Historical Review* 50 (November 1981): 387–413.

19. Nash, *Creating the West: Historical Interpretations 1890–1990* (Albuquerque: University of New Mexico Press, 1991).

20. Other similar but multiauthor collections include Roger L. Nichols, ed., *American Frontier and Western Issues: A Historiographical Review* (New York: Greenwood Press, 1986); Richard W. Etulain, ed., *Writing Western History: Essays on Major Western Historians* (Albuquerque: University of New Mexico Press, 1991; Reno: University of Nevada Press, 2002); and Clyde A. Milner II, ed., *A New Significance: Re-envisioning the History of the American West* (New York: Oxford University Press, 1996).

21. Nash, *The Federal Landscape: An Economic History of the Twentieth-Century West* (Tucson: University of Arizona Press, 1999).

22. Nash, *A Brief History of the American West Since 1945* (Fort Worth, Tex.: Harcourt Brace and Company, 2000).

23. Nash elaborates on his historiographical perspectives, as well as on those of the New Western historians, in his "Point of View: One Hundred Years of Western History," *Journal of the West* 32 (January 1993): 3–4, and Nash, "The Global Context of the New Western Historian," in *Old West/New West: Quo Vadis?* ed. Gene M. Gressley (Worland, Wyo.: High Plains Publishing Company, 1994), 147–62, 183–84.

Contributors

Marjorie Bell Chambers is professor of history and political science at the Union Institute's Graduate College of Interdisciplinary Arts and Sciences based in Cincinnati, Ohio. She earned her doctorate in recent American history at the University of New Mexico under the late Professor Gerald Nash's mentorship and played an activist role in the second wave of the women's movement.

Margaret Connell-Szasz claims the Columbia River Plateau as her homeland. In recent years her scholarship has moved from a focus on American Indian/Alaska Native ethnohistory to comparative history, as is evident in her essay in this book. Currently she is completing a book that draws links between the Scottish Highlanders and the Iroquois and Northeast Algonquians in the eighteenth century. Her publications include *Education and the American Indian: The Road to Self-Determination* (1999) and *Between Indian and White Worlds: The Cultural Broker* (1994, 2001).

Richard W. Etulain, previously professor of history and director of the Center for the American West at the University of New Mexico, is now a full-time researcher and writer residing in Portland, Oregon. He specializes in the history and literature of the American West and has authored or edited forty books. Among those volumes are *The American West: A Twentieth-Century History* (coauthored with Michel P. Malone, 1989); *Re-imagining the Modern American West* (1996); *Researching Western History: Topics in the Twentieth Century* (coedited with Gerald D. Nash, 1997); *Religion in Modern New Mexico* (coedited with Ferenc M. Szasz, 1997); *Telling Western Stories* (1999); *The Hollywood West* (coedited with Glenda Riley, 2001); and *New Mexico Lives: Profiles and Historical Sketches* (2002). He has served as president of both the Western Literature and Western History associations.

Arthur R. Gómez, a native of the Southwest, holds a Ph.D. from the University of New Mexico. An eighteen-year employee of the National Park Service, he is the regional historian for the Intermountain Region Support Office, Santa Fe. Recent publications include *Quest for the Golden Circle: The Four Corners and the Metropolitan West, 1945–1970* (1994, 2000); *Forests Under Fire: A Century of Ecosystem Mismanagement* (coedited with Christopher J. Huggard, 2001); and "Public Lands and Public Sentiment: A Comparative Look at the National Parks in the American West," in *Land in the American West: Private Claims and the Common Good,* edited by James Foster and William Robbins (2000).

Gene M. Gressley's almost four-decade, multivaried career at the University of Wyoming included All University Professor, founding director, emeritus, of the American Heritage Center, and assistant to the president. Gressley has also written/edited eight books and forty-plus articles. Among these volumes are *Bankers and Cattlemen* (1966), *The Twentieth-Century West* (1977), and *Old West/New West: Quo Vadis?* (1994).

Christopher J. Huggard is an associate professor of history at NorthWest Arkansas Community College, where he is head of the Western Civilization section and also teaches U.S. and environmental history. He coedited *Forests under Fire: A Century of Ecosystem Mismanagement in the Southwest* (with Arthur R. Gómez, 2001). He also served as editor in chief for the *Mining History Journal* from 1994 to 2000 and has authored several essays on mining and the environment in the American West in scholarly journals.

Roger W. Lotchin is professor of history at the University of North Carolina. He is the editor and author of articles, essays, and books on urbanism, war, and the West, including *Fortress California, 1910–1961: From Warfare to Welfare* (1992); *The Way We Really Were: The Golden State in the Second Great War* (2000); and a study of California cities in World War II (forthcoming).

Carol Lynn MacGregor studied with Gerald Nash at the University of New Mexico, receiving her doctorate in 1999. She teaches American history, specializing in the West, at Boise State University. Her book *The Journals of Patrick Gass of the Lewis and Clark Expedition* was printed for the third time in 2000. MacGregor is also a rancher and philanthropist in her native Idaho.

Donald J. Pisani is Merrick Professor of Western American History at the University of Oklahoma, specializing in environmental history. His most recent book, *Water and American Government: The Bureau of Reclamation and the New West, 1902–1936,* will be published by the University of California Press in 2002. His current research project is a history of land and squatter riots in California during the 1850s.

Ferenc M. Szasz is professor of history at the University of New Mexico, where he has taught since 1967. Author/editor of more than ninety articles and nine books, he concentrates chiefly on the social and intellectual history of the United States. Among his publications are *Religion in Modern New Mexico* (coedited with Richard W. Etulain, 1997); *Religion in the Modern American West* (2000); and *Scots in the North American West, 1790–1917* (2000). His best-known work is *The Day the Sun Rose Twice: The Story of the Trinity Site Nuclear Explosion, July 16, 1945* (1984, reprint, 1995).

Index